GENDER AND WELFARE IN MEXICO

NICHOLE SANDERS

GENDER AND WELFARE IN MEXICO

The Consolidation of a Postrevolutionary State

THE PENNSYLVANIA STATE UNIVERSITY PRESS

UNIVERSITY PARK, PENNSYLVANIA

Parts of chapters 2 and 3 were previously published in
"Improving Mothers: Poverty, the Family, and 'Modern' Social
Assistance in Mexico, 1937–1950," in *The Women's Revolution:
Women and Womanhood in Mexico, 1910–1953*, ed. Patience
Schell and Stephanie Mitchell (Lanham, Md.: Rowman
and Littlefield, 2006), 187–203.

Library of Congress Cataloging-in-Publication Data

Sanders, Nichole, 1970–
Gender and welfare in Mexico : the consolidation of a
postrevolutionary state / Nichole Sanders.
p.   cm.
Includes bibliographical references and index.
Summary: "Examines the political and social influences
behind the creation of the postrevolutionary Mexican
welfare state in the 1930s, 1940s, and 1950s"—Provided by publisher.
ISBN 978-0-271-04887-1 (cloth : alk. paper)
ISBN 978-0-271-04888-8 (pbk. : alk. paper)
1. Welfare state—Mexico—History—20th century.
2. Public welfare—Mexico—History—20th century.
3. Mexico—Social policy.
4. Mexico—Politics and government—20th century.
I. Title.

HN117.S26 2011
361.6'5097209041—dc22
2011008007

The Pennsylvania State University Press is a member of the
Association of American University Presses.

It is the policy of
The Pennsylvania State University
Press to use acid-free paper. Publications on uncoated stock
satisfy the minimum requirements of American National
Standard for Information Sciences—Permanence of Paper
for Printed Library Material, ANSI Z39.48-1992.

Frontispiece: Hugo Brehme, photograph of a public letter
writer and a woman holding a baby in the foreground, Mexico
(detail), between ca. 1890 and 1923. Library of Congress,
Prints and Photographs Division, Frank and Frances
Carpenter Collection [LC-USZ62-114771].

CONTENTS

ACKNOWLEDGMENTS

I am pleased and excited to have the opportunity to thank everyone who has contributed in some form to the publication of this book. While all errors are mine alone, any strengths of the project are due to the large amount of support and guidance I have received along the way.

Many thanks to Steven Topik, a model of intellectual curiosity and patience. Jaime Rodríguez provided much appreciated guidance in the intricacies of both the U.S. and Mexican academies, and Heidi Tinsman not only taught me feminist theory but served as a role model of a successful academic. Julio Moreno helped steer me though archival work, showing me how to navigate my way through a variety of archives in Mexico City. Research support was provided by the School of Humanities, the Humanities Center, and the Department of History at the University of California, Irvine. I would also like to thank the staffs of the archives I visited in Mexico City, who were very helpful and often pointed in me in research directions I had not considered. In particular, many thanks to Roberto Berestain and Enrique Cervantez Sánchez of the Archivo General de la Nación. Both were generous with their time and offered indispensable advice.

Mónica Sayrols, Olivia Silva, and Luz María Cruz have provided friendship, housing, and diversion throughout my research trips to Mexico. Mónica and Olivia in particular have been lifelong friends, and I owe to them my fascination with Mexican history. Research would not be nearly as much fun without them.

Many colleagues have read and offered helpful comments on the book in its various stages. Many thanks to Donna Guy, Margaret Chowning, Gabriela Cano, Ann Blum, Katherine Bliss, Jocelyn Olcott, Susan Gauss, Víctor Macías-González, Aaron Navarro, Anne Rubenstein, Susie Porter, Verónica Castillo-Muñoz, Patience Schell, Dina Berger, María Teresa Fernández Aceves, Gladys McCormick, Kristina Boylan, and Francie Chassen-López. I would especially like to thank Mary Kay Vaughan, who not only read many drafts but offered thoughtful and constructive advice throughout every phase of the project. I would also like to thank Sandy Thatcher, the former director of Penn State Press, for his support, and the anonymous reader engaged by the Press for his or her excellent suggestions. Additionally, I would like to thank Suzanne Wolk for her excellent editing, which greatly strengthened the book.

At Lynchburg College I have benefited from the support of Dean Kim McCabe and from funding provided through a Lynchburg College Faculty Summer Research Grant and a Virginia Federation for Independent Colleges' Maurice L. Mednick Memorial Fellowship. I also received financial help in the form of a Lewis-Hanke Award from the Conference on Latin American History. I have been fortunate in enjoying the intellectual sustenance, encouragement, and friendship of a terrific group of colleagues: Sabita Manian, Laura Kicklighter, Kirt von Daacke, Brian Crim, Phil Stump, Jim Owens, N. S. Amos, Chidsey Dickson, Kate Gray, Laura Marello, and Kathleen Vlieger, among many others. Lorna Dawson edited and re-edited parts of the manuscript at a crucial time, and for that I will forever be grateful.

I would like to thank Jonathan Shipe for help with the bibliography and Cathie Eagle for her technical expertise. This book would never have seen the light of day if not for the help of the fantastic LC library staff—in particular Ariel Myers, an amazing librarian and friend. I thank Ariel for her moral support and excellent research skills.

I'd also like to thank Amelia Lyons for many years of friendship and support. Amelia read many drafts and discussed many iterations of this book with me, in addition to serving as an unpaid therapist.

Much love and gratitude also go to Mike Masatsugu and Wiebke Ipsen. Wiebke is no longer with us, but her influence can be felt on every page of this book. She was a true friend and a gifted scholar, and she is sorely missed.

This book is dedicated to my family, who have stood by me ever since I had the crazy idea to become an academic. The memory and enthusiasm of my father have sustained me through many a rough patch. My mother, Pamela Sanders, and my brother, Jason Sanders, have always been there for me. My husband, Robert Wooters, has suffered though moves, absences, and my anxiety with grace and patience. Finally, my son, Jeffrey, arrived during my first semester on the tenure track and has grown alongside this book. He keeps me on my toes, and his excitement that his mommy is writing a book has kept me going, especially when it would have been easier to quit. My love and gratitude to all of them.

LIST OF ABBREVIATIONS

IMSS Instituto Mexicano del Seguridad Social (Mexican Social Security Institute)

PRI Partido Revolucionario Institucional (Institutional Revolutionary Party)

PRM Partido de la Revolución Mexicana (Mexican Revolutionary Party)

SAP Secretaría de Asistencia Pública (Ministry of Public Assistance)

SEP Secretaría de Educación Pública (Ministry of Public Education)

SSA Secretaría de Salubridad y Asistencia (Ministry of Health and Welfare)

UNAM Universidad Nacional Autónoma de México (Autonomous National University of Mexico)

INTRODUCTION

My meal—meat, fruit and pure milk—
Is very simple
But the meal never lacks something better than bread:
The tortilla.

I drink water rather than *pulque*,
My meals are made with clean water
And to be even more sure
I drink my water well boiled.

I like clean clothes
My underwear, my shirts
"White always, clean always"
This is the best advice.

I no longer wear huaraches
I dress my feet better now
With squeaky shoes
Which better protect my feet.

—Dr. R. Esquerro Peraza, "Yo quiero mi jacalito:
Corrido Ranchero," *El Nacional*, October 6, 1935

The lines above are from a *corrido* composed in honor of the Seventh Pan-American Child Congress, hosted in Mexico City in 1935.[1] The *corrido* itself, written by a male physician, was seventeen stanzas long and was dedicated to the celebration of good hygiene. It appeared in the pro-government daily *El Nacional* on the first day of the conference and was one of many articles that showcased the Mexican government's commitment to international standards for child and maternal health and welfare.

The *corrido* is a Mexican song roughly translated "ballad." It is particularly telling that public health officials co-opted a genre of regional folk music to highlight the beauty of Mexican culture and emphasize national unity—a unity that transcended class differences. A tribute to the Pan-American Child Congress, Esquerro Peraza's "Yo quiero mi jacalito" also showcased Mexican participation in transnational health and welfare projects. The *corrido* refers to Mexican customs and practices, such as the consumption of tortillas, and (in the eyes of the reformers) Mexicans' unfortunate propensity to drink *pulque*, a fermented beverage derived from the cactus. Yet it also emphasizes the ability of the Mexican people to overcome these bad habits and become part of a modern nation-state. The speaker now drinks boiled water, appreciates clean white clothes, and wears shoes, not huaraches—a sandal worn by most peasants.

Interestingly, both the author and the subject of the song are male, but from different classes. The author is a doctor, part of the professional urban class. The subject is a peasant, asked to change his "backward" ways and become more modern by practicing scientific hygiene. The habits of peasants, both those who stayed in the countryside and those who migrated to the cities, created anxiety for public health and welfare workers. They, and other social welfare reformers, believed that through the science of hygiene and public health these peasants could be redeemed and made part of the modern nation-state. What is elided, however, is the invisible labor needed to create these hygienic conditions. Women made the tortillas, boiled the water, and washed the clothes. The *corrido* quoted above suggests that gender discourses during this period could be complicated. Clearly, this male doctor saw men as those in need of improvement. Men would be the new citizens. Yet other reformers, both male and female, saw mothers as the conduit through which modernity could reach Mexico.

This book looks at how middle-class Mexican social welfare reformers, both male and female, used the construction of the Mexican welfare state and transnational attitudes about citizenship, motherhood, the poor, charity, and welfare to open up political spaces in which they could accomplish their goal of modernizing Mexico. Their ability to use the prestige of the Pan-American Child Congress to lobby for new policies led to the creation of the Ministry of Public Assistance (Secretaría de Asistencia Pública, or SAP) in 1937. The SAP was merged with the Mexico City Department of Health in 1943 to create the Ministry of Health and Welfare (Secretaría de Salubridad y Asistencia, or SSA). The creation of this ministry allowed both male and female reformers (doctors, nurses, social workers, lawyers, and other professionals) to work together to create what they considered a modern Mexico, in which the poor would be racially uplifted through eugenics and imbued with middle-class values. While men controlled the upper levels of power in the SAP/SSA and focused predominantly on public health initiatives, women, whether as social workers, other professionals, or volunteers, wrote and managed welfare policy for mothers and children.

Understanding how middle-class professionals gained the power to inter-vene in the lives of poor women is crucial to our comprehension of how the Mexican welfare state, part of the "Mexican Miracle," was formed.

The postrevolutionary welfare state reflected multiple influences: nine-teenth-century benevolent programs, particularly female-headed Catholic charities, the rise of eugenics, with its focus on science and child rearing, the postrevolutionary expansion of the Mexican middle class, and transnational attitudes and ideologies surrounding twentieth-century welfare. This book examines how these influences worked together to produce the SAP/SSA and its social assistance programs in the late 1930s, 1940s, and 1950s.

The social reform movement of the mid-twentieth century sprang from the violence of the Mexican Revolution (1910–17). The revolution itself was a reaction to the policies of Porfirio Díaz, liberal dictator of Mexico from 1876 to 1910, an era known as the Porfiriato. Under Díaz, power and prestige had been centralized in Mexico City, leaving out other social and political groups. Three factions emerged during the revolution, all demanding politi-cal, social, and economic reforms, led by Venustiano Carranza, Pancho Villa, and Emilio Zapata. The armed phase of the revolution lasted until 1917, with all factions fighting for political dominance. The victors, the Car-rancistas, were largely northern elites and the middle class, who greatly feared the upheaval of the revolution and the violence it unleashed. Begin-ning in 1917, the Carrancistas sought to rewrite the laws of Mexican society and consolidate their political control.

The Carrancistas contested the power of the Porfirian elite and sought to create a "modern," developed Mexico. Their ally in this quest was an expanding middle class—especially middle-class professionals—that had largely been denied political and social power under the Díaz regime.[2] The postrevolutionary government relied on a strong, centralized state and on "experts" to implement reform: lawyers drafted a new constitution and new laws, economists managed the economy, and professional social reformers sought to rewrite gender and social norms for a new society.

While doctors, lawyers, and public health officials had always enjoyed professional status, part of "updating" the welfare movement after the revo-lution meant professionalizing female reformers as well. A well-developed benevolent network existed during the Porfiriato, with men controlling the state apparatus while women volunteered in charitable, often Catholic, pro-grams. By the 1940s, however, women were earning degrees in education, nursing, and social work. The professionalization of women was thus em-bedded within the rise of the postrevolutionary middle class, and within the ascendancy of the dominant political party to come out of the revolution, the Partido Revolucionario Institucional (PRI). To understand how the

PRI maintained power and legitimacy, one must understand its relationship to the middle class, particularly the segment of the middle class dedicated to social reform.

The PRI was the prevailing political party in twentieth-century Mexico, holding power from the 1920s until it lost the presidency in 2000. The PRI began in 1929 as the Partido Nacional Revolucionario and became the party of the government, dominating popular elections and eliminating viable competitors.[3] President Lázaro Cárdenas expanded the scope of the government and renamed the party the Partido de la Revolución Mexicana (PRM) in 1938. Under Cárdenas the PRM incorporated sectors of social movements—the Confederación de Trabajadores de México (CTM, or Confederation of Mexican Workers), the Confederación Nacional Campesina (CNC, or National Confederation of Peasants), and the Federación de Sindicatos de Trabajadores al Servicio del Estado (FSTSE, or Federation of Unions of State Service Workers). The CTM, CNC, and FSTSE also had feminine secretariats that addressed women's issues.[4] The incorporation of these confederations allowed the PRM to co-opt these social movements, including women's movements, and gather political strength. The party underwent one final name change in 1946, becoming the PRI. The creation and achievements of the PRI have long fascinated scholars. This work seeks to explain the PRI's success by examining its relationship with the social reform movement.

Reformers drew their ideas not only from their own national experience but from the international reform networks of which they were a part. While the tradition of private charitable organizations continued and grew during the "Mexican Miracle," the expanded role of the state and its self-proclaimed goal of modernizing Mexico, which involved constructing the welfare state through the SAP/SSA, is the focus of this book. Other state agencies created social assistance programs, among them the Instituto Mexicano del Seguridad Social (IMSS), the Secretaría de Educación Pública (SEP), and the Secretaría de Trabajo y Previsión Social, but these focused either on workers or on children from all socioeconomic classes. The SSA's welfare programs were uniquely dedicated to the poor—those left out by the other agencies. The SSA's activities, however, should be seen against a background of many "experts" working to develop and modernize Mexico. The PRI was able to capitalize on its alliance with this group.

Many reformers, not just in Mexico but throughout Latin America, Europe, and the United States, saw the intervention of the state in welfare as the most modern and scientific way to improve social conditions. The PRI therefore gained political legitimacy from cooperating with this movement, but it was also able to draw on the international prestige and status of

Mexican welfare advocates to increase its standing both at home and abroad. SSA officials invited trade groups, teachers, and other foreign experts to its new welfare centers to showcase the government's commitment to modern scientific management of the poor. Foreign observers commented quite favorably on the new programs, and the government used their endorsement to convince Mexicans that the PRI was doing an effective job of managing the country. Mexican presidents, for example, highlighted these achievements in their speeches.

Gender, Welfare, and Transnational Influences

To professional welfare reformers, ideas about appropriate gender roles were central to modernizing Mexico. According to feminist historians such as Joan Scott, gender is a fundamental way of understanding how power works in a society. Historians of gender see it as the historically and culturally specific social construction of masculinity and femininity. Patriarchy is created through these social constructions and through the relationships between men and women. Recent scholarship has examined how those in power manipulate gender constructions in order to maintain hegemony.[5]

Classic studies of the construction of the welfare state, such as Gøsta Esping-Andersen's, are predicated on the understanding of citizenship as class-based and male. *Gender and Welfare in Mexico* builds on more recent scholarship to demonstrate that gender as a category of analysis is central to understanding the way in which welfare states have been constructed. Seth Koven and Sonya Michel outline the relationship between women's welfare activities and strong versus weak states in their classic study of the role of maternal and child welfare policies.[6] Susan Pedersen's excellent work compares Great Britain and France to demonstrate both the centrality of gender in the formation of the European welfare state and how complicated gender ideologies can be. Theda Skocpol's work on the development of the U.S. welfare state highlights the importance of treating the government as a social actor in its own right, and Linda Gordon's study of single women and welfare shows the importance of exploring social attitudes toward the poor, poor women in particular. National studies of Latin America, such as Karin Rosemblatt's pathbreaking book on the Chilean welfare state, Christine Ehrick's work on Uruguay, Ann Blum's work on Mexico, and Donna Guy's studies of Argentina, also explore the role of gender in the formation of the welfare state.[7]

While these studies provide useful models for comparing welfare regimes, they focus largely on the state as an entity removed from larger transnational forces. Certainly, the creation of the welfare state was predicated on the existence of a nation-state. The historiography, however, has tended to preserve national boundaries. This work builds on these excellent studies but demonstrates that it is just as important to understand the transnational focus of maternal and child welfare during this period. Welfare states were created not only because of national contingencies but also in conjunction with an international reform movement that made motherhood its central focus and had roots in the nineteenth century. Without appreciating this dimension of the modern welfare state, Mexico's story would be incomplete.

The structural processes of industrialization and urbanization, and the social problems created as a result, sparked an international social welfare movement at the end of the nineteenth century. Reformers sought to ameliorate the most egregious consequences—poverty, urban squalor and overpopulation, child labor, and disease—and to preserve social stability. Welfare advocates participated in a variety of international meetings, conferences, and gatherings, discussing the most effective means of dealing with social problems. Latin American reformers traveled to Europe and the United States but also took part in Pan-American meetings to formulate strategies for dealing with social problems specific to Latin America. The vigorous participation of Mexican delegates in this movement reveals that international discourse about maternal and child welfare was just as important as national political struggles and ideologies in shaping the Mexican welfare state. The international was refracted through the lens of the Mexican experience, in particular the Mexican Revolution, creating a welfare policy that responded to specific Mexican realities but also had much in common with the policies of other Latin American nations. The creation of the welfare state in Mexico did not come directly out of the revolution, nor was it imposed by the PRI, but the PRI was singularly adept at capitalizing on the international influence and the regulation of gender roles that the reform movement championed.

The construction of the Mexican welfare state also responded to transnational forces, resulting in what scholars have called the "modernization of patriarchy." Historians such as Susan Besse, Donna Guy, Karin Rosemblatt, and Mary Kay Vaughan have shown that in the twentieth century Latin American governments abandoned earlier liberal political models and moved toward stronger central states with industrial, rather than export-led, economies. The process involved many socioeconomic changes, among them changes in gender relations. With a stronger central state came restrictions on unfettered male authority in the home. Yet the result was not the end of patriarchy but its "modernization." Women, in exchange for an improved position within the family and larger society, allowed the state to enter their homes in order to monitor motherhood and dictate appropriate behavior for mothers. Women were not to be regulated or punished by their husbands but by agents of the state, especially doctors, nurses, teachers, and social workers.

Many of the programs instituted by the SAP/SSA attempted to strengthen the male-headed family. Campaigns to promote civil marriage, the establishment of family dining halls, and the implementation of a foster-care system for orphans all sought to reinforce the family and promote a specific kind of masculinity. As Vaughan observes in the case of peasants in the countryside, reformers also wanted to create a new, sanitized form of masculinity for the urban poor that would make men into responsible fathers. Women, in exchange for some new freedoms, accepted the role of "modern" mothers, although these changes did not fundamentally challenge society's view of women as "natural" caregivers.[8]

Welfare professionals realized, however, that because of either death or abandonment, some households were female-headed. Many programs implemented in the 1940s and '50s, such as mothers' clubs and maternal and child welfare centers, specifically targeted single mothers and their children. These programs provided pre- and postnatal care as well as access to medical professionals for women and their children. They also offered training and education that allowed single mothers to work from their homes as they raised their children. If a mother had to work, they provided day-care facilities for her children. Mothers were taught gender-specific job skills (and explicitly were not trained to work in the newly emerging industrial sector). If mothers could remain in the home, the family model was preserved. To take advantage of state benefits, poor mothers had to submit to the constant scrutiny of the state in the form of social workers, doctors, and other welfare professionals. The state, with the cooperation of mothers, would raise young Mexicans to fit into an industrialized nation. In the case of single mothers, welfare policy essentially sought to replace male heads of households with state agencies.[9] Since state policies were not designed to enable women to live or work on their own, state paternalism was strengthened and traditional gender roles preserved.

What is interesting, however, is the female face that modern patriarchy wore. While the top officials of the SSA were male, women nevertheless played an important role in the construction and implementation of health and welfare policy through both social work and voluntary committees. Professional women like Mathilde Rodríguez Cabo, Enelda Fox, and Francisca Acosta headed departments dedicated to maternal and child welfare and became a key force in writing and promoting SSA programs. Welfare workers in the field were overwhelmingly female and found their own work personally empowering and liberating, even as they promoted policies that reinforced poor women's dependence on men. Such workers were complicit in creating a system that sought to replicate the male-headed household and reinforce gender roles within the family, even as they managed to break free of these roles themselves.

Eugenic Thought in Latin America

Social workers exploited the "science" of eugenics to promote these changes. In fact, eugenics, another transnational ideology, shaped Mexico's national experience during this period. The delegates to the various Pan-American meetings were influenced by both their own anxieties about gender and race and their understanding of racist attitudes toward Latin America in the United States and Europe. As we will see in chapter 1, Latin American reformers in the 1930s saw the implementation of welfare policy as a marker of culture and progress, and they couched their reforms in terms of a "civilizing mission." Social activists believed that their countries were racially unfit and socially backward. In order to "uplift" their people and achieve "progress," programs were needed to educate and train children, whom welfare specialists considered the future wealth of their nations.

Latin American policymakers were well aware of their economic disadvantages vis-à-vis more developed nations, and also of their racial difference from those nations. Latin American elites knew that most Americans and Europeans considered them racially inferior—and many agreed, contending that the racial makeup of their own countries retarded their development. Plans to "whiten" their populations through European immigration at the turn of the twentieth century gave way to an emphasis on eugenics in the 1920s and 1930s. Eugenics was a popular concept in Europe and North America as well, but it took a different form in Latin America.

Latin American elites embraced a neo-Lamarckian version of eugenics, which stressed the primacy of environmental factors and held that changes in environment could improve "the race." This represented a departure from the Mendelian form of eugenic thought popular in the United States, England, and Germany, which favored a more deterministic theory of genetics, arguing that genes or "germ plasm" passed unalterably from generation to generation. Public health became important to Latin American eugenicists because it offered a positive way for their societies to become racially "civilized" that stood in contrast to "negative" North American and German sterilization policies.[10]

Through the discourse of eugenics, the poor became associated with racial inferiority rather than, as in the past, with suffering and with receiving their reward in heaven. As Nancy Leys Stepan contends, "these professionals assumed that social ills accumulated at the bottom of the racial-social hierarchy—that the poor were poor because they were unhygienic, dirty, ignorant, and hereditarily unfit."[11] Any attempts to combat poverty during this period revealed not only class bias on the part of reformers but racial bias as well. Mexican professionals often conflated social class and race. As the historian Karin Rosemblatt notes in her discussion of Mexican social scientists during the same period, "Class distinctions increasingly replaced, but also subsumed, racial distinctions in Mexican social science. Scholars considered poverty and economic deprivation as racial conditions and believed that economic uplift would do away with racial inequality."[12] Reformers saw eugenics as a scientific way to "uplift" the poor racially.

Eugenics in Mexico can be seen as part of postrevolutionary state building.[13] Mexican eugenicists emphasized the importance of motherhood, sexuality, and children to the national project of modernization. "Echoing French eugenicists," writes Alexandra Minna Stern, "Mexicans embraced puericulture, 'the scientific cultivation of the child,' and advocated a pronatalism tempered by biological selection."[14] Reformers believed that syphilis, alcoholism, tuberculosis, and other diseases had direct hereditary effects. Educational measures such as classes in puericulture (the science of child rearing) and other public health programs were thus essential if Mexico was to modernize and join the march of progress. Policymakers maintained that Mexican industries needed vigorous, healthy workers, and mothers had to be trained to raise their children appropriately, so that they could fill this need. Eugenicists' idea of "responsible motherhood" meant that mothers had to learn to avoid vice and disease so that they would not pass these handicaps on to their children genetically.

As Stern asserts eugenics offered Mexican and other Latin American elites a "scientific" way to reshape their populations and redefine citizenship along specific gender and racial norms. Eugenicists focused on reproduction and socialization, thereby increasing the importance of mothers and children to rapidly modernizing societies. As Stern points out, "This historical transformation entailed more than just a reinscription of a traditional, patriarchal view of women as caretakers—at stake was the rearticulation of all points of power within the domestic domain. Only such intimate contact could construct modern citizens and recompose existing ones."[15] The changes in Mexico and Latin America reflected a global movement toward the reform of gender relations in the interwar years.[16] Eugenics rewrote power relations within the family, giving mothers a vital role in the construction of modern nation-states. The centrality of motherhood challenged the ultimate patriarchal authority of the father, but, as noted above, it did not fundamentally challenge patriarchy, since male power within the family was transferred to the state, embodied by the predominantly male medical establishment.

Welfare Reform in Mexico

The Mexican social reformers who worked at the SAP/SSA were well schooled in the "science" of eugenics, and by the 1940s and 1950s had participated in transnational welfare networks for almost eighty years. The 1917 constitution contained social welfare provisions; article 27, part 3, for example, established state control over public and private benevolent organizations, defining benevolence broadly to include scientific investigation and education. It limited benevolent organizations' accumulation of funds and property and prohibited them from being administered by religious institutions. Article 73 created a public health authority (the Consejo de Salubridad General) that was to be controlled directly by the president.[17] In many ways, as Mario Luís Fuentes observes, these articles merely ratified key aspects of the Ley Reforma—a period of liberal reform in mid-nineteenth-century Mexico. But they also point to the importance of social health and welfare policy to revolutionary leaders. The Mexican Revolution and the subsequent consolidation of state power in the 1920s and '30s meant that reform efforts were often couched in the language of social justice. By the 1940s (the beginning of the "Mexican Miracle"), however, the relative importance of social justice gave way to an emphasis on economic development, political stability, and modernization.

The story of the Mexican Miracle itself is a familiar one. In the late 1930s the Mexican government shifted from a policy of economic redistribution to one of state-sponsored industrialization. Politicians and government economists believed that the best hope for social justice lay no longer in agrarian reform, as it had in the 1930s, but in economic growth. It was necessary, that is, to create wealth before it could be redistributed. It thus became government policy to support industrial development through the policies of "import-substitution industrialization" (ISI). The Mexican government reasoned that the economic situation created by World War II was ideal for implementing this new policy. The economy of the United States, Mexico's largest trading partner, was tied up in war production and needed to import both agricultural and manufactured goods from its neighbor to the south. The result was an expansion of Mexico's manufacturing base, the growth of both the working and the middle classes, and increased urbanization. Growth rates averaged almost 6.5 percent per annum,[18] and the PRI became the single most powerful political party in Mexico. The combination of political stability, PRI dominance, and economic growth gave rise to the term "Mexican Miracle" to describe the period from the mid-1940s through the early 1970s.

Political commentators have debated the nature of the PRI's role in Mexico's economy.[19] Scholars such as Roger Hansen and William Glade, writing primarily in the 1960s, applauded the PRI's successful interventionist model, which led to extraordinary growth rates. The 1970s saw a shift to a revisionist view that critiqued the PRI and its policies as a betrayal of the revolution. Political economists charged that the PRI's interventions during the years after World War II were responsible for the economic crises of the 1970s and 1980s. Many also criticized the PRI for abandoning the goal of social justice, some questioning whether the PRI had ever really been committed to uplifting the poor. More recent literature has tried to substantiate or refute this claim by examining the government's relationship to different social groups. The SAP was created during a period of growth in both state and private initiatives to combat poverty and modernize Mexico. State initiatives (in addition to the SAP) included not only the creation of the IMSS, or the Mexican Social Security Institute, but other measures designed to help workers, such as protective legislation, the construction of public housing, and food subsidies. These measures, however, specifically targeted workers rather than the poor in general.

Labor historians have spilled a great deal of ink looking into the connection of the PRI to organized labor in an attempt to evaluate the ways in which the PRI gained political legitimacy. Kevin Middlebrook, for example, has examined the relationship between organized labor and the state and the role it played in the long tenure of the PRI. He argues that "economic growth produced new sources of employment. . . . Active state regulation of economic affairs and an expanding public sector made it easier for major labor organizations to translate their political importance into social and economic policy gains."[20] Labor historians like Middlebrook have argued that political stability during this period came in part from the strong relationship between the state and organized labor. Because the state supplied social programs such as the IMSS, housing, and food, stability was possible and organized labor reaped the benefits.

Other labor historians, while not denying the importance of the state, have examined the ways in which workers interacted with industrialists and with labor unions themselves during the twentieth century. Historians such as Susan Gauss and Michael Snodgrass have looked at how paternalistic businesses provided social welfare provisions for employees. Companies supplied housing, schools, and leisure activities, just as the government did. These historians have also explored the gender relations embedded within these paternalistic relationships. Clearly, welfare during this period came not from state programs alone and was targeted not only to male workers. Industrialists, unions, and private charities sought to provide welfare, thus attempting to rewrite gender norms in order to promote social stability.[21]

This development took on added significance during the period of the Mexican Miracle. World War II sped up the processes that had begun before the Mexican Revolution. The migration of peasants into cities, combined with the economic retrenchment of the 1930s (caused by the Great Depression), created wider-scale, more visible poverty in the cities, particularly Mexico City. President Lázaro Cárdenas created the SAP in 1937 to centralize a hodgepodge of commissions and boards established by postrevolutionary administrations. The agency's mission was to protect "our country's inhabitants from social weakness, particularly economic weakness. The goals are to prevent, mitigate, or cure this weakness by attempting to integrate, reintegrate, or maintain as active elements of production and consumption suffering individuals, [so that] they can enjoy the best welfare possible."[22] The SAP's purpose, in other words, was to integrate marginalized populations into Mexican society.

The SAP was never the largest or the best-funded government agency, however. Scholars have downplayed the PRI's commitment to welfare during this crucial period of state formation because government expenditures for social assistance spending never represented a significant portion of Mexico's federal budget. In 1938, according to James Wilkie, 4.9 percent of government spending under Cárdenas, or 3.1 pesos per capita, targeted public health, welfare, and other assistance. By 1958 the total percentage of this assistance had fallen to 3.3 percent of the budget, although per capita spending had increased to 5.8 pesos. This was more than the IMSS received—0.7 percent of the federal budget, or 0.8 pesos per capita in 1945; those figures increased to 1.7 percent of the federal budget and 3.5 pesos per capita in 1958.[23] Moreover, most of these expenditures were concentrated in Mexico City; by 1950, 80 percent of SSA spending targeted Mexico City, where 12 percent of the country's population lived but where the urban poor were most heavily concentrated and were the greatest threat to the PRI's political power.[24]

Yet scholars have failed to appreciate that the SSA, despite its limited budget, continued to expand programs and services throughout both Mexico City and the entire country between roughly 1934 and 1963. The number of shelters, dining halls, public bathrooms, day-care centers, workshops, food and clothing distribution centers, and other forms of aid increased from a total of twenty-three in 1936 to 186 in 1963 (although the rate of increase was irregular). The number of hospitals, asylums, and rehabilitation centers increased as well, from 803 in 1934 to 1,671 in 1961. The number of privately run shelters and charities also increased during this period, calling into question some historians' assertion that the revolution died in 1940.[25] In fact, it was the role of private investment that allowed for this expansion: after 1940, the Mexican government successfully co-opted many formerly private charitable endeavors (many of them headed by women and rooted in the Porfiriato) and redirected their energies toward SAP (after 1943, SSA) agencies and programming. Scholars have thoroughly examined the relationship between private investment and ISI in the consolidation of the Mexican Miracle. But they have not looked at how private contributions also allowed for the expansion of social assistance that bolstered the PRI's power.

Their focus on the relative lack of government expenditure has also allowed scholars to overlook the social significance of the SAP/SSA. Historians are only now beginning to study the issue of how government work opened new avenues for female employment during this period. Susie Porter has shown how debates about the nature of office work, particularly government work, affected middle-class values and practices. This study builds on Porter's work by showing that the SAP/SSA was not just an agency where women could work as typists or clerical help: women in this agency held management positions and wrote social assistance policy.

In 1938 the SAP employed about 5,230 workers, 57 percent of whom were women. The secretary and various subsecretaries of the agency were men. In fact, in the 1938 labor census, men outnumbered women in the SAP's administrative category (483 versus 402), professional category (438 versus 110), and worker category (364 versus 102), although women outnumbered men in the "especialista" (specialist) category (291 versus 1,192) and "servant" category (672 versus 1,176). Interestingly, 54 percent of all women employed were single, making single women 31 percent of the total SAP workforce.[26]

Subsecretaries oversaw a number of SAP departments, and it is at the departmental level that women exercised influence. The departments dedicated to maternal and child welfare were renamed and reorganized several times over the twenty years examined in this study, but many department heads were women, among them Mathilde Rodríguez, Enelda Fox, and Francisca Acosta. SAP programs were created and supervised at the department level, and department heads managed staffs of social workers, volunteers, and clerical help. The department heads reported directly to the subsecretaries, but they also had access to the head of the agency himself, and in many cases they dictated terms to their supervisors. This agency allowed these female department heads considerable power and autonomy, markers of middle-class status. Their work in the SAP, and later in the SSA, allows us to understand the relationship between women's professional work and middle-class femininity during this period more fully.

The Middle Class

Political scientists have debated the centrality of middle-class support in the creation and maintenance of political regimes in Latin America. Peter Smith, for example, argues that political legitimacy derives in large part from the support of the middle sectors of society. D. S. Parker argues convincingly in his study of Peru that the middle class is less a strict economic category than a contested social (or socioeconomic) identity. Soledad Loaeza makes a similar claim about the middle class in Mexico. Anne Rubenstein argues that discourses of traditional versus modern in the postrevolutionary era often centered on women, particularly the idea of the *chica moderna* and her relationship to new modes of consumption. Rubenstein points out that these discourses were defined in relation to each other; the traditional informed the modern and vice versa, and both helped define appropriate behavior for the emerging middle-class women.[27]

The existence of the middle class was contested, gendered, and of central importance to the PRI's political consolidation. Ideas of what it meant to be middle class were in flux during the 1930s, '40s, and '50s, as a new modernization project changed the way wealth was created and distributed in Mexico. As Julio Moreno argues in *Yankee Don't Go Home*, consumption became an important marker of middle-class status during this period. Participation in the construction of the welfare state was a marker as well, one that has not been adequately addressed.

What was considered appropriate middle-class behavior? What did it mean to be "middle class" in Mexico during the 1940s and '50s? Attitudes toward class and social status are notoriously difficult to define because they are constantly changing. Status means different things to different people. As Rubenstein and Moreno point out, consumption—the ability to purchase consumer goods—was one indication. William French argues in *A Peaceful and Working People* that for the *gente decente* during the Porfiriato, manners and morals mattered; that is, the ability to play certain social roles was what marked one as part of the middle class. Loaeza and Porter also contend that education and the ability to practice a profession also helped define the Mexican middle class.

Social reformers were well educated and considered themselves professionals. Their writings reveal that they valued education, science, and the law, the tools with which they aimed to modernize Mexico. They defined themselves against the people they worked with, and they saw the poor as uneducated, superstitious, and lawless. But part of what differentiated the middle class from the poor was the power middle-class reformers had, through the state, to intervene in the lives of the poor. This social power, I argue, came in part from the social prestige of the "charity ladies." That is, middle-class women and the state drew on the prestige conferred by women's traditional participation in charity work to encourage women to work for the new ministry. Their position allowed them not only to be middle class but also to define what they considered appropriate middle-class behavior and standards for their clients. But because the language that emerged during the Mexican Miracle emphasized welfare as modern, scientific, and professional, women felt that they were also taking part in the construction of a new society. They either became middle class or used their new roles to bolster their middle-class status.

In many ways, the new middle-class professionals also defined themselves against the Mexican upper class. The revolution did not destroy the Porfirian elite, but the new Mexican government did seek to curb their economic and social power. Middle-class reformers' criticism of religious charities can be read as a critique of the elite and their approach to poverty. If the elite were wedded to tradition, then this new professional class would be part of the modern construction of Mexico—a revolutionary Mexico. This new professional class saw women as key to creating this new, modern nation, but, ironically, their view was rooted in the Mexican reform tradition that they fiercely derided.

The Nineteenth Century: Gender, the Poor, and Catholic Social Action

Mexicans had long held the belief that women were particularly suited for welfare work because of their "natural" moral superiority and inherent maternal characteristics, which some scholars have termed "benevolent femininity." Indeed, this form of maternalism became an important rationale in many parts of the world for elite female activity and political participation. In Mexico, Catholic social action bolstered this view, both before and after the revolution. The anticlericalism of the revolution tempered but did not eradicate this discourse. As Karen Tice explains, "As with many facets of reform practice and thinking, however, benevolent femininity did not simply disappear. It co-existed in a variety of transmuted forms embedded in ascendant scientific and professional discourses."[28] Attitudes toward social reform after the revolution reflected the influence of these new professional and scientific discourses, pairing these discourses with older attitudes regarding appropriate professional activity for women. Social work therefore emerged as a professional field believed to be particularly suited to women because of commonly held assumptions about "benevolent femininity."

Pamela Voekel argues convincingly in *Alone Before God* that attitudes about liberal modernity in nineteenth-century Mexico had their roots in Catholic ideology, although liberal discourse was officially anticlerical. I contend that these attitudes persisted after the revolution as well. Official state rhetoric was anticlerical, especially in the 1930s. Welfare workers criticized religious charity as backward and old-fashioned. And yet, as Tice explains, the discourse of benevolent femininity, which helped to justify women's participation in professional welfare work, was embedded in the new welfare state. Catholic social action, which sought class harmony, also shaped post-revolutionary reformers' attitudes about the poor. While the rhetoric of the Mexican Miracle differed from that of the Porfiriato—the poor needed to be uplifted and integrated rather than encouraged passively to accept their fate—the belief that poverty undermined the modern state persisted. Post-revolutionary modernity was tied to industrialization, consumption, and control of the violence that erupted during the revolution. Welfare workers contributed to the construction of the "new" Mexico, but the nineteenth century's gendered understanding of the poor, women, charity, Catholicism (particularly the late nineteenth-century Catholic social action), and the role of the government shaped twentieth-century welfare practices.

In 1877 Porfirio Díaz had federalized welfare by placing administration of the Junta Directiva de Beneficencia Pública under the Secretaría de Gobernación. In 1881 a new law grouped government benevolent organizations into three categories: hospitals, shelters, and centers of education and correction. Thus recipients of state aid were either the sick and infirm or those otherwise in need of state protection: the indigent, orphans, the mentally ill, juvenile delinquents, and pregnant women. State paternalism was therefore an important ideological underpinning of the provision of welfare. As article 49 of the law stated, state institutions existed for those who "really needed help and would be free only for those truly indigent."[29] The truly deserving poor would get help, but others were expected to take care of themselves.

Government officials and the middle and upper classes alike, however, viewed poverty as a social ill that had to be controlled rather than eradicated. Upper-class women focused their efforts on poor women, especially poor mothers, in order to guarantee the health of Mexican children and families. A growing middle class allowed these women to perform charitable activities as well.

Porfirian reformers, then, secularized the welfare system and placed it under federal control; but a system of private charities, under federal supervision, also emerged in the late nineteenth century. The private charities, dominated by women, were primarily religious in nature and responded to the call to take part in benevolent work issued in the papal encyclical *Rerum Novarum*. The expansion of elite women's charitable activities had steadily gained acceptance throughout the nineteenth century and took on increased momentum under Porfirio Díaz's liberal regime. Pope Leo XIII's call for social action inspired many Porfirian women and served as a continued justification for their work. This work aided the construction of the Porfirian state—a balancing act between public programs and private works. Both networks were influenced by transnational currents in welfare reform; Catholic charities in particular were influenced by social Catholicism.

Rerum Novarum addressed the social question created by the modern capitalist system and the egregious effects of industrialization. The encyclical delineated the forms of exploitation suffered by the working class. It was suffering, the church argued, that made capital accumulation possible. The encyclical also criticized "rich and opulent men" for ignoring their charitable duty. Although it defended the working class, it fiercely decried socialism and firmly defended the right to private property. Essentially, the encyclical sought to promote class harmony and conciliation. It exhorted the rich to treat the poor as human beings, not slaves—they should be paid a living wage, for example. The rich should also pay more attention to social justice and charity work. The poor, for their part, were admonished to accept their humble social position. If all classes followed these recommendations, the result would be "true brotherly love."[30] *Rerum Novarum*, then, did not recommend fundamental changes to the capitalist system; it saw the solution to social unrest and other ills of industrial capitalism as cooperation between the classes, each playing its part and treating the other fairly. If the rich would commit themselves to ameliorating the most egregious excesses of the capitalist system, and the poor learned to accept their "place," all would be well.

Rerum Novarum built upon the Latin American elite's interest in charity and welfare by advocating a particular form of social action. Charitable work gave elite and middle-class women an opening for greater participation in the public sphere. Church congresses between 1903 and 1909 outlined plans for this kind of participation, specifically the "formation of Catholic worker circles; increased Catholic presence in education; promotion of wages which would allow men to support their families; primary education and 'moral' leisure activities for the working class; and dignity for the home, family and children."[31] The Catholic congresses, which were attended by women as well as men, promoted temperance, campaigns to legitimize marriages, greater protections for women (including "fallen" women) and orphans, and educational reforms, particularly for servants.[32] Women's roles in Catholic charities increased not only in Latin America but in European Catholic countries as well.[33] Conferences in European and Latin American countries provided women an international context for their activities in Mexico. The ability of social reformers to draw on international contacts gave the reform movement, especially female reformers, a certain prestige. These contacts remained important after the revolution, as the postrevolutionary state and the middle class sought legitimacy.[34]

Middle-class attitudes toward the poor and working women helped shape the particular contours of welfare in Mexico, both public and private. As Susie Porter has demonstrated, by the 1880s industrialization had made working women more prominent in Mexican cities (especially Mexico City), and their presence produced anxiety among the middle class. Positivists like Horacio Barreda equated working women with the disintegration of the home and the disruption of class relations.[35] Middle-class reformers saw motherhood as the true calling of respectable women, and benevolent activity was largely designed to help poor and working women become better mothers. Charitable work also gave middle-class women an aura of respectability; formerly an elite activity, it was now open to middle-class women as well. The growth of government welfare services also gave newly professional men a venue for their activities. In sum, the expansion of welfare, through both religious charities dominated by women and state-run agencies dominated by male doctors, sociologists, and other professionals, helped define a new middle-class identity, a trend that continued in the 1940s and '50s.

While male officials remained largely in charge of the public welfare system throughout the Porfiriato, private benevolent organizations, especially those run by elite women, undertook many important charitable projects.[36] Mexican women's charitable organizations never had the direct political power that their counterparts in Argentina did, but they still exerted a strong social influence.[37] Prominent elite women such as Carmen Romero Rubio de Díaz, Porfirio Díaz's wife, played a large role in creating and sponsoring welfare projects. In 1887, for example, Romero Rubio de

Díaz founded the first Casa Amiga de la Obrera, a day-care center modeled on European kindergartens for the children of working mothers. She was also the honorary patron of the seamstresses' society, the Sociedad Fraternal de Costureras.[38] Romero Rubio de Díaz remained active in benevolent activities throughout her life, indeed, even in death. In 1941 she left five thousand pesos to the SAP, stipulating that the money be used to help fund improvements to the first Casa Amiga de la Obrera, which she herself had founded more than fifty years before.[39]

During the Porfiriato the number of charitable organizations founded and administered by women for women and children grew. They included such institutions as a branch of the U.S.-based Florence Crittenden homes, as well as shelters and mothers' clubs designed to educate poor and working-class women in the latest child-care methods.[40] Another important group was the Union de Damas Católicas Mexicanas, which was made up mainly of upper- and upper-middle-class women and was dedicated to Catholic charity. The group also offered a vision of what it considered "reasonable" feminism. The Damas Católicas believed that women had a moral obligation to work for the improvement of society and that this obligation transcended their religious and domestic responsibilities. In order to improve the lives of the poor, particularly poor women and their children, the Damas created centers that offered training in job skills, catechism classes, and even unionizing activities.[41]

Catholic charitable work, directed primarily at poor mothers and their children, allowed elite women to argue that their public activities were extensions of their roles as mothers. This "benevolent femininity" shaped many of the discourses surrounding the poor and social welfare after the revolution. In fact, many of the issues and concerns discussed by the Damas Católicas and the Catholic congresses became part of the rhetoric of the revolution and were incorporated into the 1917 constitution.[42]

As noted above, the welfare system that emerged from the revolution had its roots in nineteenth-century liberal ideology and Porfirian attitudes toward the poor. Postrevolutionary governments maintained state-run programs and continued to regulate private charities. Many private entities founded during the Porfiriato, such as the Casas Amigas de la Obrera and mothers' clubs, day-care centers, and school breakfast programs, continued to function after the revolution but were now administered by the government. While the Porfirian state-run public school system and other public institutions preached messages similar to those of the religious charities, it is significant that many of the religious programs were adopted wholesale by the postrevolutionary regime. Benevolent femininity did not disappear, but it became part of a new, postrevolutionary discourse.

Overview of the Book

This study relies heavily on the documents left behind by the men and women who worked in the SSA and on newspaper articles and *licenciatura* theses written by social workers studying at the national university, the Universidad Nacional Autónoma de México (UNAM). The voices of a relatively small group of people inform our understandings of gender and welfare during this period in Mexico. As these were predominantly educated professionals, they tell us more about the construction of a middle-class identity in Mexico, and the relationship of middle-class reformers to the government during this twenty-year period, than they do about the recipients of state welfare, the *clases populares*, and their understanding of citizenship and welfare rights. Where the documents permit, I have included the voices of the poor and their reactions to SSA programs. But these voices are almost always mediated by the voice of an SSA worker or volunteer.

Because the SSA memos, reports, and program descriptions on which this book is based are largely institutional, I have tried to look at other types of documents as well. The institutional reports tell us about the SSA programs that were implemented, but they do not tell us much about reactions to the programs, either from program participants or from the welfare workers "on the ground." I have thus supplemented these documents with a few letters in the archives and the writings of the social workers themselves. Sometimes social workers included their personal views in official reports; their academic theses also provide glimpses into how they saw their role in the welfare apparatus. Newspaper articles and editorials have also provided insight into attitudes toward SSA programming.

I relied as well on the official SAP/SSA monthly periodical—published either as *Asistencia Social* (social assistance) or simply *Asistencia* (assistance, or welfare)—which was distributed to SAP/SSA workers and other interested parties; the agency estimates that twenty-five thousand copies were distributed each month, beginning in the late 1930s. The periodical featured articles, primarily but not exclusively by SAP/SSA workers, on agency programs, public health, child nutrition, welfare initiatives in other countries, and so on. It was an important source of information for welfare workers and also a means of publicizing the work of the agency. Many copies went to government agencies outside Mexico City.

This book focuses on the social welfare activities of the SAP/SSA, predominantly in Mexico City and primarily in the areas of maternal and child health and welfare. As such it does not attempt to offer a comprehensive overview of SAP/SSA activities. I focus on Mexico City because the vast

majority of SSA funds were spent there, and because SSA workers considered Mexico City an example for other Mexican cities and states.

Chapter 1 looks at the Pan-American Child Congresses as significant
arbiters of international discourse on maternal and child welfare. These
congresses were certainly not the only international efforts dedicated to this
issue, but they held great importance for the Mexican reform community,
and Mexicans were able to use the prestige of this forum to showcase their
reform efforts and press for more support and funding. As Donna Guy
notes, social reformers capitalized on the momentum created by the child
congresses to implement welfare policies in their home countries. "Often,
these formal, highly public and erudite ceremonies served as a legitimating
function for intellectuals and politicians endeavoring to create political consensus on social topics," she writes. "Both before and after the Congresses—
advocates used professional authority to pressure political systems for
reform."[43] The opening chapter focuses on the Seventh Pan-American
Child Congress, held in Mexico City in 1935. It also looks at the eighth
congress, held in Washington, D.C., in 1942, where the Mexican delegation
was the largest foreign delegation to the congress. This congress is important because many of the programs discussed there became models for Mexican programs by the end of the 1940s.

Chapters 2 and 3 examine how the international discourses of the Pan-
American Child Congresses intersected with Mexican realities in the late
1930s and 1940s to construct social assistance programs in Mexico City.
These chapters look at how reformers like Mathilde Rodríguez Cabo, Enelda Fox, and others who attended the congresses translated ideologies into
practical programs for poor families and single mothers. These programs
were meant to create strong Mexican families and help mothers raise their
children in a modern, scientific manner. These chapters also examine how
discourse about the poor shifted from seeing the poor as a class in the 1930s
to emphasizing mothers and children in the 1940s and '50s.

Chapter 4 turns to the Ninth Pan-American Child Congress and the
creation of Unicef and looks at how international discourses and standards
influenced Mexican welfare in the 1950s. One important shift was a renewed
emphasis on rural welfare, and changes in approaches to the countryside
spurred by postwar discussion of maternal and child health and welfare.
This chapter also examines how the PRI used the prestige of welfare to
gain political ascendancy.

Chapter 5 looks at the development of social work as a career dominated
by women—its intellectual roots, transnational influences, and the way in
which Mexican social workers understood their role in the construction of

a postrevolutionary state. It also looks at how professional social work influenced the construction of middle-class identity and how notions of benevolent femininity fit into this construction.

The Mexican Miracle did not end poverty, leading many to question the efficacy of state-run programs. If we look at welfare in strictly class-based economic terms, such questions appear to have merit. The use of gender as a category of analysis, however, allows us to complicate the question. Professional welfare workers trained poor women to aspire to middle-class standards. Job training (albeit for very specific types of jobs) and the provision of day-care centers gave poor women a conduit into the middle class. Many social workers themselves came from working-class or lower-middle-class backgrounds and used the professional status that social work bestowed to ascend more firmly into the middle class (see chapter 5). Thus, although the welfare state did not eradicate poverty, it nevertheless contributed to the growth and strength of the emerging middle class, a group of vital importance to the PRI.

Social welfare policy in Mexico reflected the vision and determination of largely middle-class reformers. The government pointed to the significance of the middle class when the president of the Mexican Congress declared that it was of great importance to "the social fight."[44] Reformers used maternal and child welfare in part to gain political power, through the newly created SAP, but also to advance their social goals. This book examines the reformers' beliefs and politics, as well as the major programs they established in the 1930s and '40s, and shows how those programs sought to inculcate in the poor not only middle-class values but an ethic of consumption.

1

GENDER, RACE, AND THE PAN-AMERICAN CHILD CONGRESSES

In October 1935, reformers from all over Latin America and the United States convened in Mexico City for the Seventh Pan-American Child Congress. Mexican newspapers reported enthusiastically on the proceedings, listing the times, places, and titles of the lectures almost two weeks in advance. French, Swiss, and Belgian benevolent organizations declared October 3 "El Día de Benificencia" in the capital, and newspapers ran *corridos* dedicated to the celebration of hygiene.[1]

Mexican officials at the highest levels sought to link the prestige of the congress to the Mexican government. President Lázaro Cárdenas was elected "patron" of the proceedings, and former president Emilio Portes Gil attended the inauguration. Mexicans showcased their achievements, chartering buses to take foreign observers on tours of Mexican welfare centers. The pro-government daily *El Nacional* lauded the work of the congress and tied these programs to the success of the revolution itself, specifically mentioning the commendations of foreign participants.[2]

This congress was significant for Mexican reformers in many ways. Mexicans were able to show the international community their welfare programs, and the government gained valuable political capital from the congress's success. Many of the men and women in attendance went on to be policymakers at the newly formed Secretaría de Asistencia Pública (SAP) in 1937. The discussions and lectures by people from all over the Americas provide insight into the programs developed for the SAP. Almost all of the initiatives discussed at this and other Pan-American Child Congresses were implemented by the SAP/SSA by the end of the 1940s.

Who were these reformers, and what were their goals? They were doctors, teachers, nurses, social workers, psychologists, and feminist organizers, trained professionals predominantly from the middle and upper classes. Many had studied either at UNAM or at universities abroad, and had participated in international conferences on a variety of social and medical issues. Many of these reformers were women, and women played an active role in these policy debates, primarily as social workers, teachers, nurses, and feminist organizers. The reformers would become part of the growing Mexican state bureaucracy, not only in the SAP but in the Ministry of Labor, the Ministry of Education, and, after 1943, the IMSS.

While participants in the congresses advocated different tactics at different times, their fundamental goal never wavered: economic and social progress in Mexico. They believed that the way to achieve this goal was to reduce poverty and create a productive citizenry. While these goals are similar to those espoused by other political actors at the time, the attendees at this congress were unique in advocating maternal and child welfare policy as the most scientific and progressive way to achieve their goal. As one doctor from El Salvador declared during the opening ceremonies, "You will see with this Congress that men of science will collaborate in the task of improving *hispanoamericanos* who are inferior to other peoples. Poor distribution of wealth causes this inferiority, and we, men of science, should contribute our light so that there is no exploitation. El Salvador follows the example of Mexico."[3]

Like middle-class reformers all over Latin America, Mexican welfare workers saw themselves as a distinct group and used their professional status to claim legitimacy and cohesion. Many of them belonged to multiple organizations that claimed a progressive agenda, particularly a eugenic agenda. They saw themselves as modern, scientific, and above all professional. They positioned themselves as separate from and superior to elite charity workers and philanthropists and believed that their middle-class professional status, in partnership with the state, would transform Mexico's "backward" population. Women, as mothers or social workers, would be central to this transformation though the tutelage of "men of science."

Mexican reformers did, however, occasionally disagree on the ideological focus of their interventions. Many of the reformers in attendance were schoolteachers and as such may have been a part of Cárdenas's socialist education project. The conservative daily *Excélsior* reported on the reformers' alleged "Bolshevik eruptions." One schoolteacher, Díaz Cárdenas, interrupted a plenary session with demands that the congress focus on working-class children. Delegates chastised him for introducing the theme in the wrong session. Other speakers were interrupted, according to *Excélsior*, creating shouting and disorder. Díaz Cárdenas also disrupted a lecture on breast-feeding, demanding that the congress "take into account the fact that proletarian children were victims of class struggle [and thus that] they should be the focus, not other children." Dr. Martínez Báez retorted, "In science there are no class distinctions."[4] While socialists and eugenicists agreed that nurturing mothers and healthy children were crucial to national development, each group clearly saw class though different ideological lenses.

Excélsior reported that even during the closing ceremonies some participants continued to decry capitalism and U.S. imperialism, blaming both for the conditions working-class children suffered. Interestingly, *Excélsior* was the only paper to report on these disturbances; both *El Nacional* and *El Universal* made no mention of discord. *El Universal* specifically mentioned Díaz Cárdenas's talk but ignored the apparent controversy it provoked.[5]

It is difficult to tell from the reports how influential or controversial Díaz Cárdenas and his allies were. Only *Excélsior* portrayed him in a negative light. *Excélsior* also took the editorial opportunity to criticize the Mexican government, claiming that private charity was still necessary in Mexico and attacking corrupt government health inspectors.[6] It is likely that Díaz Cárdenas was part of President Cárdenas's socialist education project; if so, his ideas would not have been particularly controversial, although his tactics may have been. Moreover, as we shall see in the following chapter, Mexican reformers active in the newly created SAP articulated critiques of capitalism and imperialism until about 1940, when the focus shifted away from class struggle and toward mothers and children exclusively. It seems that eugenicists had won the ideological battle within the SAP by 1940.

The boundaries between the various professions, particularly for female professionals, tended to be fuzzy during this period. With the exception of medical doctors, professions often overlapped. Thus a teacher might also have been trained as a social worker, and many nurses performed functions that we would associate with social work. All delegates to these congresses held some sort of professional position, and most were in a position to influence, if not actually dictate, policy. All considered themselves aligned with social reform movements that advocated the health and welfare of children. This chapter thus refers to *congresistas* interchangeably as reformers, policymakers, delegates, social workers, and welfare advocates; they themselves would not have recognized sharp dividing lines between these terms.

The Pan-American Child Congresses were significant because they showcased Pan-American attitudes toward health and welfare programs for mothers and children, programs that would become the heart of the Mexican welfare state. This chapter examines two of the congresses, the seventh, held in 1935 in Mexico City, and the eighth, held in 1942 in Washington, D.C. By 1942 Mexican authorities had implemented many of the policies and programs outlined by the *congresistas* in 1935. Indeed, the Mexican delegation continued to have a large presence at the 1942 congress, with the second-largest delegation (after the United States). Mexico sent fifteen representatives, followed by Chile with eleven, Cuba with ten, and Brazil with eight.

Both congresses were dominated by Mexican social reformers, including the women who would go on to staff the newly created federal welfare agency, women like Josefina Gaona (the head of social work for the Mexico City Department of Social Therapy, Beneficencia Pública), Julia Nava de Ruisánchez (a social worker who created one of the first Mexican social work programs), Mathilde Rodríguez Cabo (director of Social Action under SAP and head of the 1942 delegation), Elena Torres (a feminist organizer), and Enelda Fox (director of the Department of Child Welfare in the 1940s). Gustavo Baz, who became the minister of the SAP in 1940, also attended. Other female reformers, such as Paula Alegría (who became chief of the Office for Women and Children in the Ministry of Labor in 1942) and Rosaura Zapata (a teacher who coordinated the education section for the 1935 congress and attended the 1942 congress as the head of the SEP's kindergarten program) would work for other government agencies in the 1940s and '50s. Their thoughts about social welfare reform are critical to understanding the development of the Mexican welfare state.

Beginning in the 1930s, many Latin American nations, including Mexico, faced severe crises as a worldwide depression fundamentally altered and exposed the dependencies of Latin American economies. In response to these crises, many governments moved toward import-substitution industrialization in an effort to make their countries more economically self-sufficient. Political and economic leaders argued for a nationalistic model of development, much to the dismay of their North American neighbor.

Historians and political scientists have studied this shift in economic priority, but they have tended to ignore reformers' assumptions about gender, class, and race, which were deeply embedded in this economic shift and were integral to the formation of a particularly Latin American discourse on development—and indeed to the creation of the welfare state that was a response to the economic crisis. While the nature of the discourse changed between 1930 and 1950 as a result of World War II and the cold war, ideologies surrounding changing gender roles, racial "uplift," and the emerging middle class remained central to Latin American policymakers' ideas about how to modernize and industrialize Latin America most efficiently. As I noted in the Introduction, their ideas about welfare in the 1930s put women, whether as mothers or as social workers, front and center.

The Pan-American Child Congresses began in 1916 as part of a global movement that had its roots in the late nineteenth century, in European and North American efforts to protect children and address racial and pro-natalist concerns. In addition to welfare provisions, these congresses in-cluded a substantial medical component that addressed children's health. As discussed in the Introduction, reformers considered the health and wel-fare of children an important marker of modernity—healthy children would assure national social and economic development.[7] The delegates also of-fered a vision of welfare linked firmly to the state rather than to religious or other private groups. In fact, Latin American governments used state-sponsored programs as a hedge against the social power of the Catholic Church and, in Mexico, of elites allied with the church and the Porfirian regime.[8] The desire to uplift the poor and make their countries competitive through the power of the state reflected, in large part, the goals of the emerging middle class.[9] In Mexico, this segment of the middle class used the congresses to assert power within the newly emerging state apparatus.

In October 1935 representatives from twenty-two countries in North and South America met in Mexico City for the Seventh Pan-American Child Congress. Katherine Lenroot, a noted U.S. child welfare advocate, recom-mended Mexico City, declaring, "For me it is a high honor that the Seventh Congress will take place in a country that has done so much to protect children, that has conserved its Spanish heritage while overcoming its indig-enous roots," adding, "this country is also important because it is the point of contact between the Latin civilization and the Anglo-Saxon civiliza-tion."[10] Underscoring the racism prevalent during this period, Lenroot em-phasized Mexico's white European heritage, while praising Mexican reformers for attempting to educate the indigenous population in the ways of modernity.

The participants at the seventh congress argued that it was the state's responsibility to bring Latin America up to the economic, social, and racial standards of the United States and western Europe through policies that focused on children, the future wealth of the nation. *Congresistas* contended that Latin America could civilize itself and become like Europe and their northern neighbors if this resource could be properly harnessed. Children needed to be trained to be future workers and to improve the racial stock of the nation, and delegates argued that it was the state's mission to oversee this transformation. This was not to be a transformation brought from abroad; it was a "civilizing mission" created by Latin American elites and imposed on their own populations.[11] Policymakers believed, moreover, that the state would succeed by working in partnership with women.

This concern for public health and welfare was in part a response to rapid population growth in the cities at the turn of the century. In Brazil and the southern cone nations, immigration from Europe spurred urban growth, while in other countries internal migration to the cities caused concern. Rapid urbanization came with costs. Cities needed to control living and working conditions in order to avoid health problems. As Asunción Lavrín points out, "Desirable as this growth was, it was plagued by alarming health problems that reflected badly on nations wishing to join the mainstream of Western 'progress.' One way of demonstrating 'civilization' was to control the embarrassing social and medical problems affecting their cities."[12] Part of the "civilizing mission" involved turning this population into a stable workforce that would allow Latin American countries to catch up economically to other Western nations.

Because public health became so important for racial improvement and economic development, projects focused on the young. Children had to be taught proper hygiene and receive medical treatment to ensure the future racial health of the nation. Policymakers saw mothers as crucial to this mission, as they were so vital in the early years of a child's upbringing. Mothers therefore had to be specially trained. And because someone had to train mothers, social workers became integral to the success of the mission as well. A focus on mothers and children allowed the reform movement to modernize patriarchy rather than supplant it.

Professional Social Workers, the State, and Social Transformation

Public health and welfare came to be accepted by the beginning of the twentieth century, when women lacked the vote and other legitimate means of joining political life in Latin America. Reformers viewed women's participation in programs targeting children as a natural extension of their role as mothers. Indeed, policymakers considered women ideally suited to social work, for they were seen as kinder, more caring, and more ethical. As Marisabel Simons, a Mexican teacher, put it, "The country needs a woman, a woman who is above all an optimist who knows how to overcome the most difficult obstacles that present themselves, who has a strong character, a firm will, and who knows how to win the hearts and confidence of the poor, who is sweet and caring, energetic and firm as the circumstances dictate."[13]

Because the task could be so daunting, policymakers and social workers alike maintained that the women who entered the profession of social work had to have very special characteristics, characteristics that were inherently feminine. "The social worker should be an observer," Simons continued, "prudent, serene, discreet, altruistic, dynamic and impartial, intelligent . . . she should be serious and happy."[14] According to Jénaro V. Vázquez and Gilberto Loyo, prominent Mexican demographers and eugenicists, the social worker would serve as an investigator, educator, counselor, and social engineer. She would be perfect for working with other women and children, since, they and others argued, women naturally possessed the qualities of understanding and tact necessary to enter people's homes and provide poor families with moral guidance.[15]

Ironically, while reformers considered women "naturally" fit for work in the field of public health and welfare, they nonetheless had to be properly educated and trained to perform this role. With the new emphasis on the role of the state in social transformation came an increased emphasis on social workers' professional training. By the 1920s several Latin American countries had established professional schools of social work that had produced a professional cadre of female social workers by the 1930s.[16]

One part of this civilizing mission involved economic development. As mentioned above, Latin Americans were painfully aware of the gap in economic development between their countries and North America and Europe. Simons argued that this gap in living standards could be explained in part by North Americans' commitment to social service. Simons lamented the fact that although workers' wages were no higher in the United States than they were in Latin America, the American poor and working class nevertheless enjoyed a much higher standard of living, so she claimed. Although this was not in fact the case, it allowed Simons to blame Latin American poverty on workers' lack of scientific training rather than on structural economic factors. Simons pointed to the transformational nature of social work, arguing that social workers had trained Americans to improve themselves and work harder. "Social work there [in the United States] has realized its main goal," she maintained; "it has transformed the masses, made them civilized, and has made their daily fight for life that much easier." Social work in the United States had created model workers, and it could do the same in Latin America. Simons called for the creation of more schools of social work in Latin America, noting the paucity of such schools there compared with the number in Europe and North America.[17]

Before social workers could civilize and modernize Latin American society, however, older notions of philanthropy had to be overcome. Traditional forms of charity like giving alms, reformers claimed, hurt the poor more than they helped. "Many times alms are given," Simons wrote, "being moved by a feeling called charity, but the task of the social worker is to battle against charity. Once a pauper has spent what was given, and usually spent poorly, his labor, which should be constructive, is harder." Simply giving handouts to the poor did not teach them how to work for their living; in fact, it rewarded them for begging. In addition, reformers maintained, the poor were poor in part because they did not know how to manage money. Beggars were more likely to spend their money on drink than on necessities like food and shelter. Social workers had to teach the poor to work. "One should prepare the poor [los miserables] not to live off handouts," Simons continued, "but through their own efforts. We know that almsgiving does absolutely nothing to ameliorate the causes of misery. Rather, it temporarily hides the symptoms of the social maladjustment of the individual and contributes to the slow but sure transformation of that individual into someone without shame, without their own initiative, who lives materially and morally at the expense of the rest of us."[18]

Furthermore, reformers argued, handouts would create a permanent class of poor people who would rather beg than work. A nation could not progress economically if it could not train its citizens to be good workers. Government officials and welfare advocates alike believed that well-trained workers would ensure the demographic health of the nation, enhance industrial productivity, and contribute to national development.[19] Workers had to show discipline and initiative in order to improve themselves and their country. This was especially important as Latin American nations shifted from an economic model of exporting raw materials to one based on industrial production.

Reformers' attitudes toward the poor reflected a complex set of social changes. The older conception of poverty saw the poor as a group that would always exist and understood their poverty as a reflection of their moral failures. Catholics could improve the moral state of their own souls through almsgiving and other good deeds. The poor could not be redeemed but had to be controlled, and any aid they received was best handled by private charities or the church. This view began to change in the late nineteenth and early twentieth centuries, giving way to a belief that the poor could be redeemed through properly applied scientific methods. Reformers derided older forms of charity as inefficient and problematic. Even so, some of the older attitudes toward the poor endured. Although the poor could be redeemed, middle-class welfare workers did not see them as social or "racial" equals. If they were to be redeemed, the poor would have to submit to tutelage, much like the children to whom middle-class reformers compared them. Simons's description of the poor as los miserables—literally, the miserable or despicable ones—reflects the class bias with which reformers approached the poor.

By the 1930s the increased role of the state and the professionalization of social work reflected a new scientific emphasis. Child welfare specialists argued that, as Simons put it, "social service was the scientific and modern form of altruism."[20] It was clear to reformers that traditional forms of charity had done nothing to eradicate poverty. Almsgiving was at best a temporary solution. Social workers, therefore, would scientifically tailor treatment to each individual case. Only after discovering the root causes of poverty and recommending individualized treatments could the material and moral standards of living rise.[21] *Congresistas* contended that modern scientific programs would combat poverty at its source: the home. A visit to the home was a necessary first step in recommending a solution for a poor family's economic and social condition.

Visiting and trying to educate the poor was not an easy task. Welfare workers had to combat resistance from sectors of society that supported older notions of charity, and many poor people resisted the incursion of the state into their homes and resented professional advice. "Generally social work is not well understood," Simons wrote; "a social worker is viewed as having bad intentions. She is seen as a propagator of dissolute ideas, as one who is encourages children against their parents. Finally, they feel her investigation is intrusive. Almost always her labor is poorly received."[22] Many social workers came from middle-class backgrounds and did not understand the reality of life in a poor neighborhood. Mothers in a working-class neighborhood in Mexico City complained that the teachers in the Casa Amiga de la Obrera, a vocational school run by the SAP for the children of working mothers, punished their children for infractions by suspending them from school for the day. Where were their children supposed to go, the mothers asked, if they themselves were working and could not be at home with them?[23] Child welfare advocates often recommended unrealistic solutions to poor people's problems that failed to take into account the material realities of their lives.

It was the social worker's primary task to enter the home of her clients and offer professional diagnoses and treatment for the socioeconomic challenges the family faced. Delegates to the child congresses viewed these specialists as a crucial link between the home, teachers, and doctors. As Simons wrote in her paper on social workers, "She ensures that mothers receive proper pre- and postnatal treatment. It is she, who with an intuition all social workers should possess, guides the mothers to avoid infant mortality. . . . It is necessary that the social worker prepare mothers, showing them how to care for their children so that a strong, healthy, prepared and active generation can be created for the betterment of the country."[24] Social workers also worked with doctors to make sure that children were treated for illnesses, and they taught mothers not to fear doctors. This was especially important in populations unaccustomed to visiting medical doctors, relying instead on folk cures and midwives. Social workers sought to ensure that mothers and children received "appropriate," that is, "modern and scientific," medical care—although ironically they were to use their intuition to guide poor mothers, a suggestion that perhaps middle-class intuition was superior to the poor's reliance on "superstition." Policymakers viewed infant mortality in particular as a failure on the part of the state to protect future generations. By 1930, delegates noted with alarm, the child mortality rates of most Latin American countries still compared unfavorably with European rates.[25]

Welfare specialists also tried to teach mothers to avoid vices and in-structed them on the benefits of a proper and healthy marriage.[26] Neo-Lamarckian eugenic thought claimed that alcoholism, drug use, and syphilis damaged a country's racial stock. Not only could the fetus be damaged by a mother's addiction or disease, but, eugenicists believed, these defects could be passed on to future generations. It was of the utmost importance, there-fore, that mothers avoid such vices. *Congresistas* also maintained that a strong family was the foundation of the nation, and they sought to persuade moth-ers to seek and remain in stable, state-sanctioned marriages.

Training Mothers

Congresistas, who influenced the ways in which welfare reform would be instituted in their home countries, viewed mothers as the key to healthy children. As Judith Rivera de Rangel, a Mexican teacher, commented, "Of course, everyone, prudent men and women alike, are interested in the lives of children; but it is in the first seven years of life that the little one is exclusively in the hands of women."[27] Training poor mothers to raise their children using modern scientific techniques became the primary goal. Re-formers paid special attention to working women, believing that their physi-cal working conditions would create unhealthy offspring. Their approach reflected their class and racial biases; needless to say, none of the training programs targeted middle- or upper-class women.

Educators held that it was no longer appropriate for mothers to raise children using traditional methods. Enelda Fox, the prominent Mexican social worker who went on to serve as an administrator in the Mexican SSA in the 1940s and 1950s, wrote that it was "necessary to prepare mothers for the correct protection of their children. Our civilization has arrived at a state where it is necessary to recognize that the animal instincts humans possess are not enough to give confidence in the mother—she cannot depend on these instincts to guide her in raising, protecting, and educating her children. The maternal instincts a mother has in common with animals are not sufficient as a preparation for a civilized life."[28] It was no longer enough for women to rely on "natural" instincts or traditions. Indeed, Fox suggested that the poor were not much better than animals.

Fox condemned practices that could produce mental and physical defects in children if they were not raised according to modern scientific methods. In order to facilitate the work of training mothers in proper child-rearing techniques, Fox contended, specialists should keep statistics and records on children that would show what methods worked best. "From an economic point of view," she wrote, "modern societies consider that this continued vigilance of the child constitutes the most economical program for the health of the country."[29] Once again, racial health and economic growth were explicitly linked. The state would compile statistics (requiring an increased bureaucracy and more active government role) to facilitate progress. Modern record keeping also privileged a certain kind of knowledge: that of scientific statistics over traditional local knowledge passed down through the generations. For the civilizing mission to work, poor mothers had to be taught to care for their children scientifically.

Most policymakers advocated training in both high schools and mother-child centers, where poor mothers could receive medical care for themselves and their children and participate in programs designed to teach them child care and other domestic skills. Future mothers needed to be taught not only how to care for babies but how to create clean and hygienic homes. If girls did not learn these skills in high school, social workers agreed, then mothers should be encouraged to take classes in puericulture (child care) at mother-child centers, where many received medical care for their babies anyway. This way mothers would receive the modern training necessary. Elena Torres, a Mexican teacher and feminist organizer, even suggested creating youth brigades to train mothers.[30] She foresaw a Mexico that within a generation would be filled with children who would contribute positively to the country's economic and social development.[31]

As noted above, social reformers also worried that working women would inadvertently harm their babies because of the nature of their work. "A decreased birth rate," wrote Nieves Hernández, "is generally a fact in countries that have achieved a state of advanced civilization. In our country the birth rate is decreasing and depends not on the infecundity of the race but on the nefarious influence of modern civilization and its inconveniences."[32] Thus, although civilization brought many advantages, modern industry came with disadvantages as well.

Policymakers believed that women's work in factories was one particularly dangerous effect of industrialization, especially for pregnant workers. The repetitive nature of factory work and the exposure to toxic chemicals imperiled both mothers and fetuses. Social workers cited fatigue as another danger, asserting that exhaustion from both the job and work in the home caused accidents and predisposed women to illness. Studies suggested that working women regularly delivered unhealthy babies with low birth weights. They were also more likely than middle- and upper-class women to abandon their babies when they returned to work. *Congresistas* in particular were disturbed by the disease and death rates of working-class children, which were higher than the rates in any other social class.[33]

Social workers advocated several measures to combat these problems. For one thing, they believed that pregnant workers should not be allowed to work during the last three months of pregnancy and for a month after delivering the baby. They also argued that a woman should be paid for this maternity leave, even if complications in the pregnancy forced her to leave work before the last trimester. According to welfare advocates, special doctors should be scientifically trained to help working mothers. Centers for working mothers should be provided for healthy recreation; nursing centers should be set up in all factories that employed more than fifty female workers, so that mothers could nurse their children for the first year. And if a mother worked in a factory employing fewer than fifty women, she should receive extra pay to compensate for not being able to nurse her baby.[34] Most policymakers agreed that mothers should stay at home and care for their children if at all possible. But *congresistas* understood that many mothers had to work. Since working mothers were at increased risk for illness and premature death, many reformers argued that they should be regulated. Modern science would have to ameliorate the ills of modern civilization.

Reformers saw education as the key to the dissemination of the scientific method and the creation of future generations of healthy children, which would ensure national economic and social development. The Seventh Pan-American Child Congress therefore proposed the following:

> The VII Pan-American Child Congress, taking into account the urgency with which cooperation between the home and school is needed, submits for consideration to all the countries represented the following: (1) A child's education should start in the cradle and it is therefore indispensable that mothers have the necessary preparation; (2) it is necessary to procure through as many means as necessary the security and training of the family in order to fulfill its corresponding

social functions; (3) the education imparted in the home should corre-
spond to that of the schools, and parents should cooperate with the
teachers whenever necessary; (4) secondary schools need to teach children how to become good future parents, directing the education of
their own children and efficiently and rationally cooperating with the
schools; (5) it is desirable also that women's schools organize special
classes for current and future mothers. Also, radio stations should
organize conferences to illustrate for the woman her possibilities and
responsibilities with respect to the education of her children and the
well-being and progress of her family.[35]

These recommendations encapsulate reformers' vision of the partnership
between the state and the properly constituted family. The state would
train mothers to fulfill their social role as a progressive force within the
family. Scientifically and rationally trained mothers, in cooperation with the
state, would raise productive citizens. And what better way to promote this
new partnership than through the modern technology of the radio?

Over and over again, doctors, teachers, and social workers exhorted
women to take special classes where they would learn these new techniques.
While the mother was considered the most influential person in a child's
life, welfare workers also recognized the importance of the father. Children
should be raised in a two-parent family, they argued, because only in such
a family could all the benefits of education and support be maximized.
Policymakers denounced men who abandoned their families and who did
not live up to their responsibilities. Educators focused not only on training
parents but on educating children for the sake of the families they would
one day start.

(Re)Constructing the Family

Clearly the mother was the central figure in a healthy family. As one reformer put it, "the protection of the child is rooted in the protection of the
mother. The two cannot be separated because this endangers their health
and life." But a mother could do her job only if the father of her children
supported her adequately. Many social workers, doctors, and educators argued that the father's abandonment of his children represented the gravest
threat to their health and welfare by leaving the mother "poor and unprotected."[36] Some reformers wanted legislation that would force fathers to take
economic responsibility for their families; others advocated an educational
program that would school young men in the dangers of abandoning their

children, whether legitimate or illegitimate. If the father could not be forced to support his family, some maintained, then the state should take over his role.

A. Sainz Trejo, a doctor from Veracruz, Mexico, conducted a study in which he discovered that almost half of all children born in Veracruz were illegitimate. Arguing that although single mothers tried their best, illegitimate children lacked the advantages of other children, Sainz Trejo linked this crisis to the nation's future: failure to support these children would lead to racial degeneration, thus endangering Mexico's future. It was imperative that all children have access to adequate resources and support. "What should this support be?" he asked. "According to the Civil Code, not only food, clothing, assistance in the case of illness, but also the necessary financial support for a primary education and for the child to learn a job skill or profession: this is what a legitimate child has a right to. The illegitimate child should have a right to this support as well."[37] Others argued that the courts needed to protect single mothers—and to force men to fulfill their obligations. Policymakers also maintained that a child had a right to his or her paternal surname, and that single mothers had a right to the moral and financial support of the father.[38] Once men faced their responsibilities, proper families could be created, and children would be healthier and happier. Some looked to the Soviet Union as a model of the effectiveness of forcing men legally to recognize all of their children. Legal enforcement would have a liberating effect on women, who would no longer have to bear sole responsibility for their children, and would reduce child poverty.[39]

In addition to abolishing the distinction between illegitimate and legitimate offspring, policymakers argued that children had a right to know who their parents were. Cuban lawyer and feminist organizer Ofelia Domínguez Navarro proposed reformation of the legal codes to allow for the investigation of paternity, so that the legal status of legitimate and illegitimate children would be the same.[40] Forcing fathers to support all of their children would go a long way toward alleviating childhood poverty, she argued, which threatened the strength of the nation. This position pitted reformers not only against the poor, who tended not to marry formally, but often against socially prominent men. Enforcing paternity would mean that many men would have to admit to marital infidelities, and that illegitimate children would have the right to paternal support and inheritance. In fact, in Mexico, the issue had been raised at the 1917 constitutional convention and voted down. Men feared that public naming of paternity would tarnish their honor and embarrass them in front of their wives and families. Reformers challenged middle- and upper-class men's unfettered sexual access to women.[41]

While policymakers urged that men be held legally accountable for their children, they also advocated educational projects to teach men to be good fathers. Children, they said, especially young girls, needed to be taught child care and hygiene. Boys needed to be taught to respect women, so that they would not abandon their responsibilities when they became fathers. But policymakers did not limit these projects to the school. Taking into account the large illiterate population in Latin America, they also urged that other methods of education be employed, including traveling expositions, primers, flyers, conferences, practical demonstrations, and movies.[42]

Finally, many realized that no amount of legislation or education would reduce the number of illegitimate children to zero, or anything like it. These children still needed to be fed and protected. Policymakers therefore concluded that it was the obligation of the state to care for them. As Sainz Trejo put it:

> The state has the unavoidable obligation to protect illegitimate children. First, the state should, by any means possible, attempt to determine paternity. The state should also modify laws to assure that illegitimate and legitimate children have the same right to support. If it is impossible to determine paternity, the state should take charge of the protection and care of illegitimate children, as well as their education. Their education can be provided through foundling homes, orphanages, etc. The state should put all of its resources into studying these circumstances, being always a guide for the resolution of these problems.[43]

In sum, the participants in the 1935 congress crystallized a view of child welfare that put women front and center, whether as mothers or as social workers. Latin American social reformers, concerned about what they saw as their countrymen's racial and economic inferiorities, championed the role of the state in "civilizing" these "backward" peoples. These concerns persisted throughout the late 1930s and 1940s, although the outbreak of World War II changed the geopolitical reality of the region. The outbreak of the war allowed Latin American policymakers to reshape the discourse to suit wartime contingencies.

World War II and the Eighth Pan-American Child Congress

The Eighth Pan-American Child Congress was held May 2–9, 1942, in Washington, D.C. Themes relating to the war dominated the conference, and delegates modified their speeches to address the circumstances of the war. Some of the themes discussed seven years earlier still had currency, but the terms of the discourse had shifted. The 1942 congress sought to promote a partnership between the Latin American countries and their northern neighbor. While delegates still stressed the importance of social work, maternal education, and the legal responsibilities of parents, particularly fathers, the themes were now discussed in terms of strengthening Latin American countries for the war effort. Latin American delegates acknowledged that their countries still suffered from severe social and economic problems, but they no longer couched their rhetoric in terms of inferiority. The demands of World War II forced the United States to pay more attention to Latin America, and changing international conditions subtly changed Latin American perceptions of their region's place in the international order. Latin American political and economic leaders believed that the war would allow them to pursue economic growth; reformers maintained that this growth had to be coupled with social welfare measures.

World War II had a dramatic impact on Latin American economies and societies. Economic changes—starting with the economic crises of World War I and the Great Depression—brought social change as the older export-led model of economic growth gave way to a model that emphasized industrialization and resulted in large-scale migration from the countryside to the cities; the average urban growth rate in Latin America between 1950 and 1980 was 4.1 percent.[44] The newly urban population was hit hard by the high rates of inflation that characterized the wartime economy. Urbanization and wartime propaganda also led to greater popular demands for democratic social reforms.

Many factors influenced Latin American leaders' decision to support a shift from an economy based on exports to one based on industrial production. One was simple expediency: the U.S. and European economies were directed to production for wartime needs, and Latin Americans could not import manufactured goods. This ability of the United States and Europe to harness their industrial capabilities for the war effort impressed Latin American leaders, who saw in Latin American industrialization the promise of greater economic independence. Many Latin American governments thus began in the late 1930s and early 1940s to expand their national manufacturing capabilities, making industrialization official state policy. The process of Latin American industrialization was characterized by interventionist governments. As one Argentine leader declared, the state was "no worse or more bureaucratic an administrator than a company that possesses a monopoly." Latin American leaders now saw state-led industrialization, rather than the European immigration liberal positivists had advocated earlier, as the best path to modernization.[45]

The expansion of industry coupled with rapid population growth intensified migration to the cities. The working class grew in size and became more diverse. In the early 1930s workers had been concentrated in the service and transportation sectors as well as in mining, food processing, and textiles; by the end of the war the urban industrial base had expanded to include many more occupations. In Mexico, workers in the manufacturing sector increased from 568,000 in 1940 to 922,000 in 1945, and in Brazil the number increased from 995,000 to 1,608,000.[46]

Because of the war, Latin American imports of manufactured goods fell, but there was an overall increase in its export sector. The import shortages, rising shipping costs, and large balance-of-payment surpluses combined to create rapid inflation, which hurt urban workers and created political instability. As rural agricultural workers poured into the cities, and as more food was exported rather than consumed at home, urban populations in Latin America faced food shortages, which only contributed to urban unrest. In Mexico the number of urban strikes increased from 98 in 1942 to 766 in 1943 and 887 in 1944, dropping off in 1945 to 220.[47]

The contingencies of the war allowed Latin American social reformers to reshape the concept and discourse of social welfare. No longer hampered by an inferior self-image, policymakers began during the war to view their relationship with the United States and western Europe as a partnership. The Allies needed strong Latin American countries to provide goods for the war effort, and Latin Americans saw the war as an opportunity to promote protectionist economic policies. But policymakers could not ignore the social problems plaguing the cities, a cause of increasing concern. Economic growth, they argued, had to be coupled with health and welfare programs. Government spending on such programs would guarantee future success and modernization. It was in this context that the Eighth Pan-American Child Congress convened in 1942.

Wartime Concerns: The Eighth Pan-American Child Congress

Perhaps because the Eighth Pan-American Child Congress was held in the U.S. capital at the height of the war, North American reformers took the lead in setting the agenda. Congress organizers asked delegates at the last minute to rethink their addresses and to emphasize the needs of children in wartime. The head of the Mexican delegation, Mathilde Rodríguez Cabo, observed that the shape and content of the congress's *Acta Final*, the document outlining and summarizing the goals of the congress, was determined by the U.S. delegation. This document, according to Rodríguez Cabo, was based largely on the 1940 White House Conference on Children in a Democracy and the subsequent *Declaration of Principles Relating to the Care of Children During a War*.[48] While the United States might have taken the lead in determining the agenda of the eighth congress, the U.S. delegation nevertheless had to keep Latin American needs in mind. The result was a call for a renewed emphasis on maternal and child welfare that echoed the concerns discussed seven years earlier in Mexico City.

Policymakers still believed that welfare policy could transform the nature of Latin American society. With the wealth that would come from economic development, more money could be dedicated to child and maternal welfare programs. "In spite of the state of emergency that is engulfing the world right now," Rodríguez Cabo maintained, there was a great need "to push, amplify, and complement the services of Child Protection as the only way to save future generations from social, economic, and moral bankruptcy." She also spoke of "the urgent need to search for new ways of life in which greater social equality will guarantee work for all, with sufficient salaries to allow them to fulfill their and their families' needs in the face of future contingencies."[49] Rodríguez Cabo articulated the view that economic expansion had to be coupled with social reform. Economic growth was not enough; it had to be responsible economic growth.

The eighth congress's *Acta Final* recommended several means of increasing economic growth. Planners sought to encourage production for both internal and external markets and asserted that the social costs of economic expansion should be mitigated by government programs. The state, in short, should protect those hurt most egregiously by inflation. They agreed that national production had to be stimulated with the goal of reducing the high cost of necessities, and they maintained that the state should intervene when necessary to regulate and distribute these goods. Delegates saw the role of the state as positive; the government would do its best to promote growth yet contain inflation. If that was impossible, it would make sure that the public had access to the basic necessities at a reasonable price. Policymakers also believed that the state should have an increased role in industrial planning and labor policy.[50]

Policymakers agreed that workers had to be placed in the industries necessary for national production—either for the war effort in the United States or for industrialization in Latin America. They argued that preference should be given to heads of the family, whether male or female; that is, female heads of households had to be guaranteed full participation in the new industries. This guarantee reflected wartime realities in the United States: many women had to work to support their families while their husbands were overseas. It also reflected conditions in Latin America, where paternal abandonment resulted in a large percentage of female-headed households. While most social reformers maintained that women's primary duty was to remain in the home, participants in the eighth congress, like those in the seventh, recognized the necessity of women's work and advocated measures designed to protect working mothers, including job training, work rations, a living wage, and clean and hygienic housing for workers.[51]

Delegates supported a census of all individuals enrolled in the armed forces or occupied in war-related activities or national industries. This census would be invaluable for economic planning both before and after the war. Participants argued that after the war these soldiers and workers had to be relocated as quickly as possible to industries dedicated to national reconstruction. In addition, these people, especially the agricultural workers, needed to be returned to their original towns or regions, in order to prevent massive urban unemployment and agricultural labor shortages.[52] Mass migration to the cities as a result of industrial policy had already created surplus labor there, and the corresponding shortage of agricultural workers had already begun to create food shortages, urban unrest, and political instability.[53] Failure to relocate workers after the war would only exacerbate these problems.

In an attempt to deal with these issues, policymakers had called for centralized maternal and child welfare spending during the war. They also argued that wartime spending needed to be redirected in the postwar era to health, welfare, and education. This spending would help mitigate some of the social and economic problems created by the war. Because state spending would not reach the levels necessary to meet national needs, delegates also called for volunteers and private investment to help further these programs.[54]

Maternal and child education was to be at the forefront of this battle to promote economic growth with social reform, although the emphasis shifted from maternal training and child care to children's rights to health care, education, and workplace protections. Reformers agreed that children needed certain protections if they were to develop into productive citizens. Every child should have access to "the essential elements of a healthy and correct life: nutritious food, healthy recreation, sufficient rest and physical, emotional, and intellectual development, not just for his/her own development but also for the development of those who surround the child." It was no longer sufficient to tend to a child's physical needs. Children also needed the resources that would allow them to explore and develop their interests and skills, and learn to live productively within a community. This new emphasis reflected a move toward greater professionalization of education, social work, and maternal training. Children could not be allowed to simply "fritter away" free time; their recreation now had to be "expertly directed," and their time would serve educational purposes as well, and would help reformers in their goal of creating a population better suited to modern life.

The proposed education would be more useful for a child growing up in an urban, industrial setting than to a peasant. A modern economy required workers of all types; therefore educators maintained that all children should have the opportunity to train themselves "according to their own aptitudes, which would be age appropriate." Educators acknowledged the diversity of children's talents and advocated a curriculum that would allow each child to develop his or her own unique talents. Policymakers agreed that children should be trained to take part in society at all levels, to "be able to take part in activities that convert the primary material of human life into creations of utility or beauty, as an artist or artisan, as a worker in the countryside, the mine, workshop or factory, as a member of the institutions organized for the improvement of society, like a man of letters, science, or spiritual guide." Interestingly, this training was not class specific—each child had a right to enter any profession he or she chose. A proper education would guarantee that a child would learn his or her strengths and weaknesses and would choose a profession based on his or her skills. What was important was that the child become a productive member of society. This plan for a reformed education also reflected policymakers' zeal for a planned economy. If children could be taught at a young age to develop their skills, they could more easily be integrated into the new economy—an industrial capitalist economy based on a division of labor.

Reformers also acknowledged reluctantly that children might have to work and that they therefore needed special training and protection. If they had to work, then at least they should be taught in ways appropriate "to their age and capability, employing measures such as: teaching the child responsibilities for life commensurate with age." Reformers advocated laws that would set a minimum employment age, limit the workday to fewer than six hours, and establish an obligatory register for all employed children under the age of sixteen. Once again, delegates maintained that the state should play an active role in regulating and monitoring child labor. While this policy may have been unrealistic in areas just beginning to create a strong central government, it nevertheless reflected delegates' concern that economic growth be coupled with social responsibility.[55]

Although children might have to work, educators argued that play was equally important to a child's development. A child had to be able "to use his creative faculties during part of his free time, to learn and practice his aptitudes, thus dedicating time to activities of his choice, individual as well as social." Free time also had to be used to teach children to interact within a social group. Delegates proposed day-care centers and kindergartens along the lines of those established in Germany at the turn of the century. In all of these ways, policymakers maintained, a child would be taught to become a productive participant in a democracy. Once again, the assumption that children had free time and that it could be regulated reflected the reformers' middle-class background. The whole concept that poor and working-class children had time for organized recreation and inner self-development, and that these things would eventually help them find good jobs and become productive, enlightened citizens, said much more about the reformers themselves than it did about the targets of their benevolent good works.

The document that resulted from the eighth congress envisioned the "opportunity for every child to incorporate himself into the life of the collectivity. With this proposal it is necessary to stimulate the conscience of the child to realize his obligation to contribute to the progress of the community and to prepare him for the responsibilities of citizenship, and also to learn at an early age that the rights enjoyed in a democracy impose an unavoidable obligation to enjoy these privileges without being egoistic or anti-social." Social skills were of great importance at a time when many had fled the countryside for the city and urban ills were creating political instability. If all worked according to their abilities and toward the goal of improving the community, argued delegates, many of these social ills could be alleviated. The eighth congress placed great importance on the idea of community. Welfare workers did not see citizenship as based on individual autonomy but on the relationship between the citizen and the community. Indeed, this vision expanded the theme of cooperation between the family and the state. Policymakers also continued to stress the importance of the family, explicitly linking the health and economic stability of the family to the economic and political stability of the nation. It was thus the obligation of the state to ensure an adequate standard of living for all. Delegates recommended increased social service spending and the creation of social security programs in order to guarantee this minimum standard.

Social reformers worried about abandoned children, and their recommendations shifted from placing children in large shelters and orphanages to advocating systems of foster care. Children should remain with their families if possible; an institutional setting was seen as a last resort. Maternal indigence should not cause a child to be separated from his or her mother. Rather, the state should assume responsibility for the child in a foster home until the mother could resolve her economic difficulties. In addition, reformers maintained that welfare could provide the mother with a pension while her children were in foster care; this would facilitate her economic recovery. Foster care would allow children to grow up and participate in a family. Foster families had an added advantage: the state could monitor foster parents in a way that it could not oversee a natural family.

Documents such as the *Actas Finales* produced by these congresses show a remarkable amount of homogeneity in attitudes toward gender, race, and the role of the state in welfare and economic development. What accounts for this level of consensus? In large part, the desire of the reformers to remake gender roles within a reconstituted family and to improve "the race" reflected middle-class aspirations for increased social and political power. The ability to call oneself "professional," and to have access to the education and training it took to be "professional," allowed the middle class to differentiate itself from the working and lower classes. It also allowed this group to position itself as distinct from and superior to the traditional elite, aligned with the Catholic Church and conservative traditional values. The desire to frame one's work within the discourse of professionalism, scientific professionalism (through eugenics) in particular, created a remarkable consensus and solidarity within the professional community. Socialists and eugenicists may have disagreed about class analysis, but they shared the view that children were the country's future wealth and therefore needed modern, scientific education and training.

Mexican reformers were an integral part of the international maternal and child welfare movement. Mexican teachers, doctors, social workers, and other professionals attended Pan-American and other international meetings and helped shape the discourse of gender, race, class, and the role of the emerging welfare state in Mexico. They also helped shape Pan-American views on maternal and child welfare. The Pan-American Child Congresses influenced the ways in which national reformers developed and implemented welfare policy. Latin American nations implemented many of the reforms discussed at these congresses, among them mother-child centers in Mexico, Chile, Argentina, and Brazil; family dining centers in Mexico and Brazil; and schools for professional social workers in Chile (1925), Mexico (1933), Brazil (1936), and Peru (1937). As we shall see in the next chapter, the principles set in the 1935 congress would shape the development of Mexican welfare policy, even as Mexican reformers shaped the way other Latin America reformers would view child welfare.

2

WELFARE REFORM IN MEXICO:

Stabilizing the Family

After the Seventh Pan-American Child Congress in 1935, Mexican welfare reformers began in earnest to implement the policies and programs they had proposed. They took their lead not only from international welfare models but from the reality of an increasingly urban population. Poverty, inflation, and the perceived disintegration of the family worried Mexican government leaders, who turned to social reformers to help mitigate some of the more egregious effects of urbanization. As government economic experts pushed the economy to industrialize through import-substitution industrialization, social experts sought to shore up and stabilize Mexican families so they could contribute to the nation's economic progress. Beginning in 1937 with the creation of the SAP, welfare workers implemented a variety of programs and campaigns designed to ameliorate poverty and begging and to reinforce a middle-class idea of what a "modern" family should look like. Not surprisingly, their model of the family consisted of a married couple, with a hardworking father who supported his wife and children. Programs like the campaigns to promote civil marriage, the creation of family dining halls, and the shift from large orphanages to a foster-care system reflected their vision.

As we saw in the previous chapter, both parents were targeted for education in modern child-rearing practices. Mary Kay Vaughan and others have shown how both the Cultural Missions of the 1920s and Cárdenas's socialist education project of the 1930s attempted to "domesticate" rural men. Educators tried to persuade men to give up drinking and gambling, to work hard and support their families. As Vaughan argues, this attempt modernized patriarchal family relations, as the roles of fathers and mothers were revamped. SAP programs promoted a form of masculinity for working-class men in the cities considered appropriate for a modernizing country.

Despite the antichurch rhetoric of reformers in the 1930s, many of the new welfare programs had their roots in the Porfiriato. Older programs and services were retooled and combined with eugenic aims to create "new" kind of welfare that would transform Mexican society. And while their ideology regarding race was similar to that of the *indigenismo* movement, welfare reformers nevertheless thought that racial improvement would best be achieved through the creation of strong families and the education of mothers. *Indigenistas* such as Manuel Gamio, a Mexican anthropologist who headed the Inter-American Indian Institute from 1942 to 1960, insisted in the 1940s that indigenous Mexicans were not biologically inferior; rather, it was their culture that retarded their development. Gamio believed that national progress could be achieved through the Westernization of the Indian. Welfare reformers, including prominent eugenicists, agreed. But there was a fine line between race and culture, and it was unclear exactly where this line should be drawn. Despite the "scientific" rhetoric of welfare reform, many welfare advocates saw poverty, at least in part, as the result of racial inferiority. Most reformers thought that poverty could be alleviated by educating the poor, while some *indigenistas* saw the solution in miscegenation.[1]

Cárdenas and the National Institutionalization of Welfare

The U.S. stock market crash of 1929 set off the Great Depression in the United States, negatively affecting Mexico's economic situation. Between 1929 and 1932 the Mexican GDP declined by 17.6 percent as the unemployment rate grew by 350 percent. In addition, the rapid population growth and urbanization that had begun in the 1920s continued. Mexico City's population grew by 67 percent between 1921 and 1930, as the Depression exacerbated problems of population growth and migration to the cities.[2] Lázaro Cárdenas took office in 1934 during this bleak economic period.[3]

Historians disagree about the nature and depth of the Cárdenas administration's reforms. One thing seems clear: *Cardenismo* was characterized by a growing government role in social and economic matters and increased government spending. Politically, the government embodied a variety of social groups, all jockeying for political power and influence. Cárdenas's supporters backed the administration's labor and agrarian reforms, economic nationalism, socialist education, and progressive foreign policy.[4]

Many of these supporters were loyal to this political vision; others may have been more opportunistic. In any case, middle-class welfare reformers need to be understood within a context of shifting coalitions.[5]

President Cárdenas took office after a decade of political uncertainty and violence, which had diminished the faith of the Mexican people in the revolutionary government. The Cristero Rebellion (1926–29), an armed rebellion against President Calles's attempt to enforce provisions of the 1917 constitution's restrictions on the church, had challenged the government's legitimacy.[6] Cárdenas moved to consolidate his political power along social democratic lines, incorporating both labor and peasants into the Partido Nacional Revolucionario (the predecessor of the PRM) and launching a socialist education project—provoking the dismay of powerful elites in Mexican society, including landowners, business owners, financial leaders, and the Catholic Church. His economic policy sought to redistribute wealth along socialist lines. Cárdenas's creation of the SAP was part of this campaign.

The creation of the SAP was informed by both national and international factors. Economic depression and the increasing visibility of the poor on the streets of Mexico City pressured the government to come up with remedies for social ills. Of course, social welfare advocates had been working since the revolution to increase the government's commitment to social welfare policy, but economic crisis now worked in their favor. Elevating the SAP to the federal level gave Cárdenas a valuable political ally—middle-class reformers. As Susie Porter points out, the creation of this federal agency did more than simply elevate the fight against poverty to a higher and more prestigious rhetorical plane. A federal agency also provided plum positions for reformers who associated a government job with improved economic and social status—markers of the middle class.[7] It allowed Cárdenas to renew the fight against poverty, giving him a way to commit Mexico internationally to a goal of modernization, progress, and racial uplift.

It is therefore not surprising that Cárdenas's regime made the fight against poverty and begging one of its priorities.[8] While Mexico City's Beneficencia Pública had mounted campaigns against mendicancy throughout the early 1930s (indeed, antibegging campaigns had been conducted since colonial times), the SAP, because it was now a federal agency, was able to lend more resources and prestige to the fight. According to SAP leadership, the poor were victims of capitalism. They were forced into mendicancy not only because of their poverty but because Mexico's Catholic tradition encouraged begging and almsgiving. Thus the SAP's critique of begging allowed the government to confront the authority of the Catholic Church, which had challenged the new revolutionary government in the Cristero Rebellion.[9]

In order to combat the twin evils of poverty and the Catholic Church, the SAP launched a campaign against "old-fashioned" charity and philanthropy, arguing instead for "scientific" and "modern" social welfare programs, echoing calls for the modernization of philanthropy made at the Seventh Pan-American Child Congress. At the heart of this campaign was a critique of both poverty and older forms of social relief. In its first years the SAP saw welfare as protecting and integrating the lower classes into society. SAP policymakers also saw programs like mother-child centers and day care as a way to educate and acculturate the rural population that was beginning to flood Mexico City.[10]

Explaining how poverty was the direct result of unfettered capitalism, Francisco Palacios, an SAP official, wrote in 1938:

> Why now do the ambitions of the proletariat scare the bourgeois gentlemen? Do they not remember that their most powerful technologies have caused millions and millions of victims? Surely they want to forget their victims halted on their highways, crushed with their cars, struck down by their airplanes. . . . Dying of hunger at the closed doors of Beneficence, of cold in the atriums of the churches, of sickness in front of hospitals, dying from sinful ways in brothels, of tuberculosis, sadness, and desperation in the prisons. . . . As the old nobles thought that these crimes were the price of progress, so now the bourgeoisie believe the same; the bourgeoisie in the face of this desolate picture claim that they love their culture, and will take care of justice, they will exact modified justice. They are the bearers of God's will.[11]

SAP officials maintained that the concentrated wealth of capitalism created poverty and begging, and they also criticized the technological accoutrements of capitalism: highways, automobiles, and airplanes. Because the wealthy, both the "old nobility" (the Porfirian elite) and the newly rich bourgeoisie, spent too much time accumulating wealth and playing with their new toys, they were neglecting their responsibilities—welfare centers, churches, and hospitals were underfunded, yet brothels and prisons remained open. This socialist appraisal of capitalism and its ills was not unique to Mexico during the 1930s. Palacios's reference to sin and God, however, shows the Catholic roots of the Mexican reform movement that did not entirely disappear with the ascent of the newer discourse of science and modernity. And, significantly, this critique may have given Cárdenas the leverage he needed over other political elites by allying him with the concerns of the middle-class reform movement.

Many welfare advocates blamed poverty and begging on Mexico's religious heritage—on the idea that almsgiving would benefit the giver by ensuring his place in heaven. This belief had its roots in colonial times, and it reinforced the view that the poor would always remain poor, and that all social groups should know their places. Miguel A. Quintana, a professor of economics and social sciences, argued that old-fashioned charity only reinforced social distinctions, to the detriment of both rich and poor, for the poor could not help but feel slighted by it. He called for a modern form of social welfare that would integrate the poor into society.[12]

Because charity was a temporary fix, reformers argued, it not only failed to solve the root cause of poverty—namely, capitalism—but even exacerbated the problem. Only the application of the scientific method could diagnose and cure social ills.[13] Mexican policymakers echoed their international compatriots in their demands for a more scientific form of social assistance, and joined in other Latin American reformers' attacks on the Catholic Church.

Since poverty and mendicancy were the direct results of unfettered capitalism and old-fashioned religion, it was the responsibility of society to address them through government programs. An editorial in the SAP periodical *Asistencia Social* argued that economic liberation for *campesinos* and urban workers alike was possible only through state intervention. "Public health is not possible," the editorial asserted, "when workers live in filthy places, because theirs is a starvation wage that does not permit them to have a good home."[14] The SAP leadership emphasized social justice rather than developmentalism, and championed the equality of all classes.

Welfare reformers' critique of unfettered capitalism marked a departure from older attitudes toward the poor, the so-called dangerous classes. During the Porfiriato the poor were seen as a threat to society that had to be controlled.[15] "Modern" social assistance sought not to control the poor but to uplift them and integrate them into society. Whereas the role of the state previously had been to regulate and police the lower classes, the government now saw its role as protecting the "socially and economically weak." The SAP's critique of the Catholic Church and unregulated capitalism represented one faction of the revolution, one shared by some middle-class reformers.

By the late 1930s the focus of welfare had begun to shift from integrating workers into society to protecting the family, particularly women and children, so as to ensure that future generations could be spared the most egregious harms of the capitalist economy. At the same time, reformers hoped that government protection would instill in poor families a sense of loyalty to the state. In 1939 the SAP subsecretary Silvestre Guerrero called in a radio address for the creation of a national "mother and child" committee. "Considering that many Mexican children live abandoned and unprotected," he said, "it is an unavoidable obligation of those inhabitants of this country who are in a position to do so to collaborate together to place more attention on mothers and children."[16] Mexican mothers needed help in raising their children, so that they would not suffer harm through self-sacrifice on behalf of their children. Embodied in this outlook was also a critique of lower-class men who abandoned their families. This new focus of welfare reform was complete by the time President Ávila Camacho took office in 1940.

What influenced this shift from integrating workers into society to protecting them from economic devastation? It may be useful to think of the class-based discourse on welfare during the early years of the SAP as an aberration, an exception to the rule. Welfare reformers had always argued that mothers and children were central to their goal of economic and social progress. The Seventh Pan-American Child Congress in 1935 and the ideology of eugenics influenced these ideas about mothers and children. This attitude also had roots in Catholic Porfirian welfare ideology—Catholic social action looked to women's charitable work as a way to smooth over class tensions and emphasized the role mothers played in the creation of model citizens. The emphasis on class conciliation reappeared in the 1940s, as the Mexican government moved away from the overt socialist message of the Cárdenas regime. More traditional notions of women's role in charity work merged with the "scientific" discourse of "progress" and eugenics to create a powerful social role for mothers, women, and welfare workers.

Pronatalism, as we have seen, was another component of the new approach to welfare, and it reflected demographic concerns both in Mexico and in Europe. The Mexican Revolution was violent and created much social upheaval. The Mexican population dropped from 15,160,369 in 1910 to 14,334,780 in 1921.[17] While the population had rebounded by the 1940s, many reformers still feared a decrease in population growth. These fears also reflected European, particularly French, anxieties about population decline caused by World War I. As Nancy Leys Stepan has shown, French scientific and eugenic thought influenced Latin American thought about science in general and eugenics in particular. The renewed emphasis on mothers and children reflected Mexican policymakers' concerns with the health and education of children, and by extension their mothers. Stepan argues that eugenics officially lost its legitimacy after the horrors of Hitler's final solution were exposed after World War II.[18] Yet in Mexico, *Eugenisia* and *Puericultura*, two pro-eugenics magazines, continued to be published until the early 1950s, which suggests the popularity of eugenicist thought in Mexico even after the war.

The men and women charged with running the SAP in the 1940s came from a eugenics background. Particularly after 1943, when the SAP merged with the Mexico City Department of Health to become the Secretaría de Salubridad y Asistencia (SSA), male doctors ran most of the programs. And the women who made up the middle tier of management came from either a medical or a eugenics background as well. For example, Mathilde Rodríguez Cabo was a prominent psychiatrist and was active in feminist and socialist causes (she was a member of the Frente Único pro Derechos de la Mujer) and in the eugenics movement. In the 1930s she served as head of Mexico City's Departamento de Readaptación y Previsión Social and spoke out about prostitution.[19] In the 1940s she headed up the SSA's Department of Social Action. Likewise, Enelda Fox, the director of the SSA's Department of Child Welfare, had a PhD in psychology from the University of London. Dr. Margarita Delgado worked at the SSA in the 1940s and 1950s and was also president of the Pan-American Medical Women's Alliance, the first meeting of which was hosted in Mexico City. Delgado, like Fox and Rodríguez Cabo, was highly educated, came from a medical background, and would have considered herself a professional.

Women like Rodríguez Cabo and Fox worked alongside male reformers (mostly doctors and lawyers) to write, enact, and oversee Mexican welfare policy in the 1940s and 1950s. Both women had been active in the Pan-American Child Congresses and other transnational feminist movements and came from middle-class backgrounds. Their advanced degrees marked them as professionals. Their views influenced the way the SSA interacted with poor Mexicans and the programs the agency offered them. Their movement into the upper echelons of management in the SSA (along with the new minister, the physician Gustavo Baz) allowed them to promote programs and policies that reflected their eugenics background and goals. They successfully shifted the discourse away from viewing the poor as a class to seeing welfare as offering protection to Mexican families.

The 1940s saw the implementation of civil marriage campaigns, *comedores familiares* (family dining halls), and foster homes dedicated to protecting and bolstering the family in partnership with private charitable institutions. These programs allowed the state to intervene directly in the lives of the poor in order to create and privilege certain kinds of families—those favored by middle-class reformers. When a family lacked a father, the state stepped in to play the paternal role. What is significant about this "modernization of patriarchy" is the role played by women, as high-level administrators, social workers, and volunteers.

Welfare Policy and World War II

Manuel Ávila Camacho became president in 1940. His election is generally understood as signaling a shift to the right politically, and as a consolidation of the PRM. His administration began to dismantle some of the previous administration's more "revolutionary" measures, such as land and labor reforms. He also intensified Cárdenas's industrialization goals, aggressively pushing for a model of modernization known as import-substitution industrialization.[20] This policy encouraged the domestic manufacture of light consumer goods, which had previously been imported from the United States and Europe, and aimed at the eventual domestic production of both intermediate and capital goods.[21] The state played a dominant role in the economy, fostering both industrial and agricultural production. The government also contributed heavily to developing an infrastructure of improved transportation and communication networks through the construction of roads, airports, railways, and ports.

The Ávila Camacho administration opted to support rather than compete with private industry, and it heavily promoted private-sector industrialization. Nacional Financiera (NAFINSA), the state-run development bank, in addition to promoting parastatal firms such as Petróleos de México, engaged in extensive long-term lending to the private sector and formed investment partnerships with both private domestic and international firms. By 1961 NAFINSA's investments were supporting 533 industrial firms, and its long-term investments were twice as large as the sum of such loans deriving from the private banking system.[22]

Just as Ávila Camacho increased state support for the economy and infrastructure, he reiterated his government's commitment to welfare and to motherhood and the Mexican family. Speaking in 1941, he tied the strength of the Mexican family, particularly rural families, to the strength of the nation: "The peasant knows that the furrow in which he labors not only provides the harvest for his family, but also provides a basis for the prosperity of the country. These men need to be safeguarded as the future of the nation, which they will help construct with energy and perseverance. Men, along with the enthusiasm of the children and with women in the breast of the home, will ensure the unity and strength of the nation."[23] In explicitly linking the strength of the home to the health of the nation, Ávila Camacho echoed welfare reformers. But, like those reformers, he was talking about a particular type of family, one headed by a hardworking father who sup-ported his family and enabled his wife and children to stay at home.

The emphasis on industrialization strained urban infrastructure. Under Ávila Camacho and his successors, Mexico saw even more urban migration from the countryside, especially to Mexico City, where many of the new factories were located. Between 1940 and 1960 the percentage of the Mexican population living in metropolitan areas doubled, increas-ing from approximately 8 percent to 15.8 percent. By 1970, a mere decade later, fully 50 percent of Mexico's total population lived in Mexico City, the federal districts, and ten states surrounding the city.[24] The govern-ment encouraged large-scale agriculture in the countryside, in part to feed the burgeoning cities and in part for export to the United States. World War II also placed new demands on the economy. Railroads shifted to shipping for export, which created bottlenecks in food shipments to the cities. The result of these bottlenecks was increased inflation and a lower standard of living, especially for urban consumers, many of whom were newly arrived migrants.[25]

In the midst of these deteriorating conditions, Ávila Camacho named Gustavo Baz minister of the SAP in 1940.[26] The president's first cabinet was a study in the balance of forces, as Ávila Camacho tried to mediate between different factions of the revolution. Several of his cabinet officials supported Cárdenas and his policies and represented the left-leaning side of the revolution. Other officials were clearly more conservative.[27] Baz himself may indeed have become more conservative by 1940; his calls for private investment in welfare programs seem to indicate a conservative bent. Yet he had fought for Zapata and, according to his memoir, felt unwavering admi-ration for the man. While he may have had complex, sometimes contradic-tory political views, Baz's appointment served several political purposes. As a former revolutionary general and governor, Baz was loyal to the PRM. As a doctor, he also represented and was part of the professional welfare reform movement. Although his views may have been more conservative than those of his anticapitalist predecessors, Baz still believed that if Mexico was to modernize, the government had to sponsor programs that reinforced the Mexican family, especially targeting poor mothers and children.

While NAFINSA's economists called for increased cooperation between the government and private companies, Dr. Baz and his policymakers advo-cated a similar partnership in the area of welfare, on the grounds that Mexi-co's welfare needs could be met only through a combination of state and private funding. The SAP maintained throughout the 1940s that the gov-ernment had primacy in protecting Mexican families and integrating them into the industrial economy. But SAP officials also argued that the private sector had an important role to play and saw SAP programs as complementary. "SAP, through the Dirección General de Asistencia Infantil, has intensified private investment in favor of childhood, to be coordinated with official action," wrote Mathilde Rodríguez Cabo. "Because ultimately the whole of society has responsibility for the conditions of misery and abandonment in which thousands of children are born and raised. The possibility exists that with the help of different sectors of society, child welfare can be implemented in a fuller and more effective manner."[28] Editorials and op-eds in the Mexico City daily *El Nacional* echoed the idea that welfare was society's responsibility, and that private citizens should work in conjunction with the government to help the most needy.[29]

Many of the programs instituted in the 1940s were remarkably similar to the programs created in the 1920s, which themselves had parallels to programs and ideas circulating during the Porfiriato.[30] Private charity groups had continued their work throughout the 1930s, and many resented the SAP's critique of private charity promulgated in the 1930s. Conservative groups lauded Baz's calls for greater cooperation between the state and private benevolent organizations. One editorialist lambasted the Cárdenas administration, declaring:

> Private benevolence cooperated for many years in this capital, but the intransigent "politicians" appeared with their cries for "centralization," which hobbled private charity. They impeded the continuation of private initiatives, viewing the noble works of ladies as a "backward" ideology, or as reactionary. The authorities of public benevolence were the first to place obstacles in the way of private relief, and these obstacles caused many groups to dissolve, or to work under very precarious conditions. . . . Yet nevertheless these self-sacrificing ladies continued to work![31]

With the SAP's call for private cooperation, many of these "self-sacrificing ladies" felt vindicated, and they began to participate in the SAP's voluntary committees (discussed in chapter 3). Voluntary committees expanded throughout the 1940s and 1950s, providing a way for upper-class women to continue their charitable work under the supervision of the SAP (after 1943, the SSA). The voluntary committees also represented a resurgence of older Catholic attitudes toward women, work, and the family.

Deteriorating conditions in the cities increased the need for social spending. Inflation and unemployment created by the wartime economy worried policymakers, who saw no respite with the end of the war. In fact, one SAP official argued that the end of the war would cause a jump in unemploy-ment, as *braceros* returning from the United States sought scarce jobs. He estimated that as many as 150 million could be affected by unemployment and the resulting poverty.[32] Yet the Mexican government did not have the necessary resources to devote to programs for the poor.[33] A partnership with private organizations seemed to be the perfect solution. The Mexican constitution mandated that the state control private benevolent organiza-tions. A partnership would allow increased funding for the SAP/SSA, and at the same time assure reformers that their vision of welfare policy would remain intact.[34]

Baz's calls for increased private funding resonated with the government's commitment to state support for private industry. This new "spirit of coop-eration" also allowed critics and editorialists to continue to take aim at Cárdenas's vision of welfare reform. An editorial in the conservative daily *Excélsior* declared, "Especially in Mexico, which is a poor country with a poor state, this cooperation [between public and private] in much more necessary than in countries that have a higher standard of living and better social programs. We have had a great tradition of generosity, which previous disorganized and unscrupulous administrations have killed."[35] Critics also pointed to what they believed to be large-scale corruption at the SAP. Many faulted distributors for charging higher prices than necessary to the SAP, while others pointed to the regular siphoning off of funds intended for the poor. One op-ed accused the SAP of corruption at every level.[36] Charges of corruption and disorganization allowed conservatives to claim the mantle of welfare as their own and to advocate programs focusing on women and children, not on the redistribution of wealth. This focus on generosity to mothers and their children echoed older notions of charity, which relied on the spirit of the giver, rather than "modern" social assis-tance, which stressed the responsibility of the state.

In August 1943 the SAP sponsored the First National Congress for Public Welfare. The previous minister of the ministry, Silvestre Guerrero, planned the congress and promoted its theme: problems relating to the improvement of social, medical, and educational conditions for children and abandoned mothers.[37] Participants at the congress also discussed the global implications for social welfare created by the war and reiterated the call for greater private assistance in the field of social welfare.[38]

The themes of the congress reflected many of the concerns created by the effects of World War II in Mexico. As noted above, the renewed em-phasis on industrialization, necessitated by the war, created inflation and social unrest in the cities—1944 saw a high of 887 strikes involving 165,744 workers. In addition, the presence of U.S. Ambassador George Messers-mith and President Ávila Camacho indicated the importance of social wel-fare to both the Mexican and U.S. governments. Messersmith reiterated the importance of cooperation between the two countries, noting that "the progress Mexico has achieved in recent years has been extraordinary and [I would like to] honor those government officials, economic entities, scien-tists, and professionals who have worked for this progress. . . . The mutual interest of Mexico and the United States requires broad cooperation be-tween our two countries and peoples."[39] Messersmith's call for greater politi-cal and economic cooperation reflected the U.S. desire to secure Mexico as a partner in the war effort—not only for strategic military reasons but because Mexico could export valuable products that the U.S. wartime econ-omy desperately needed.

The First National Congress for Public Welfare also articulated concerns for child and maternal assistance that echoed the concerns of the 1935 and 1942 Pan-American Child Congresses. Mathilde Rodríguez Cabo, who had participated in both congresses (and was head of the Mexican delegation to the 1942 congress), spoke of the need to bolster the family as the social unit that could best guarantee the care and education of children. She argued that economic conditions had to be improved, and she advocated a mini-mum wage. She also contended that in order to improve the living condi-tions of families, the state needed to increase agricultural and industrial output for both the internal market as well as for export. These concerns dominated the Congresos Panamericanos, where welfare policymakers from all over Latin America clearly linked child and maternal welfare policy to industrial development and responsible modernization—that is, moderniza-tion that acknowledged the ill effects of development, such as child poverty, and took steps to ameliorate them. According to these welfare advocates, improved standards of living would accompany greater economic modern-ization. This in turn would improve family life and create better economic, social, and medical conditions for children. Improved conditions for chil-dren would translate into healthy workers for the newly developing econo-mies. The First National Congress for Public Welfare voted to support the resolutions passed at the Eighth Pan-American Child Congress, with its emphasis on creating and nurturing model families. And the first step in creating a model family was legal marriage, which meant legitimate children.

Civil Marriage

Nineteenth-century liberal reformers throughout Latin America had chal-lenged the Catholic Church's monopoly on conducting marriage ceremonies by creating civil marriage. The civil codes that were updated in the nineteenth century sought to secularize Catholic religious norms. While many scholars view nineteenth-century liberalism as a positive force in Latin America, feminists such as Silvia Arrom, Elizabeth Dore, and Asunción Lavrín question liberalism's benefits for women. The secularization of marriage abolished the privileges and protections that married women enjoyed under the monarchy. Under Catholic doctrine, for example, adultery was considered equally sinful for both husbands and wives, and ecclesiastical courts often judged husbands and wives equally. Nineteenth-century reforms legalized adultery for men but made it a capital offense for women. So-called crimes of passion—a husband's murder of his adulterous wife, for instance—were legalized when committed by men. Women, by contrast, could not use infidelity even as grounds for divorce unless it took place in their marriage bed or created a public scandal.[40]

In the late nineteenth century, feminists began to organize to press for reform of some of the more egregious reforms of the civil codes. In particular, women demanded greater property rights, control over their children (*patria potestad*), and greater access to divorce. Although male liberal reformers sought to diminish the authority of the Catholic Church in matters of the home and family, their reforms made access to divorce no easier for women. Female reformers fought for divorce as a means of achieving female equality before the law and to address issues such as spousal abuse.[41]

The 1917 Mexican constitution had legalized divorce, but male legislators had done little to reform other marriage laws. In particular, *congresistas* sought to protect men from paternity suits, which would have allowed women to sue their partners (who were often married men) for economic support of their illegitimate children, thereby causing them public embarrassment and impugning their honor.[42] Middle-class legislators opposed taking this kind of responsibility for their own actions, but they supported imposing it on the poor.

Welfare reformers, that is, sought to establish a system of civil marriage based on class. Legitimate marriages were the bedrock of the nation, so long as this didn't mean *their* marriages. *Amasia,* or common-law marriage, was common among the popular classes, and welfare advocates believed that this practice had to be eradicated on the grounds that civil marriage protected wives and children from paternal death or abandonment. Legal civil marriage meant that a woman could sue the father of her children for economic support that would be difficult to enforce without a marriage contract.[43]

And, as we have seen, reformers believed that legal marriage promoted social order. Both parents had responsibility for raising the children, but it was the mother's task to do the housework. A woman was expected to live with her lawful husband, unless he was not in Mexico or lived somewhere "insalubrious." While reformers also believed that a man should have the right to his wife's earnings, the primary intent of civil marriage was to "improve the legal and moral situation of the children, and, principally, of the woman."[44] In addition, reformers sought to break up the "traditional" home, which included extended family members, and replace it with the "modern" family.[45] Grandparents, who in the past had helped with child care, were not seen as part of the model. Child care was to be the province of the wife and mother.[46]

This vision of family and home also reflected the concerns of women active in Catholic social action before the revolution. According to Catholic doctrine, all family members should know their place; if men and women played their appropriate roles, society could prosper. Social Catholicism also preached class harmony, arguing that the poor should know their place as well. By ignoring problems of middle-class men's infidelity, reformers implicitly condoned the regulation of the poor's sexuality, but not that of their own class.

In order to preserve and strengthen the two-parent nuclear family, the SAP's Department of Legal Assistance launched the first campaign against *amasia* in 1940. Legal marriage was the goal, and reformers spent much time and effort trying to convince the poor that civil marriage was one way to improve their lives. The campaign began in Mexico City, where in 1942 two thousand civil marriages were performed at the SAP; according to SAP statistics, six thousand children became "legitimate" as a result. In fact, *Asistencia* and SAP reports to the president often contained photographs of mass marriage ceremonies conducted in SAP offices and of mother-child centers. Legitimate children could sue their fathers for support, just as their mothers could sue their husbands. SAP/SSA professionals hoped to expand the program to the provinces.

Social reformers continued encouraging legal marriage throughout the 1940s and 1950s. Official statistics show that in 1946–47, the SSA celebrated 390 marriages, thereby legitimizing 1,086 children.[47] This number increased over the years, the SSA noting that in 1955–56 the Civil Registry reported to the Secretaría de Economía that it had performed 1,259 marriages and legitimated 3,412 children.[48] In the 1950s the SSA moved to give abandoned or divorced wives some form of material aid, usually in the form of food pensions. This assistance reinforced the message that legal marriage conferred financial benefits—an abandoned or divorced wife merited help, whereas a single mother would not get the same kind of aid.[49]

How did the poor react to efforts to encourage legal marriage? While the archival record remains relatively mute on the subject, other traces of their voices have survived. Manuel Sánchez, one of Oscar Lewis's subjects in his anthropological work on a poor Mexico City family in the 1950s, stated, "I had never thought of going through a church wedding, it simply never occurred to me, and that is true of most of the men and women I know. I always assumed that if the woman loves me and I love her and we wish to live together, then the legal papers and things like that are not important. . . . There is also the matter of being poor. If one begins to examine what a marriage comes to, a poor man realizes he doesn't have enough money for a wedding." Manuel did not see the point of legal marriage. "Besides," he continued, "a poor man has nothing to leave to his children so there is no need to protect them legally. If I had a million pesos, or a house, or a bank account or some material goods, I would have a civil marriage right away to legalize my children as my legitimate heirs. But people in my class have nothing."[50] Manuel acknowledged that a civil marriage was not as costly as a church wedding, but he also rejected the responsibilities that came with legal marriage, even seeing it as an affront to his masculinity. Legal marriage would tie him down, he said, and in any case he did not need the law to force responsibilities on him that he would shoulder willingly out of love. Reformers tried to change such attitudes. Although they succeeded in conducting thousands of civil marriages, poor men and women had their own reasons for rejecting an institution they viewed as impractical, unnecessary, and outside their cultural traditions.

The campaign against *amasía* reflected both national and international attitudes toward legitimate marriage. As noted above, Mexican reformers since the Porfirato had campaigned to promote civil marriage and the rights of children, even if illegitimate, to know and receive support from their fathers. Child welfare advocates maintained that the rights of children to an adequate upbringing trumped the right of a man to engage in extramarital or irresponsible sex. International reformers campaigned on the issue as well. As we saw in chapter 1, Ofelia Domínguez Navarro spoke out in Cuba in the 1920s on the difference in legal and social status between legitimate and illegitimate children and was jailed several times for her "radical" political views. In 1933 she was exiled to Mexico, where she stayed for the year with her parents. In 1935 she returned to Mexico City to speak on the issue of child legitimacy, along with Mexican and other Latin American delegates, at the Seventh Pan-American Child Congress.[51]

Civil marriages also had the advantage of allowing the government to monitor a growing population more accurately. With formal marriage, officials could better keep track of residences, number of children per family, and the size of the population. As reformers tried to manage urbanization "scientifically" and to racially uplift the population, this knowledge helped them plan programs for the poor.

If fathers could not fulfill their financial obligations to provide for the family, then mothers could work outside the home. SAP officials, however, sought to provide programs that would allow the father to fulfill his role within the family, thereby ensuring that the wife could stay at home. Their primary means to this end was the *comedores familiars*.

Family Dining Halls

The SAP created the first family dining hall in 1941, claiming that this initiative "constitutes a transcendental work that will achieve the most favorable transformation of the physical health of the country's inhabitants, strengthening their bodies so that they can provide the maximum amount of work and effort for themselves and for the country in which they live, and so that they can successfully fight the battle against sickness and death, saving themselves for the country [and living] useful lives full of promise."[52] Here again the physical health of the family was explicitly linked to the economic health of the nation, echoing the concerns of reformers all over Latin America in the 1930s. Only with healthy, happy workers could Mexico and other Latin American countries industrialize and become modern. The family dining halls were designed to guarantee proper nutrition.

The dining halls had to be organized in such a way that they could not be construed as charity. The poor needed help, but they also needed to be able to help themselves. Reformers therefore created the family dining halls as public facilities that families paid to use. Reformers calculated very carefully how much money a poor family spent on food and charged them that amount to eat at the family dining hall. As one welfare worker declared, "This is not about heads of families spending less on food; rather, it is about allowing them to improve the quality of food their families consume while spending the same amount of money." Another advantage of the dining halls was that they "liberate[d] the mother from the slavery of the kitchen, allowing her to dedicate herself to remunerative work that will help the family."[53]

The family dining halls were part of a larger movement across Latin America designed to provide nutritional benefits to the region's poor. This movement had its start in the League of Nations Hygiene Commission. Welfare professionals in Mexico modeled their program on other family dining halls created in Peru, Argentina, Uruguay, and Chile.[54] Reformers were also impressed with the system of dining halls in Brazil, inaugurated in 1941 by the Servicio de Aposentaduria e Previdencia Social. Like the dining halls of Mexico, the goal of the Brazilian program was to improve the nutrition of the working classes in order to "conciliate the interests of capital and the workers, of the *patrones* and their employees . . . procuring for all well-being, comfort, hygiene, and a healthy life for all of the Brazilian population."[55]

Such nutritional programs were created throughout Latin America in the late 1930s and early 1940s, their goal explicitly linked to industrialization. "The hygienic and sanitary work done in the dining halls produces economic benefits because it favors the progress of industry for better yield and quality of work" by reducing absenteeism due to illnesses linked to poor nutrition, according to a 1941 article in the SAP's *Asistencia*. "It is known that well-fed people get sick less often, that the duration of their illness decreases, that they suffer fewer work-related accidents, and that the yield is greater."[56] Reformers also linked the dining halls to democratic ideals, the president of the Mexican Nutrition and Family Dining Halls Commission declaring, "In an ideal democracy it is not that the rich and powerful should eat on the floor with their fingers, but that the poor should eat at a table with decency. . . . The ideal democracy is an ideal of dignity."[57] Once again, welfare workers articulated a class-based understanding of hygiene—the only proper way to eat was at a table with utensils. The poor did not have to "know their place"; they could learn to behave like the middle class, even if they did not enjoy middle-class incomes.

The first family dining hall in Mexico was located near the center of Mexico City, near the poor neighborhoods of Tepito, Morelos, and La Lagunilla.[58] The objective was not only to provide nutritious meals to the poor but to train the patrons of the hall to have improved (middle-class) hygienic habits, such as washing one's hands before eating and brushing one's teeth afterward, wiping one's mouth with a napkin (rather than with the back of the hand or a shirt sleeve), and eating at a table with a fork and knife. The intent, again, was to "improve family life."[59] Family dining halls therefore were constructed with stations where clients could wash their hands before meals and brush their teeth afterward. Each dining hall also had a doctor on staff, and clients were required to visit the medical staff periodically to make sure they were healthy and were practicing good hygiene.[60] Finally, in order to preserve family unity, families were seated together, instead of separating adults from children.[61]

Reformers had high hopes for the efficacy of the dining halls, and they set out even before their inauguration to encourage a number of families to participate in the new program. Unfortunately, the family dining hall did not prove to be as popular with its target audience as it was in the professional welfare community. In order to be permitted to use the dining halls, each family had to undergo a socioeconomic interview performed by a social worker, nurse-dietician, and doctor to make sure the family qualified.[62] But in order to complete the interview, families had to be persuaded to come to the dining hall.

Social workers reported that their efforts to reach the poor were often met with resistance. As one of them put it,

> After the hard labor of applying all of the arguments possible, the social worker and the nurse dietician finally penetrated the wall of suspicion surrounding the Mexican family of humble origin. There were many, maybe 25% of the families visited, who would not listen to us, did not trust us, and slammed their doors in our face. Another 25% allowed us to enter the humble room that was their home but would not be inscribed, for multiple reasons—no money being the primary reason—or they were not used to eating outside of their home, the husband and children only liked the wife's cooking, it was too much trouble to go to the dining hall three times a day, and they feared that they would not like the food at the hall and would be stuck paying for it. . . . Other people heard us coldly, almost with indifference. We passed by their room with an application. They would give us the information to fill out the application and, after much vacillation, tell us to come back when their husbands would be home, because they could not make any decisions without him.[63]

In an era before fast food or even popular restaurants, eating in the home was often the only option available to most Mexicans. Accustomed to women cooking in the home, the poor were suspicious of social workers' attempts to bring this activity into a public arena and often frustrated welfare workers' attempts to usurp the privacy and autonomy of the home, as they saw it. Social workers at the Pan-American Child Congresses had noted that they were often given a hard time during their home visits. It is not difficult to imagine, in a society where the popular classes regularly suffered indignities or abuse at the hands of their middle- and upper-class employers, that they would be hesitant to offer up their homes to the scrutiny of reformers, no matter how well-intentioned. Refusing to participate in the SAP's vision of modernity may have also been a "safe" way for the popular classes to resist the processes of modernization in which they had been swept up. For families perhaps recently arrived from the countryside, or experiencing the rampant inflation and overcrowding of the cities, the home may have been their only refuge.

After spending months trying to persuade families to subscribe, social workers succeeded in enrolling approximately two hundred families. Yet problems continued. Some families did not show up because they had moved, or they decided they did not want to eat at the *comedores* after all, or they had lost their jobs and did not want to spend the money. Others simply gave no reason for changing their minds. So social workers tried a different route to publicize the dining halls, working through the local schools and parents' associations. Interestingly, they also solicited the help of local priests, asking them not only to help locate eligible families but to persuade them to come, indicating perhaps a relaxing view of the church on the part of welfare workers.[64] These workers declared that they "had to overcome a traditional population, used to their habits of eating at home."[65]

Once the first *comedor* had been established, SAP workers conducted a statistical analysis of the population served. Surprisingly, many of the patrons served were middle-class families with more than eleven members, the elderly, widows of professional men, "good" families fallen on hard times, and recent arrivals from the countryside. For these people, the dining hall was like a "blessing from Heaven."[66] Silvia Arrom notes that in the first half of the nineteenth century, many women of good families fallen on hard times lived at the Mexico City Poor House. The Poor House, maintained by the Mexican government, represented a "respectable" form of charity. It seems that this tradition may have continued in the system of family dining halls, with middle-class families down on their luck patronizing the halls, seemingly without embarrassment.[67]

The SAP deemed the first dining hall a success and opened a second. The popularity of the two *comedores* soon inspired requests for additional dining halls, targeted to specific populations—for example, school dining halls. One such facility was requested in 1945 by the principal and parents' association of school V-XV.-93, the Manuel E. Villaseñor school. This group maintained that the facility was needed because of the number of children begging in the area, and because the dining hall was viewed as "responding to all the noble propositions and elevated ideas that inspire and feed this profoundly human and incredibly redemptive work," in the words of the director, José Heliodoro Bravo. The new dining hall was inaugurated in April 1945, with half of the school's eight hundred children attending. Its slogan: "After bread, education is the first need of the people."[68]

The goal of the dining hall system was the socioeconomic rehabilitation of the Mexican family through nutritional, medical, and social services. To achieve this goal, the system had to prioritize the clients seeking aid. The

SAP/SSA assigned youth top priority, stipulating that at least 60 percent of the population served in each *comedor* had to be children. This would allow doctors, nurses, and social workers to monitor the children's diet and health. The agency also made families a priority, although policymakers preferred healthy families, which they believed could be "rehabilitated" more quickly than sick families. Pregnant wives with small children were also favored. Finally, officials ranked other clients: families with a working father and a mother working in the home with three or more young children; families with three or more small children in which the parents lacked stable work but where one or the other could be trained for something more remunerative; single mothers with three or more small children; families whose only social assistance was the *comedores*; and families who needed only temporary social assistance in addition to the dining halls. Other cases were left up to the discretion of the authorities. Policymakers intended families to use the facility as a temporary measure and therefore reevaluated each family's situation every three months.[69] Regular evaluation also allowed the SAP/SSA to intervene consistently in family life to guarantee that "proper" values were maintained.

Welfare workers were proud of their dining hall system. This pride extended to the Mexican president, who often invited international observers on tours of the facilities. In a report to Ávila Camacho, agency officials wrote up the positive comments of the international delegates to the Confederación de Trabajadores de América Látina, a U.S. medical team, prominent PRI leaders (such as Vicente Toledano), and social work students and their teachers. Many of the international observers lauded the Mexicans for their achievements and compared the Mexican *comedores* favorably with those in their home countries, or expressed the hope that their own countries would create similar dining halls.[70]

The SAP established the dining halls in order to preserve families and allow male heads of household to provide for their families during hard times. Thus the centers were meant to bolster a specific type of patriarchal arrangement, not to undercut patriarchy. Reformers encouraged men to embody a certain kind of masculinity—one that emphasized care and commitment to wife and children. As teachers in the countryside sought to discipline male peasant behavior, urban welfare workers sought to inculcate a disciplined, rational masculinity in poor male heads of household as well.[71] The social workers who recruited families in the poor neighborhoods, staffed the dining halls, and monitored the families were largely female. Women were the face of official state patriarchy.

Foster Care

In order to ensure that all children were exposed to middle-class family values, the SSA also instituted a foster-care system for the children of the poor. Like the dining halls, foster care also allowed employment for women, either as foster mothers or as the social workers who monitored the foster families. As Ann Blum has shown, the Catholic Church established the two largest orphanages in Mexico City, the Hospicio de Pobres and the Casa de Niños Expositos, in the late eighteenth century. This system was in place throughout the nineteenth century and remained fundamentally unaltered until the 1940s. By the time of the Porfiriato, the orphanages offered moral and practical instruction to ensure that the children could become functional members of society after they reached the age of majority. An expansion of private charity also created a parallel system of institutions that allowed "respectable" families to place their children in orphanages that did not serve the poor. State welfare, therefore, catered almost exclusively to poor clients.[72]

The Hospicio and Casa de Niños orphanages housed not only orphans but the children of parents who could not support them. Many parents left their children for short periods of time and recovered them when they could. In many cases, mothers interned their children because they themselves worked as domestic servants, and employers preferred to hire women without children.[73] The practice allowed women who worked at least part of the time some flexibility in their child-care arrangements, especially if other family members were unavailable or unwilling to look after the children.

Welfare professionals objected to this practice. Legal abandonment allowed the state to assume parental rights and obligations. Welfare authorities, intent upon training children to become proper citizens and workers, decried the interference of parents, because the practice interfered with their aspirations, creating a tension between the goal of creating stable families and the goal of having properly trained children. It also interfered with the ability of orphanage directors to place young girls in domestic service. Blum notes that most of the training girls received was for this type of work, which paralleled the growing middle class's desire to differentiate themselves from laborers and the poor through their ability to employ servants.[74]

Blum further notes that in the 1930s doctors began to notice a condition among children who lived in orphanages that they called "hospitalism," characterized by depression and slow development. This condition improved when the children went home to their families for a visit. Medical journals thus began to recommend that orphanages create a homelike environment—or else place children in foster care. Child welfare experts responded by turning away from the older model of large-scale orphanages and moving, by the 1940s, toward implementing a system of foster care that would improve a child's self-esteem, damaged by parental loss, separation form siblings, internment, or neglect.[75] Welfare professionals outlined the advantages of a foster-care system in which no more than six children would be placed with a foster family. Reformers argued that a foster family would provide children with more individualized attention than they got in orphanages, even if family life was "more disorganized" than the regimented life of the orphanage.

Orphanage officials understandably responded defensively; their large orphanages were supposed to be an exemplar of modern, scientific management of children. Children in the orphanages were closely monitored: they had specific diets, their educational and recreational time was structured, and they regularly saw medical experts. Yet the sheer number of children in the orphanages challenged the efficiency of the system. Welfare workers noted that some of the more "street-smart" children formed gangs and tyrannized the other children. According to workers, the gangs were a frequent source of indiscipline and agitation in the orphanages. Because they could not always be supervised, children also commonly developed what welfare workers considered "vices," indulging in petty theft or in sexual "perversions" like homosexuality, or they became sexually precocious. Orphanage officials also noted that the children also often developed mental "complexes" and other bad habits, such as lying, hypocrisy, rancor, and insolence, and that they displayed a lack of respect for their superiors and for society in general. In short, these children were not engaging in what reformers considered appropriate middle-class behavior, even though they had not had particularly stable experiences—on the contrary, many of them may have suffered abuse of one kind or another. Finally, the administrators of the state welfare programs noted a lack of coordination between various departments and services and felt that reorganization would improve efficiency.[76]

In October 1941 the SAP's Department of Social Welfare authorized the dismantling of the large orphanages and began to distribute children in small groups to foster homes. In early 1942, because there was not enough time to enroll the children in schools, the SAP created *hogares colectivos*, or collective homes, to serve as a transition from the large orphanages to the small foster homes. Officials created sixty-six collective homes, with unisex groups of twenty children who lived with a family, a couple, or a single woman who wanted to help raise them.[77]

Welfare workers saw both advantages and disadvantages in the collective homes. On the one hand, the smaller numbers allowed the children to receive greater individual attention, which resulted in better personal hygiene, weight gain (because of better food and medical attention), and improved school performance (because the foster mothers guaranteed that the children got to school on time and did their homework, and communicated regularly with the teachers). On the other hand, social workers noted that the homes still had too many children to feel like a "proper" home environment, and that the children continued to persist in the "vices" of homosexuality, petty theft, and gang activity because too many beds still filled a room. It was also difficult to find suitable families, houses large enough to accommodate the families and the children, and landlords willing to rent to the collective homes. Reformers were also dismayed by what they saw as the corruption displayed by the foster families in the collective homes. These families got a house from the SAP/SSA as well as electricity, phone service, cleaning supplies, food, and salaries for themselves and servants. Social workers received complaints that many of these families sold off the supplies and food for profit, or forced the children to do the housework, pocketing the money allocated to pay for servants. Workers were appalled by reports that some of the *señoras* running the homes could not even identify all of the children in their care by name.[78]

The SAP/SSA therefore moved quickly to establish the foster-care system. The foster homes were put on individual contracts in an effort to avoid excessive bureaucratization and to give the agency more flexibility in contracting families and terminating contracts. The program also provided sixteen home inspectors and two psychiatrists. The inspectors were to help train the families as well as to report to the agency on the condition of the homes. One inspector was devoted entirely to the schooling of the children. The psychiatrists trained the mothers in dealing with problem children and reported on their progress to the SAP/SSA. They also offered courses to the mothers in psychology, psychopedagogy, sexology, and "mental hygiene."[79]

Much like the older, large-scale orphanages, the foster homes were dedicated to serving orphans and children whose parents had chronic contagious diseases, moral problems, or problems that preventing them from working to support their children.[80] As with the Hospicio de Pobres, parents had to pay a monthly fee and provide clothing for their children, even if they were in foster homes. If they failed to fulfill these responsibilities, their children would be expelled from the system.[81] When parents failed to pay the fee, social workers went looking for them to find out why the support was not being paid. Sometimes the parents could not be found, so officials would move to change the child's legal status.[82]

Child welfare experts lauded the foster-care program, once again noting the superiority of the "homelike" environment. Because only six children were fostered per family, each child received far more individual attention, resulting in better health, psychological improvement, and the eradication of vices. Officials also noted less corruption among the families, attributing this, in part, to the middle-class status of almost all of the foster families. The middle-class families also provided advantages to the orphans, who were exposed to "a better atmosphere." Children's time was better structured, and the children displayed a more confident attitude. Social workers also reported fewer runaways.[83]

Mexican schools of social service trained social workers to monitor the foster homes. Workers visited the homes of applicants to evaluate their suitability and expected that foster families be middle class. One welfare professional reported that an applicant lived in an unsuitable location and advised her to look for a house in a middle-class *colonia* such as Roma, Navarte, del Valle, Industrial, or Santa María la Rivera.[84] The same social worker critiqued the house of another pair of applicants (two sisters), saying that the entryway had a "bad aspect" and was cold. On the ground floor was a garage that the social worker found unsuitable. While the apartment was large and well lit, she noted, the applicants explained that in order to afford the rent, their widowed sister would be moving in with her three children. The social worker thought that would make the apartment too crowded and recommended that the applicants be rejected.[85]

Once selected for the program, foster families had to attend special classes designed to train foster mothers in proper child care. In 1941 these classes included child hygiene, with instruction in how to create a schedule for the child, how to care for the child's personal hygiene (including the child's "digestion, evacuation, and urination") and his or her clothing, health, and habits. Classes in home hygiene focused on how to run a home and included tips on proper ventilation and lighting, cleaning, laundry, how to secure potable water, accident prevention, and heating. Classes on domestic economy included advice on budgeting, food expenses, care for personal clothing and home, and distribution of household chores. Mothers also received training in medical treatment, diet and nutrition, and child psychology.[86] Foster mothers were expected to attend all classes; if they did not, they were sent a reminder from the head of the foster-home program.[87] Ironically, while presumably they came from the middle class, the mothers nevertheless had to take special classes in proper mothering, reflecting both national and international views of scientific motherhood. No longer could women rely on innate or "natural" skills; they had to be trained to care for children.

Social workers made regular visits to foster families and reported to the SAP/SSA on the condition of the foster homes and on whether the families were following instructions. They were particularly emphatic that children learn proper middle-class habits. One social worker reported after a home visit that while the children appeared healthy and were beginning to learn to eat with silverware, she was disappointed that they were eating in the kitchen rather than with the family, thus undercutting the goal of integrating children into family life. The mother responded that the children's manners were so poor that she felt they would improve more rapidly if they ate apart so that she could monitor them more carefully. The mother also reported that she still had to supervise the boys at night because they continued to display "bad habits." Finally, the social worker commented that when she arrived at 1:30 in the afternoon, the mother was just beginning to clean the children's room, stating that the children had been there all morning because of the cold. The worker recommended that the children should be up and breakfasting no later than 8:30 A.M., and that the mother should clean the bedroom immediately, even if the children had to go back there because of the cold.[88]

The same welfare worker reported on another inspection, noting that the children were clean and that she had arrived while they were eating their breakfast. The food was ample and the children finished everything, did not chew too loudly, and behaved well. The mother commented that she and her cook always watched over Javier, one of the boys, because he never chewed his food and ate everything whole.[89] The presence of a servant marked the mother and her family as middle class and thus as able to inculcate proper values. The attention to Javier's eating habits also points to the social worker's concerns with proper middle-class etiquette and hygiene. Certainly eating without chewing would cause digestive problems, but it was rude as well. The social worker's concern with schedules reflected a general trend in child welfare advocacy toward a more structured agenda for children. As we saw in chapter 1, delegates to the Pan-American Child Congresses believed that even play should be highly regulated. The demand for more structure, supervision, and regulation of children coincided with the increasing state supervision of mothers. It also coincided with a desire to train children toward a more regimented ideal of "factory time," the better to adapt them to their future as urban laborers.

Child welfare advocates frowned upon corporal punishment. During a visit to one foster home a social worker witnessed one brother bite another, who began to cry. The worker instructed the mother to hug and console the child, which the mother refused to do. The lack of affection disturbed the welfare professional, who suspected that more serious abuse might be taking place. On the pretext of rearranging the child's clothing, the social worker checked to make sure there was no evidence of corporal punishment.[90]

Social workers carefully monitored children's sexuality as well. In addition to being concerned about homosexuality, social workers and foster mothers wanted to eradicate what they called "the vice" of masturbation. In one case the doctor recommended that in order to prevent this vice the child in question should take daily sunbaths and work harder. The sunbaths did not appear to work, as the foster mother later reported that she had cured the little boy of his "vice" by tucking in his blankets in such a way that he could not put his arms underneath.[91]

Children sometimes confounded social workers and foster mothers. One social worker reported that a child had been wetting his bed every night, creating decidedly unhygienic sleeping conditions and creating much extra work for his foster mother. At the suggestion of the social worker, the foster mother took the child to the doctor, who could find no medical problems. The child then confessed that he wet the bed because he was "too lazy" to get up at night and use the bathroom.[92]

The practice of monitoring the homes sometimes created clashes between the social workers and foster mothers. Welfare professionals often expected foster mothers to comply with standards of cleanliness and organization that must have been difficult with six small children in their care. Social workers could also be biased in the assumptions they made not only about the children but about the foster mothers as well. One social worker wrote of a foster mother that she was "of humble origin" and that "her manners and language reveal very little culture and education; she still has a very provincial style, but seems very friendly and attentive."[93] Most middle-class reformers, particularly those who believed in eugenics, would assume that someone from the countryside and of humble background would be racially inferior, since eugenicists tended to conflate class and race.

Foster mothers, not surprisingly, did not always appreciate the advice proffered. One woman, apparently annoyed by the social worker's frequent visits, answered her with "irony and despotism." According to the worker, on another occasion the foster mother behaved like a despot, and on a third occasion she criticized the SSA and was "indifferent" to the orders sent.[94] It is not clear from the report what upset the foster mother, but foster mothers were subject to intense scrutiny not only by the social workers but by the doctors and other professionals with whom they came in contact.

Doctors criticized the way they cared for their charges. For example, Bernardo Sepúlveda, director of the Department of Welfare, wrote to one woman in charge of a collective home, "I have received the Medical Inspector's report about your home and I am saddened to hear that the hygienic conditions are detestable. This results in prejudice against the children and affects the prestige of the program. From now on, please take particular care with the personal hygiene of our students."[95]

This scrutiny may not have been appreciated, especially if the mother considered herself well educated and middle class. In fact, in response to a similar complaint, one mother replied, "In answer to your memo, I must protest that only one student was found with a parasite in her hair, and this does not mean that all of the girls were to be found in detestable and unhygienic conditions. However, while lamenting the incident that brought this complaint against me, I will try in the future to maintain the home in the conditions which you desire."[96]

Nevertheless, the foster-care system allowed SSA officials to monitor their charges carefully and ensure that the children were being cared for in a "proper" manner. Officials reported that children attended school more regularly and that their health improved. The system also gave middle-class women respectable employment, allowing them to work within their homes. Child welfare advocates claimed that the system was important because "all countries that have well-organized welfare programs use foster homes. It has proved to be the cheapest way to do this, from an economic point of view, and most beneficial for the moral and intellectual development of the abandoned child—giving him a normal life that he would not have otherwise had."[97] Indeed, the system received attention from the United States. Fernanda Jones-Vargas, of New York City's Union Settlement, lauded the Mexican program, noting in particular the training program for foster mothers. She declared that the Mexican standards were on a level equal to those in the United States, if not higher, and she requested information on the curriculum of Mexico's schools of social service, with special attention to the program for fieldwork and classroom instruction.[98] Other programs organized tours of Mexican facilities, advertising them in U.S. social work journals.[99]

The SAP/SSA introduced the foster-care system in order to place children in a middle-class family setting. The hope was that these children would in time absorb middle-class work and consumer habits. Social workers exercised great control over foster homes, visiting foster families on a weekly basis and providing feedback and professional advice to the foster mothers. If a child's relatives wanted to see the child, it was up to the social worker to approve the visit. The SAP/SSA thus used female social workers to create specific family norms that bolstered the modernization of patriarchy in Mexico.[100]

For many years historians treated the family in Latin America as a trans-historical fact. According to these scholars, the family had always been male-headed and patriarchal, with women having few or no rights. More recent scholarship has debunked that myth, showing that many families in Latin America have been female-headed, and that women have had more agency within the family unit than previously acknowledged.[101] Recent feminist scholarship has also shed light on how the ideal of the bourgeois family was created by liberal elites in order to advance their modernization projects. Liberalism shifted power from the church to the state, and to male heads of household. This power shift was reflected in civil codes, labor laws, and, as this chapter has shown, in public health and welfare policy.

Mexican reformers, like their counterparts in Chile and Brazil, sought to shore up the family.[102] They believed that the economic dislocations of the Great Depression and then industrialization made it difficult for men to support their families. If a man abandoned or could not support his family, this hurt his wife and children; without economic resources the family could not educate their children. Reformers therefore sought to legalize marriage, to make it easier for men to support their families, and to provide a proper upbringing for children. Creating modern Mexican families was a central goal of the SAP/SSA, as was inculcating in Mexican children the middle-class values of hard work, hygiene, and responsible citizenship. The following chapter examines programs designed to help mothers, particularly single mothers, raise these model Mexican citizens.

3

SINGLE MOTHERS AND THE STATE

Mexican reformers saw social assistance as a way to bolster what they viewed as the appropriate family structure. Ideally, hardworking men supported their families, while their wives stayed home and raised their children using "modern" techniques. As hard as they worked to achieve this goal, however, reformers noted that many families were female-headed.

While SAP officials maintained that stable families were of the utmost importance to welfare policy, reformers recognized that mothers, in particular single mothers, were important to its mission as well. In fact, SAP statistics for 1941–42 showed that 34.9% of all people seeking social services were abandoned mothers, and 12.4% were widows. Thus 47.3% of all welfare recipients did not live in a male-headed household.[1] In 51.6% of all cases, the mother supported the family financially, although it is unclear whether these were single or married women.[2] The largest percentage of working mothers (27.1%) reported that they derived their income from domestic chores; another 18.3% worked as household servants and 14.7% as washerwomen. Others worked as seamstresses (5.7%), office workers (6.7%), waitresses (0.4%), industrial workers (3.2%), tortilla makers (5.4%), or in small businesses (3.5%); 11.5% were unemployed. By contrast, 46.8% of male heads of household were *obreros* (industrial workers) or *artesanos* (artisans).[3]

In order to protect mothers and children in female-headed households, the SAP sought to create programs that would help all poor mothers. Single mothers (either abandoned or widowed), who made up 47.3 percent of the SAP clientele, were especially targeted. The SAP aimed to serve as a surrogate father in fatherless homes, providing training and other guidance for the single working mothers and monitoring their children in schools and day-care centers.

A number of mother-child health centers were created to provide health care for these women and their children and were intended to reach the maximum number possible. Policymakers repeatedly referred to the poor as the "weak" class, presumably alluding to their earning capacity, though this term may also have referred to their perceived racial inferiority. As we have seen, the upper and middle classes generally saw the poor as racially unfit and ridden with vice and disease. Their alleged "weakness" could thus have referred to their physical health, their morals, or both.

The idea behind mother-child centers reflected the convergence of many different welfare discourses circulating in Mexico in the 1940s. The program was very similar, in some cases identical, to programs initiated by private, female-headed charities during the Porfirato. Unlike the programs of the 1930s, however, the centers did not aim to uplift or integrate women into an industrial economy. Instead, their goal was to train women as mothers and to help them find work they could perform within the home while caring for their children. The centers aimed to reconfigure the Mexican family so that it remained, in essence, a nuclear family—a family that produced "modern" (that is, hardworking and domesticated) citizens. The importance placed on mothers, particularly on mothers' health issues, also reflected eugenicist goals.

The centers' activities were directed primarily toward prenatal hygiene—care for mothers during pregnancy so that they could give birth to the healthiest possible offspring. Particular care was given to the food they consumed. The centers also immunized children against childhood diseases and launched campaigns to place homeless children in shelters or other programs.[4] The mother-child centers conformed to a new philosophy that required the direct and personal attention of all the technical personnel who staffed these centers; reformers believed that more efficient service could be provided if all of the activities were monitored and coordinated in one center. The centers also offered continuing education classes for nurses, social workers, and other personnel, and held weekly meetings to resolve problems.[5]

For example, the SSA founded the General Maximino Ávila Camacho mother-child center in 1945 and dedicated it to providing services for child protection "from the moment of conception until adolescence." Services included immunizations, medical care (which reduced maternal mortality rates from childbirth to zero by arranging for births to take place in hospitals or clinics), a breast-feeding nursery, a room for a mothers' group within the nursery, and mental hygiene classes for doctors, nurses, social workers, and day-care teachers. The classes were approved by UNAM and were also attended by foreign professionals, highlighting Mexican reformers' ties with international developments in health and welfare.[6]

The center's name reflected the cultural significance that the government attached to it. Maximino Ávila Camacho, the president's brother and the former governor of Puebla, died in 1945. Naming the center after him linked the highest levels of the PRI with the most modern of welfare services. Soledad Orozco de Ávila Camacho, President Ávila Camacho's wife, along with the wives of other prominent PRI leaders (among them the SSA minister's wife, Elena Díaz Lombardo de Baz, the president's sister, and Lázaro Cárdenas's wife), headed voluntary committees and established connections between the highest echelons of government and welfare activities and establishments that cemented the importance of welfare to the postrevolutionary government.

The center also provided hygienic and medical assistance to children from conception to adolescence, medical and hygienic assistance to mothers, social and educational assistance to preschool children, social assistance to families with children in need (as determined by on-site social workers), sanitation services to the area around the center, and training and professional development for the doctors, nurses, and social workers through participation in these services. In addition, the center created a facility to train mothers to breast-feed properly in order to assure healthy babies, which functioned as a day-care center for working mothers.[7] The mother-child centers used radio, flyers, and other means to advertise their services.[8] In order to supplement the professional welfare personnel at centers, the SAP/SSA turned to volunteers. Private cooperation helped the agency expand its services throughout this period.

Volunteer Committees

Gustavo Baz and his successors maintained throughout the 1940s that the state still held primacy in the fight to protect Mexican families and integrate them into the body politic and economy. They argued that the state, not the Catholic Church or other institutions, should educate and support proper Mexican families. But the SAP/SSA also argued that the private sector had an important role to play. In order to maximize support for its programs and policies, the agency created a parallel organization of voluntary committees for child welfare. The SAP/SSA saw their role as complementary in the fight against poverty. As one 1941 internal memo put it, "SAP, through the Dirección General de Asistencia Infantil, has intensified private invest-ment in favor of childhood, to be coordinated with official action, because ultimately the whole of society has responsibility for the conditions of mis-ery and abandonment into which thousands of children are born and raised. With the help of different sectors of society, child welfare can be imple-mented in a more full and effective manner."[9] Voluntary committees would provide money, staffing, and prestige to the ministry. They also allowed the SAP to tap into older charitable networks and redirect their energies toward state goals.

The SAP had previously divided Mexico City into a number of zones,[10] and it attached each of these committees to a zone, where it helped with the maintenance of the zone's mother-child center. For example, the Liga Femenina, a precursor to the voluntary committees, inaugurated its first welfare center in Tacubaya in 1938.[11] The new center consisted of a small bank, storeroom, pantry, and wardrobe. It provided emergency assistance to members of the community and sought donations of money as well as necessary goods such as work materials and medicine. The women hoped, however, that the center would provide not only emergency aid but educa-tion and training to the community according to the principles of the SAP. The SAP organized these committees with certain ground rules. First, they had to be composed of members who agreed to cooperate with the SAP in the development of programs for mothers and children, working to achieve the physical, mental, and social improvement of future generations. Second, although they were private entities, each committee was required to abide by SAP policy and make periodic reports to the SAP. In addition, SAP social workers and visiting nurses would provide the majority of the staff for these programs.[12]

Middle- and upper-class women made up the bulk of the membership of the committees. Although these committees had to create programs that followed SAP policy guidelines, they still functioned autonomously. The committees focused their energies on their welfare centers, promoting edu-cation for poor women. They also devoted themselves to fund-raising, often throwing lavish parties at some of Mexico City's top nightclubs to raise money for their programs. According to the SAP, Mex$59,000, a significant amount of money, was raised in this way in 1942.[13] Mathilde Rodríguez Cabo estimated that the construction of a new mother-child center in Co-lonia de Peralvillo had cost about Mex$47,289 thus far and that another $17,000 was needed.[14] Thus the money that private committees raised could go far in new constructions or in expanding services in existing centers.

In many ways, the women who staffed these committees were the "char-ity ladies" of the Porfiriato in the 1920s. These women viewed charity work as important but did not seek to transform society. They were not professionally trained, like the social workers and visiting nurses. Nevertheless, their resources were necessary to the SAP/SSA as it sought to expand welfare programs throughout the period.[15] These women provided an important source of manpower as well as money. *Asistencia* ran photos of well-dressed volunteers interacting with poor mothers and their children. One caption read: "Gifts for mothers—from time to time private cooperation, growing every day in the country, is felt in the Mothers' Clubs. We present the altruistic ladies of the Committees, as they distribute clothes, toys, candy, etc."[16] These women played an important role in expanding child welfare programs, even if they no longer had control over the nature of the policies and programs that their services allowed.

Each zone not only had a mother-child center; many also had a *casa de la madre*, or mothers' club, specifically devoted to the needs of mothers. By 1941 twenty-one voluntary committees existed, staffing and raising money for the clubs and centers. The mothers' clubs, according to their own statistics, registered ten thousand women. By 1955 there were thirty-eight mothers' clubs in Mexico.[17] In a letter asking the electricians' union for a donation, the head of one voluntary committee described the purpose of these centers as the provision of medical assistance for children, aid in cases of emergency, and breakfasts for preschool children. Centers also trained women in *pequeñas indústrias* such as dressmaking, glove making, manual labor, and practical cooking, as well as in problem solving. "Naturally," the writer stated, "the improvement of the mother reflects directly on that of the child."[18]

These programs taught women very specific types of job skills. Women were not being trained for the higher-paying skilled positions that characterized industrial labor. Middle-class reformers considered women unsuitable for that type of work. They preferred to teach the women *pequeñas indústrias* because this kind of work made use of women's supposed innate capacity to perform highly repetitive tasks, and of their allegedly innate ability to complete detailed work because of their smaller and more dexterous hands. The new job skills, however, were marketable, many could be performed in the home, and they allowed mothers to work and support their children.[19] These programs were similar to the SEP's vocational education programs of the 1920s and did not fundamentally challenge the idea that women's primary place was in the home.[20]

The *casas de la madre* aimed to conserve or reintegrate the family into society, acting to reconcile both individual and collective interests. These programs were divided into two types: casework for the individual, and programs for groups. Programs for individual women reflected the fact that the individual was not isolated but was part of a family as well as a larger community. These programs focused on teaching women to solve their own problems. It was hoped that women, thus assisted, could adapt and become "a useful element in the social environment." Thus each woman was assigned a caseworker, either a social worker employed by the SAP or a voluntary club member, who would investigate her circumstances and offer aid and training.[21]

The caseworker first went to the home of the applicant, inspected the dwelling, and offered advice on how to improve hygienic conditions and better manage the family's resources. The applicant, if chosen, could then be allowed to work in one of the *casa*'s workshops, her background and domestic responsibilities permitting. Women who worked in these workshops could also place their children in a *casa*-run day-care center. The day care was available to all working women, not just participants in the workshops, although they had to be registered members of the *casa*. In fact, by the late 1940s, voluntary committees were focusing almost exclusively on the creation of new day-care centers.

It was only after an applicant had been assessed by an SAP/SSA caseworker that emergency aid could be given. This aid could come in the form of money or in the form of clothing or breakfasts for children. Women were also offered places in shelters, where they could remain temporarily until they found new housing. These women were homeless because of either abandonment by their husbands or their own inability to keep up with rent payments. Group social work focused on education. Women were allowed to participate in the workshops only temporarily, so that workshops could train the largest number of women possible. These workshops were designed to teach women skills that they could then use in their own lives to improve their individual situations. The articles made in these workshops were then sold and the proceeds were reinvested in the *casa*; an unspecified portion was given to the women themselves, "as a stimulus."

The SAP/SSA designed these classes for mothers to complement the National Literacy Campaign and to teach women domestic and child-rearing skills. Classes included grammar, writing and computation, puericulture, and cooking with modern appliances. Finally, the *casas* offered recreation, such as a lending library and children's theater. The *casas* also sponsored camping trips for children in the countryside so that they would get exercise and fresh air, a goal that reflected eugenic ideas about promoting strong, healthy children. The camping trips may also have been intended to tie these children to the government—it was, after all, the government that provided these opportunities, and reformers may have seen this as creating loyal citizens.

While some child assistance centers contained *casas de las madres,* others organized mothers' clubs, which served much the same function as the *casas,* providing members with education and training in care of the home and family, vocational and productive activities, and social, pedagogical, and artistic activities.[22] They took classes four or five days a week, from 4:00 to 8:00 P.M. "Care of the home and family," or domestic economy, aimed "to give mothers and their daughters basic knowledge in order to manage and improve their homes and family's hygiene." Domestic economy classes had eight complementary components; they taught mothers how to manage the family's finances and schedule and how to resolve certain financial difficulties on their own. Mothers were taught the principles of sound nutrition and how to manage their kitchens, with particular attention to cleaning and preserving foodstuffs and purifying water. Home hygiene classes taught women the importance of sunlight, fresh air, potable water, and indoor plumbing. Teachers also stressed housekeeping and taught mothers how to clean washing machines, bathrooms, and furniture, how to make beds, how to kill insects, how to clean and disinfect floors, how to prevent accidents, and how to put out fires. They also showed women how to arrange and decorate their homes economically. Finally, classes taught how to machine-wash clothes, iron, mend clothes, cook, and do carpentry. The carpentry class was designed to complement the home decoration class, since the mothers learned there how to build their own furniture.[23] Many of these classes seemed designed to help families adjust to an urban environment and to participate in a capitalist economy. They taught women how to use modern appliances like washing machines and how to manage money. For women who had recently arrived from the countryside, this may have been the first time they entered into a cash economy, and learning how to manage a household's budget would have been important.

Women also participated in workshops that again focused on promoting *pequeñas indústrias,* making curtains, dolls, toys, insecticides, salsas, candies, sweaters, and socks. Classes also taught dressmaking, weaving, and how to preserve fruit and vegetables. These workshops taught women valuable vocational skills that allowed them to participate in the workforce, supporting themselves and their families. They also showed women how to sell the products they made for profit, reinvesting the profit in the centers themselves.

In some cases, interest in these products came from as far away as New York. In 1942 a Mr. Fred Leighton, an American in the import/export business, contacted the SAP about the possibility of importing Mexican handicrafts made by the mothers' clubs into the United States. He was particularly interested in the hand-woven curtains then being produced by some of the clubs. With the SAP's approval he sent an American expert to Mexico to show the clubs how to improve the efficiency of their workshops and to give them tips on current U.S. fashions and tastes. Mr. Leighton made another trip, under the auspices of Mrs. Baz (the wife of Dr. Gustavo Baz, the head of SAP), who backed the project very enthusiastically. Mr. Leighton had ambitions to import other items as well, such as Mexican handcrafted toys, which were particularly in demand since the United States was not producing toys owing to the war effort, as well as fruit preserves and honey, attractively packaged in "typical Mexican style." Enelda Fox, the head of the SAP's Department of Child Welfare, expressed the SAP's support: "These industries promise to have good success; it is always possible to be on the right track. The United States wants to buy large quantities, perhaps hundreds if not thousands. It would be a good opportunity to take advantage of the war situation and win for Mexico some new industries whose products can be sold to improve the economic conditions of needy mothers."[24] It is not clear whether the deal came through, but it is indicative of the general trend in Mexico toward manufacturing products for export to the United States, whose economy was tied up in war production.

Clubs also organized recreational activities for mothers, such as socials and excursions to the countryside. In addition, they sought to help mothers help themselves, as women came together to form mutual aid societies and placed their savings in club-run savings boxes. Women also took reading and arithmetic classes as part of the National Literacy Campaign.[25]

These clubs taught poor women skills designed to allow themselves to support their children, but, again, they did not fundamentally challenge the idea that a woman's primary responsibility was motherhood. The clubs also gave upper-class women a role to play. This elite desire to "uplift" poor women was not new in the 1940s, but the combination of private-sector volunteerism and state social work was.[26] As with the family programs, the intent was not to "liberate" mothers but to update motherhood through the construction of a modernized patriarchy. And like Catholic social action, reformers aimed to ameliorate poverty but not fundamentally to challenge the existing social system. These programs also allowed the SAP/SSA to intervene directly and consistently in the homes and lives of poor women. In order to participate in the centers, mothers and their children had to be regularly examined by the medical staff. Mothers also had to allow regular home visits by social workers or visiting nurses, in order to ensure that they were implementing what they had learned in their classes. This intervention allowed the state to usurp the father's role in caring for and protecting his family.

While archival material gives us only a glimpse of how women understood these programs, and of how they applied—or failed to apply—the lessons learned to daily life, some records indicate that mothers did find these clubs useful and that they organized to demand the services these clubs provided. Letters to the SAP/SSA from various mothers' clubs asked for more classes and centers. One woman wrote Gustavo Baz in 1943 to ask if he "would favor our humble *colonia* with a hygiene center," explaining, "we need this assistance because here there is neither a doctor or pharmacy. We would also infinitely appreciate a recreation center and park for the children, as they have no place to play; right now they play in the middle of the street, in constant danger of suffering an accident, and also we would like approval for water at the school, as well as breakfasts, because the children are very poor and they go to school sometimes without breakfast, begging water from the neighbors." The petition was successful; the SSA sent someone to help set up the requested center.[27]

Another mothers' club petitioned the ministry in 1946.

> We, the women forming the "Mothers' Club Joel Luévano," mothers of children who attend the breakfasts, students and ex-students of the different classes, and we mothers who have received the benefits of the consultations with Doctors Luís Sánchez Mejía, Alberto Origel, and Alfonso Urquijo, implore you, after having the honor of your visit to our center, and knowing as you do the complete history of the founding of our casa de la madre . . . by a voluntary committee. Well, we have known that we are in danger of losing our casa de la madre and we know that this is because the SSA thinks that it should not pay rent for a center that only administers some breakfasts. But the casa does more than just that, and for our casa we beg you . . . we do not deserve to have our casa closed. We have a right to have aid for pregnant mothers, for food for nursing mothers, for guidance for child rearing . . . like in other centers in the DF, those that we cannot attend because of their distance from our Tlalpan and the cost of the journey.[28]

We can surmise from these two examples that some women in Mexico City not only used the diverse services provided by these welfare centers but came to believe that they had a right to these services in the immediate vicinity.

Other letters came from middle-class women's groups requesting services on behalf of the mothers. Feminist organizations like the Bloque Nacional de Mujeres Revolucionarios organized to petition for more services in poor neighborhoods. This group asked for day-care centers for the children of women who sold things in the markets of the Ixtapalapa, Xichimilco, Milpa Alta, San Gregorio, and Jamaica neighborhoods.[29] Not all requests came from poor neighborhoods. A letter from the Sociedad de Padres de la Escuela "Alberto Correa" noted that although its school was located in the affluent Colonia Roma neighborhood, many of the students were the children of domestic servants, artisans, or tortilla makers who worked in the area. These parents, the letter said, "earn a meager salary that does not allow them to spend for their children, not just for their clothing but nor can they provide adequate nutrition." The letter requested that the SSA provide school breakfasts, as the Sociedad de Padres, which had been providing them at its own expense, could no longer afford to do so. The letter estimated that 150 students were affected (see map for an illustration of which neighborhoods had centers, both SAP/SSA-run and private, that distributed free breakfasts in Mexico City in 1943).[30]

While most of the time things ran smoothly between the SAP/SSA and the voluntary committees, confusion sometimes arose over which entity paid for which services. For example, Isabel J. de Domínguez, the president of the Mexico City Central Committee, wrote to Guillermo Lechuga, the vice president of the National Executive Committee for the Pro–Mother and Child Campaign and subdirector of the SAP's Department of Child Welfare, that "some difficulties have arisen between the voluntary committees and the mothers' clubs, with respect to the classes offered." She attached copies of meeting notes stating that a representative of the SAP, Dr. Viniegra, had promised that the agency would pay for the classes.[31] Lechuga replied that the SAP would no longer pay the salaries of those teaching classes in the mothers' clubs. De Domínguez wrote a second letter to Lechuga, again pleading her committee's case. According to de Domínguez, the SAP had told her that paying the teacher salaries "was one of the functions for which private cooperation was created." "Private cooperation cannot be rigid in its direction," she wrote, "however noble that may be. Voluntary committees should do what is necessary in the present." The letter was signed by seventeen members of the committee.[32]

Confusion may have arisen, at least in the early years, because the SAP professionals coordinating the voluntary committees were often overextended. In 1938 Enelda Fox, then office manager for the SAP's Department of Child Welfare, wrote to her supervisor, "All of the work done in coordinating the mothers' clubs is done by three people, Dalina Salgado, Carmen Jara Vda. de Cuesta, and Rosa Maria Carnaco, with the help of a typist. They are behind in their work because they do not have the time to complete everything. They are willing and able to do the work but need help—I

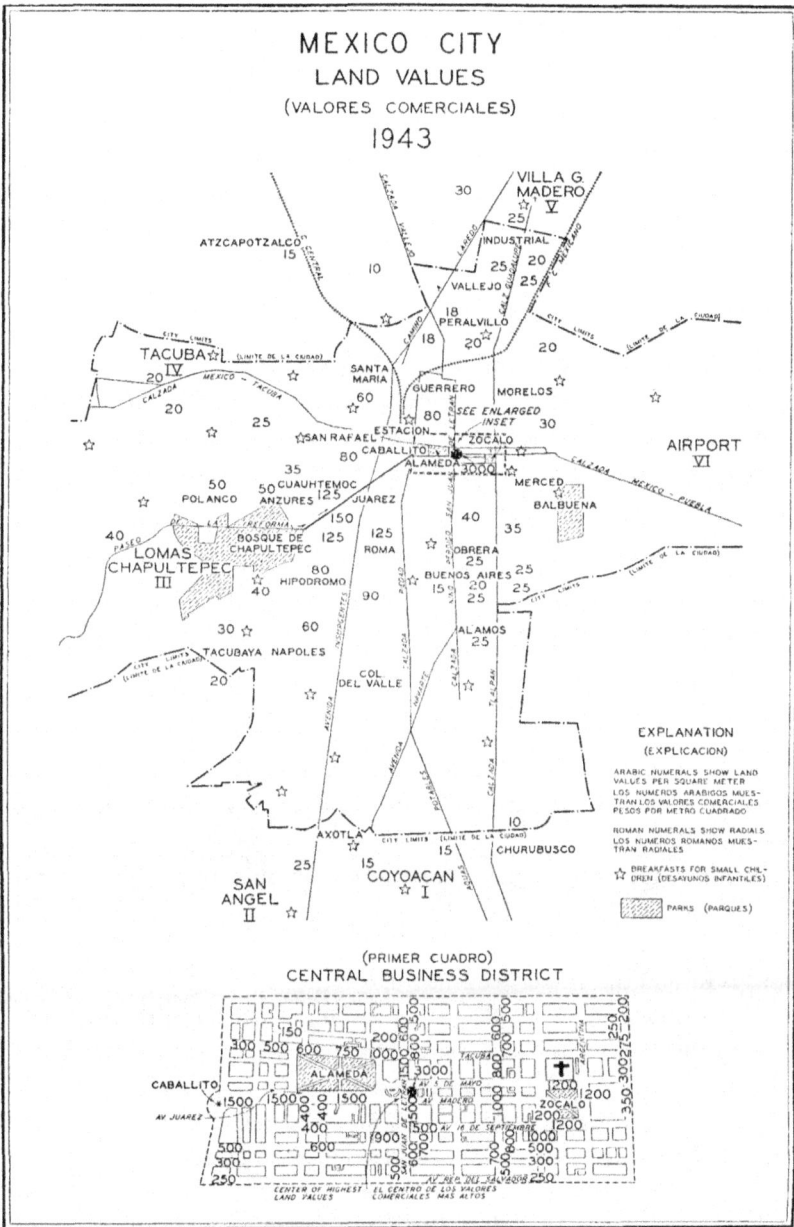

Map 1 Land values and locations of welfare centers (public and private) in Mexico City

Source: N.S. Hayner, "Mexico City: Its Growth and Configuration," *American Journal of Sociology* 50, no. 4 (1945): 302. © University of Chicago Press. Used by permission of the publisher.

would like to request three more personnel to train in order to help direct the activities of the mothers' clubs. It is urgent that this important labor not disintegrate for a lack of attention and control." Fox also requested more trained social workers for other sections of the office, noting the increase in requests for aid and the corresponding need for more staff. "I very caringly beg you to choose persons with the right preparation," she wrote, "or at least a sufficient educational level, with an aptitude for learning and a desire to work, without egoism or laziness but with devotion."[33]

These welfare centers empowered women to make claims upon the Mexican government before they had legal right to vote. These women didn't just take advantage of government programs; they believed that it was their right to have them conveniently located. The centers allowed women to participate in society through their roles as mothers. They also gave the Mexican government a means of integrating women of all classes into its modernization project, to the immeasurable economic and political benefit of the nation.

The Casa Amiga de la Obrera: A Discursive Intersection

One case in particular demonstrates how these goals played out in the daily lives of women in Mexico City and shows how both reformers and poor women understood their rights in postrevolutionary Mexico. This story centers on the Casa Amiga de la Obrera, a product of the Porfirian welfare movement.

The first Casa Amiga de la Obrera was established in 1887 by Carmen Romero Rubio de Díaz, the president's wife, who maintained and managed it until 1915. The Casa functioned as a school for the children of working mothers. In 1916 the school reopened under the administration of Mexico City's Department of Public Benevolence. The school was intimately connected to the community, and the children themselves participated in its administration. The students organized many groups and performed many services; for example, they published a school bulletin and wrote letters for illiterates in the community. They also developed cooperatives and business committees and organized a union for street vendors (comerciantes ambulantes). The students created moral organizations as well, including a committee for truth (to combat lying), a group for the defense of correct speech, and a cleanliness committee. Finally, they ran a teachers' bank and a literacy group for indigents.[34]

By the 1930s two Casas Amigas de la Obrera were in operation. According to the Department of Benevolence, their mission had "a social character"; they sought "to help women who need to work, making it impossible to care for their own children." The department argued that the Casas should be considered the women's "home, waking in the children a spirit of initiative and inventiveness, teaching them to have self-confidence in order to participate in the social process, conscious of their responsibilities." The students attending the Casas Amigas were all children of women workers, between the ages of seven and fourteen. The mothers dropped off their children at the school at 7:30 in the morning, before they went to work. The children were given breakfast, and classes began at 8:30. After morning classes, the students received a "hygienic and nutritious" meal, with "the goal of preparing healthy and strong men" (although both boys and girls attended the school). A typical meal consisted of rice or pasta, meat, salad, and vegetables, or an egg, beans, fruit, and bread—what reformers would have considered a nutritious and well-balanced meal. The students worked in workshops all afternoon and left school at 5:00 P.M.[35]

Reformers believed that children attending the Casas Amigas would have access to better education, nutrition, and health care than children of working mothers who did not attend a comprehensive school. Their goal was to integrate these children of the "weak classes" into the national project through the school's intensive services, focusing in particular on vocational education. Like the foster-care system and the family dining halls, however, this was not charity. Parents were expected to pay for the schooling, although admittedly at a subsidized rate.

School administrators believed that students had the right to a formal education, and to receive books and school supplies free of charge. They also asserted that the children had the right to health care and sufficient food. They agreed that the children should be treated with dignity and respect, so that they would develop into "virtuous citizens." But administrators also maintained that the students had obligations as well. They were expected to attend all classes and be punctual. They had to complete all of their homework assignments and any chores necessary at the school. Finally, the students had to be "scrupulously" clean at all times and were expected to help keep the school spotless as well.[36] In order to encourage cleanliness, school officials held "cleanliness contests."[37] Teachers held arithmetic and drawing competitions as well, to encourage learning. They also planned social activities, such as literary and musical performances and events like the "day of the tree" and "day of the soldier." The school took children on field trips to museums and parks and organized civic clubs like the Tree Society.[38]

While the Casas Amigas seem to have been committed to a progressive pedagogy and did their utmost to integrate students into Mexican society, problems still arose. One letter in particular sheds light on the competing values and aspirations of teachers, students, and parents. On May 13, 1937, three representatives of the Casa Amiga de la Obrera No. 1's Mothers' Society wrote to Beneficencia Pública (soon to become the SAP), and sent a copy to the president, complaining of improprieties committed by the new director of the school, Ignácia Calderón, a teacher, Paz Gallardo, and the school's cook, Maria Luisa. The mission of the school was to help working mothers support their families, the letter began, and to turn out "moral and materially useful individuals," not "social parasites." This mission had been compromised by the incomprehension, foolishness, and bad faith of the three school workers.

According to the Mothers' Society, the previous director of the school, María de La Luz Arías, had done an excellent job, encouraging a spirit of organization and cooperation in her students, who, with the help of the Mothers' Society, started a school store and organized fourteen workshops, all at no cost to the SAP. The workshops and school store were run by cooperatives, which enabled them to remain self-sufficient. Under the leadership of Ignácia Calderón, however, the store, workshops, and cooperatives functioned irregularly and sometimes not at all, and teachers had resorted to old-fashioned pedagogy. Moreover, the letter charged, Calderón was extremely hostile to the Mothers' Society. The mothers complained that the students were being punished unfairly and that staff members were behaving inappropriately. If a child was late, unkempt, had dirty clothes, or had not completed homework assignments, he or she was suspended from school for the day. This kind of punishment was excessive, the mothers complained, and was contrary to the school's goal of preventing juvenile vagrancy. Other punishments were also extreme, they alleged; for example, if one youngster spilled water at lunch, no one was allowed to drink water at lunch that day.

Children of Mothers' Society members in particular were singled out for persecution, the letter alleged. During the previous year several students had broken a window while playing. Calderón had suspended all twenty-three children for the day and told them they could return when each child paid twelve centavos to replace the glass. One student could not come up with the money and was told to go sell baskets in the plaza until he raised the twelve centavos. His mother, a member of the Mothers' Society, complained to Calderón about this treatment, and the following year Paz Gallardo, one of the teachers, expelled the boy, declaring that he needed to be whipped by a man. The mothers saw this as retaliation for his mother's challenging the director. The letter gave other examples of children of Mothers' Society members being expelled or treated poorly by the director and her staff. One

girl, who had ten siblings and whose mother did not work, was not permitted to enroll in the school because Calderón accused the mother of running
a brothel. The child was not allowed to attend classes until a doctor certified
that she was a virgin.

In addition, the mothers alleged, Calderón and all of the teachers got
drunk during a field trip to Ixtlahuaca, setting a very bad example for the
children. They also claimed that Paz Gallardo had bragged that she could
do whatever she wanted because she knew someone important and could
not be fired. Finally, the mothers accused Calderón of embezzlement, as
funds collected from the mothers and the profits from some of the workshops could not be accounted for. The mothers demanded that Beneficencia
Pública fire the director and her staff and return the school to the state it
had enjoyed before Calderón took over as director. They also asked that
their children be protected from retribution if Calderón was permitted to
stay. The agency would perform a great public service, they said, if it reformed the school.[39]

The response to this letter, if there was one, could not be found in the
archives, but a report by Ignácia Calderón on the activities of the school in
1939 suggests that she was not removed from her position. It is nonetheless
significant that the mothers wrote to the government. They articulated a
solid understanding of the school's mission, and they saw themselves as
integral to that mission. They clearly derived a sense of pride from a well-
functioning school, and they saw it as beneficial to their children. We cannot
know whether their allegations were accurate, but it is interesting that the
mothers framed their charges in such a way that they would attract the
attention of professional welfare workers. They accused the teachers of
using "old-fashioned" pedagogy, of engaging in corporal punishment, of
abusing their power, and of getting drunk on the job. The director had even
challenged the morality of a young girl. All of these accusations challenged
the efficacy of welfare reforms, which aimed to bring modern techniques to
welfare and education services. As the director of another Casa Amiga
wrote, "The teaching program that we follow . . . has as its end the development of programs of practical utility, based on scientific laws and principles,
and on Article Three of the Constitution."[40] Expelling students, closing
workshops, and threatening to beat children was neither modern nor scientific pedagogy. The mothers clearly understood the goals of the school and
complained when they saw their rights and the rights of their children being
violated. These women, like the members of other Mothers' Societies, saw
themselves as an integral part of postrevolutionary society. This sense of
participation had its roots in the Porfiriato, when the Casa Amiga and

mothers' clubs were founded. The letter reflects the intersection of the local and the international, the old and the new.

As I argue throughout this book, the intervention of the state in family life—in particular its assumption of paternal duties when fathers were absent—updated and modernized patriarchy. The SAP/SSA acted as a father figure in female-headed households, offering assistance through health and welfare programs that presumably would have been provided by working fathers. It is noteworthy that modern patriarchy wore a female face. While the head of the SAP/SSA and its top officials were male, women nevertheless played an important role in the creation and implementation of health and welfare policy through social work and voluntary committees. These women were complicit in creating a system that sought to replicate the male-headed household. While social workers and volunteers may not have seized the historical moment and implemented more radical social change, we must realize that many women saw themselves as involved in a significant social movement. Professional social work or participation in a voluntary committee gave women a political voice and a role in creating a modern, progressive society.

Steve Stern, though his concept of the "patriarchal pact," argues that women acquiesced in the patriarchal system—that they remained in situations that we may see as difficult or abusive—because they received certain benefits from doing so.[41] We can look at welfare policy in this light as well. Middle-class women did not rise up to challenge social conventions because they received tangible benefits from helping to restructure patriarchal social relations in a more progressive way. Participation in this system gave these women political access during a period when they lacked the right to vote. And poor women arguably received more services and better education for themselves and their children than they had under previous regimes.

This transformation took place in the context of rapidly changing social roles for all Mexicans. As Anne Rubenstein argues in *Bad Language, Naked Ladies, and Other Threats to the Nation*, rapid migration from country to city and economic and demographic expansion re-created gender roles for women, linking "modern girls" (*chicas modernas*) with consumption. In much the same way that welfare reformers used "modern" welfare reform to criticize the "traditional," advertisers and social commentators used the categories of modern and traditional both to sell products and (in the case of conservative commentators) to condemn the consumption. As Rubenstein argues, the traditional and the modern were categories that developed *at the same time*; one could not exist without the other.

"Modern" women were asked to be consumers. Welfare reformers also saw the modern in the construction of a male-headed family. If, in the eyes of advertisers and other arbiters of consumer culture, a *chica moderna* was independent, from the perspective of social reformers a "modern" woman was a scientific mother, living in a properly formed family and training hardworking, disciplined children. Both were new roles for women and both deliberately played on middle-class assumptions of what it meant to be modern.

The ultimate beneficiary of these changing roles was the PRI itself. With the ideal of a male-headed family firmly in place, the PRI enjoyed political stability and began to create an educated workforce for its industrial project. In the 1930s and 1940s many of the programs focused on Mexico City. After World War II (and after the merging of the SAP with Salubridad to form the SSA), reformers looked to the countryside in their efforts to modernize Mexico's population. The next chapter examines the SSA's efforts to expand both urban and rural welfare work after the war. It also explores the relationship between the PRI, gender, and welfare during the cold war.

4

THE POSTWAR YEARS:

Disease Eradication, Sanitation, and Development

In "The Biggest Treasure," a story published in *Salud*, one of the SSA's periodicals, a young street vendor named Fernando wins the lottery. He moves his wife, Margarita, and young son to a middle-class *colonia* and buys a Buick. He loves the Buick and spends most of his time taking care of the car—washing it, changing the oil, and fixing any small problems that arise. One day a doctor visits, and he and Fernando discuss the Buick and Fernando's extensive care for the car. The doctor then notices the little boy. He examines the child and discovers multiple health problems. The boy is malnourished, the result of snacking on candy all day and not having regular meals. The doctor chastises the parents—Fernando for spending more time caring for his car than for his son, and Margarita for not taking advantage of the local child welfare center, where the boy could receive free medical and dental care and where she could learn to care for him properly. Fernando and Margarita thank the doctor and vow to become more responsible parents.[1]

By the mid-1940s, SSA programs designed to help Mexican parents like Fernando and Margarita raise healthy children were well established. Mexican politicians and international reformers alike lauded Mexico's progress. "The Biggest Treasure" is in some ways self-congratulatory. The doctor can point Fernando and Margarita to free government-run health and welfare services. But the story also reflects middle-class mores. The doctor, a professional, is portrayed as an expert; the mother needs his tutelage. And the poor family, now suddenly well off, exhibits what the middle class might consider appropriate consumer behavior—they buy a house in a good neighborhood and purchase an American car. The only problem is that they do not know how to take good care of their child, a problem that could be remedied with government help.

The Ninth Pan-American Child Congress was held in Caracas, Venezuela, in 1948. Mexico does not appear to have sent a delegation to this congress, although the reports and other notes on the congress appear in the Mexican archives. The SSA sent delegations to various international sanitation meetings in 1948 and hosted several in Mexico City as well. The Mexican government forged a partnership with Unicef in 1954. It is clear from the policies initiated in Mexico that even if an official delegation was not present, Mexican reformers were still in dialogue with their Pan-American counterparts regarding maternal-child welfare in the postwar era. Fernando and Margarita's story reflects shifting transnational ideas about child health, welfare, and nutrition that circulated in the Pan-American Child Congress and other international venues. These concerns about class, race, and gender shaped Mexican policy.

The SSA continued to expand services throughout the 1950s, in large part through partnerships with private entities (like volunteer committees) or international organizations such as Unicef. This chapter examines the consolidation of urban services in Mexico City and some of the rural initiatives spearheaded by Mexican reformers' involvement in transnational discourses surrounding public health and the international renewal of interest in the countryside. It also looks at how the PRI capitalized on the work of the SSA to consolidate its own authority during the late 1940s and 1950s.

President Miguel Alemán took office in 1946 and continued the industrialization policies he inherited from his predecessor. He also inherited economic problems from the previous administration. Inflation continued, and the policy of agricultural production for export led to continued food shortages in the cities.[2] In addition, the Mexican government had to contend with the U.S. government's lack of interest in Latin America. While World War II had forced the United States to treat its southern neighbors as partners in the war effort, a destroyed European economy now preoccupied U.S. policymakers. The U.S. government refused to create a Marshall Plan for Latin America, and economies such as Mexico's suffered from decreased U.S. demand for exports.

Postwar contingencies continued this trend and changed the role of women in reform discourse. Unicef's priorities and the rhetoric of the Ninth Pan-American Child Congress redefined women's role to emphasize women's biological function. Mothers were important, and health-care programs targeted them through pre- and postnatal care programs, but only to ensure that they had physically healthy offspring. Their role in social motherhood had all but disappeared, as the state moved in to guarantee what it considered a child's legal rights. While delegates no longer spoke of maternal-child welfare in terms of a civilizing mission, that is, with a focus on eugenics and racial uplift for the poor, their beliefs nevertheless persisted throughout the 1950s. They believed that the poor in Latin America prevented sufficient national development because of their "backward" attitudes. They would have to be trained and educated if Latin America was to progress. But postwar reformers saw the state, rather than mothers, as responsible for this training.

In Mexico, however, a tradition of rural welfare work begun after the revolution mitigated this trend in the Mexican countryside. As Mary Kay Vaughan argues, the violence of the revolution worried the new government. According to reformers, the poor, particularly the rural poor, had to be "domesticated" in order to fit into postrevolutionary society.[3] The government's newly created Secretaría de Educación Pública (SEP) sent cultural missions to the countryside to teach peasants proper health and hygiene and to show *campesina* mothers proper child-rearing techniques. In the 1930s the SEP's socialist education project continued the work of the missions. Socialist education sought to rework the *campesinos* as modern participants in a capitalist society.[4] Thus, by the 1950s, Mexican reformers had been working in the countryside for roughly thirty years. Their work built upon existing Mexican programs rather than creating new ones, as other Latin American nations began to do. New programs shifted away from social motherhood and toward disease prevention and the health of mothers and children.

The shift reflected the reality that many maternal-child programs had been implemented successfully across Latin America. It also reflected new cold war conditions. Increasing state power combined with anticommunist rhetoric rendered movements advocating social change and transformation suspicious, if not dangerous. Women across Latin America had achieved suffrage by the end of the 1950s as well. Finally, any postwar international funding for child-maternal welfare came largely through Unicef, an organization that shifted emphasis away from social change to vaccinations and sanitation projects. Cold war contingencies encouraged Latin American reformers to emphasize legal child protections after World War II rather than risk the displeasure of both the United States and their own governments by advocating "radical" changes in economic redistribution or education.

The Ninth Pan-American Child Congress and Unicef

If relations between the United States and Latin America were couched in terms of a partnership during the war, the postwar years were characterized by U.S. neglect. Latin American nations called for greater American aid to help their economies develop and capitalize on economic gains made during the war. Latin Americans, in short, wanted a Marshall Plan. U.S officials, on the other hand, called for greater private investment and an end to nationalistic economic policies in Latin America. These divergent positions manifested themselves in the Dumbarton Oaks and Chapultepec conferences, held in 1944 and 1945, respectively.[5]

During the war and immediate postwar period, the United States had supported greater Latin American democratization, but this support diminished with the creation of the United Nations and in the face of Latin American nationalism. In addition, the United States cancelled many of its contracts for supplies and materials immediately after the war. This move had no immediate impact on Latin American economies, because dollar reserves built up during the war allowed these economies to continue to import goods from the United States. But by 1947 Latin American countries had depleted their reserves and faced balance-of-payments deficits. By this point the cold war occupied U.S. attention, and no further funding was promised to the region. As Rosemary Thorp comments, "Aside from the Communist world, in 1951 Latin America stood out as the single regional bloc that was not covered by a U.S aid program; in 1945–1951 Belgium and Luxembourg together received more aid than the whole of Latin America."[6]

Because they saw Latin America as relatively safe from the Communist threat, U.S. officials decided to suspend government aid to the region. The result was a slowing of import-substitution industrialization and rampant inflation. By the end of the 1940s Latin American governments were contending with an increasingly urban population, significant inflation, and, as during the war, food shortages.[7] These conditions, along with the establishment of Unicef in Latin America, prompted a shift in the discourse. Unicef's concentration on rural areas was the product of its history in Europe and Asia. After World War II, economic conditions in both rural and urban areas in Latin America, as well as Unicef's own emphasis on the countryside, prompted policymakers to focus on rural areas.

The Ninth Pan-American Child Congress and Children's Rights

The Ninth Pan-American Child Congress sought to institutionalize several of the programs and policies discussed during previous congresses, as the emphasis shifted to protecting the legal rights of children and to forming a Pan-American standard for the protection of those rights. Policymakers focused on mother-child centers, childhood education, and the protection of children and families through the court system. For the first time, delegates began to stress the importance of international rather than purely Pan-American alliances for aid. After the war the international scene had changed, and policymakers saw Latin America as part of the international postwar movement for maternal and child health.

Reformers attending the ninth congress reiterated the importance of mother-child centers, calling for construction of more of them throughout the region and the consolidation of child services into them. Delegates felt that services for maternal and child health needed to be integrated at the local level, and that these services should be complementary and should include sanitation, health services, rural medicine, mental hygiene and dental services, nurseries, school lunches, child care, and milk programs. Policymakers continued to emphasize that the social and economic health of the family had to be maintained in order to guarantee proper childhood development. They advocated programs that would treat the family as a whole and would "uplift" a family impoverished by economic difficulties, physical impediments, or social maladjustment. Child nutrition in particular was stressed because, as one delegate put it, "given the importance of the problem for the future well-being of American nations, it is recommended that the theme of child nutrition and the illnesses associated with the lack of proper nutrition be treated."[8]

Child nutrition gained in importance in part because of Unicef's efforts in Europe and also because of greater understanding in the Americas of the health problems in children associated with poor diet. Policymakers agreed that the government should guarantee that all children had a proper diet and that the provision of food, provided free of charge to children in need, should be a top priority. They even held that failure to provide children with a proper diet should be considered a criminal act. A qualified social service employee, in conjunction with the civil court system, would determine need "as quickly as possible, with priority given to the determination of need over any other civil business."[9] Once again, this policy advocated an increased role for the state and the need for a professionally trained bureaucracy. It was no longer sufficient for parents to simply declare that their children needed more food; this need now had to be determined by welfare professionals.

Policymakers also continued to emphasize the central importance of childhood education. Delegates moved toward guaranteeing proper education at all levels of society, not just in the schools. Of particular interest was the protection of a child's intellectual, physical, and moral development, especially in the realm of recreation. Educators called for the establishment of children's theaters, libraries, and sports leagues, all of which were to focus on children's moral improvement. To this end, delegates advocated the prohibition of reading material that a central censorship committee deemed inappropriate for children. Also forbidden were public lectures, plays, and other cultural offerings considered a threat to the health and moral development of children.[10]

After two decades of emphasis on urban education, delegates to the Ninth Pan-American Child Congress began to focus their attention on rural education and services—perhaps because of Unicef's emphasis on rural programs in Europe and, especially, Asia. This shift to the countryside also reflected government planners' renewed emphasis on agricultural exports to help their balance-of-payment situation. Educators argued that children in rural areas deserved the same educational opportunities that urban children enjoyed, and they advocated state-sponsored primary education to wipe out illiteracy in rural areas. Rural education was to be tailored to the needs of peasants, acting as a "guide and force to propel the progress of the area, developing positive values that peasants and their communities possess, as well as working to change the negative values."[11] Presumably these values were hard work and discipline, since rural areas produced food for the cities, where food shortages were provoking urban unrest, as well as for export.

Policymakers also emphasized rural health and sanitation services, which were integral to maximum agricultural production. "The governments of America should interest themselves in resolving, in a just and scientific manner, the economic and sanitary problems of peasant communities," the delegates maintained. "Economic and legal agrarian reforms are essential to the educational mission."[12] No less than urban workers, rural workers had to be trained and disciplined to do their part for the developing economy. Like their urban counterparts, peasants would be more productive if they lived in economically stable and healthy families. It would be the state's educational mission to train peasants to be "better," that is, modern, farmers, just as mothers had to be trained to be better mothers.

Not only were Latin American nations industrializing, but their economies relied increasingly on agricultural exports. Latin American governments viewed efficient agricultural production as a means of bringing in desperately needed foreign currency.[13] Thus rural development in Latin American nations in the 1950s was linked to the rise of agribusiness. Governments advocated a more "efficient" system of agricultural production, in essence forcing peasants off their own plots of land and onto large farms geared to the export market. These moves were not uncontested, and many peasant movements called for more just agrarian reforms. Certainly this was not a new trend; large landowners had been systematically alienating peasants from their land for centuries. In the context of the cold war, however, Latin American governments saw campaigns for peasants' rights as a dangerous move toward socialism that would only encourage the Soviet Union's desire to expand. Education, health, and welfare services would make peasants more productive and at the same time combat peasant insurgency. Rural teachers would teach peasants from an early age in order to ensure the "rational cultivation" of the land.[14]

Educators emphasized the importance of preschool education. It was not enough that children attend primary school and, when possible, secondary school; education had to begin as early in life as possible. They envisioned programs in educational centers that would teach small children skills commensurate with their age and also provide medical and welfare assistance. These programs, they argued, would reduce high death rates among young children. Needless to say, the teachers who worked in these centers were to be specially trained; in fact, they were to have at least as much training as their counterparts in primary and secondary schools. The preschool centers were to be located in areas where many mothers worked; in addition to educating the young, these centers would offer working mothers child-care classes. Finally, policymakers called for the creation of private organizations, under the aegis of the state, to fill children's medical and welfare needs. This also reflected Unicef's call for private funding, given the lack of aid from the United States.[15]

Once children entered primary school, policymakers argued that they needed to have a "progressive education" inspired by "the democratic philosophy that harmonizes one's individual liberties with fair social relations."[16] Reformers also called for the creation of a Latin American educational center that would bring teachers together to discuss pedagogy and coordinate activities across the region. This emphasis on democracy reflected the cold war conviction that development was important not only so that Latin America could progress but also to curtail communist activities.

As mentioned above, delegates to the 1948 congress also began to advocate the establishment of a legal system to guarantee the rights of the child. While this was not new, the ninth congress gave it greater emphasis than previous congresses had. Delegates now made more detailed suggestions about how and when legal institutions should be created. Specifically, policymakers called for the establishment of a special court system for children and the codification of children's legal rights. Of special concern was the legal status of abandoned children.

Delegates at the 1948 congress argued that the "modern state should allocate the largest possible amount of economic resources to combat child abandonment. Social security measures and other laws aimed to improve the life of the popular classes should be important factors in the reduction of child abandonment."[17] If at all possible, children should be left in their homes, but if this was impossible, they were to be placed in foster homes or institutions arranged to mimic family life. Delegates also wanted a special tribunal solely for children that would enforce the laws established by the children's code. This body of law, they argued, would be inspired by the general principles of the rights of children and should follow a technically formulated plan. Specifically, this code was to "formulate, regulate, and protect the right of children to live in conditions that will allow them to grow and develop physically, intellectually, and morally to the best of their ability."[18]

> This code should cover all children in each country, regardless of their nationality, race, religion, or socioeconomic condition. All nations, when possible, should also work to protect their children who reside outside the borders of their own state. The code should promulgate the right of the child to know his/her parents; have the state guarantee health and welfare; not be exploited or maltreated, either morally or physically; enjoy an education that promotes democratic values; be protected by special laws and courts; not be considered delinquent; have equal access to justice under the law no matter the child's economic status; not be separated from his/her family except in cases when the child would suffer grave danger; not be forced to practice or be taught religions other than the one practiced in the family home; not suffer humiliating judgments because of illegitimate birth.[19]

Under this code the state was obligated to care for a child until the age of eighteen if the parents proved unfit, and to create institutions to provide this care. In addition, delegates maintained, the state should coordinate public care with private institutions in order to guarantee that children's needs were met most efficiently. Finally, they argued that the state should "stimulate and provide for the well-being of the family as the best way to promote the moral and material well-being of the child."[20] The reference to freedom of religion was new and reflected UN doctrines regarding religious freedom and toleration. While the idea of a children's code and the establishment of a separate court system for children was not new, the ninth congress's emphasis on legal and judicial protections was. Previous congresses had called for greater state intervention, but in 1948 delegates got down to specifics.

It was suggested that a special coordinating institute be established. "The state should protect children through the means of a central institution," delegates averred, "whose main objective is the care and coordination of state and private organizations dedicated to the mother and her child and the study of their medical-social problems."[21] This institute was to be autonomous, but it would also conform to the laws of each country. All programs, both public and private, were to follow a general plan that this institute would formulate. It was to be provided with its own funding, which would be spent on its own programs or on private programs that promoted the well-being of children.

There was general agreement on establishment of a separate court system for children. Juvenile courts would handle adoptions, questions related to *patria potestad*, the determination of need for free meals, family placement, children in irregular situations, and antisocial behavior. These courts would guarantee that if a child was convicted of a crime, the punishment would not be excessive. The courts were to be run by doctors, social workers, and psychiatrists with special training in child welfare. Policymakers also maintained that a public ministry for children should be created and serve as an appeals court.[22]

Representatives at the ninth congress lobbied for the introduction of Unicef to Latin America, and the following year Unicef decided to fund programs in the region.[23] Unicef officials cited rural-urban migration patterns and increased industrialization as the causes of some of the misery found in developing nations. As one Unicef pamphlet declared,

> This drastic change in the traditional patterns of rural societies and the social sanctions of communities where everyone knew everyone else has created a need for more organized community services. It has meant a large number of collapsed marriages, temporary unions, broken homes and cases of child neglect. (In one South American country 250,000 children, out of a total child population of about 4.5 million, are without parental protection of any kind.) Overcrowding, unemployment, underemployment, and conditions of extreme poverty further weaken the stability of the family and the home.[24]

Unicef officials, like the congressional delegates, viewed family and home stability as crucial to a child's development. To provide for these children, Unicef's board of directors, which included Latin American members, decided to focus on child nutrition, disease eradication, and basic maternal and child health.[25] Unicef's own history shaped its solutions to Latin American issues.

The History of Unicef

The United Nations created the UN Relief and Rehabilitation Administration in 1941–42 to provide relief for the war-ravaged countries of Europe, and it was in operation by 1944. By 1946 the UNRRA had moved basic foodstuffs, clothing, materials for shelter, medical and dental supplies and equipment, vaccines, hospital equipment, seeds, fertilizer, and agricultural equipment to more than twenty European countries.[26]

The UNRRA soon fell victim to cold war politics, however, as the United States objected to providing relief to Communist nations. In 1946 the UN dismantled the UNRRA and created the UN International Children's Emergency Fund, or Unicef. The UN intended this fund to be temporary, to care for children affected by the war in Europe. One of the advisors to the creation of Unicef was Katherine Lenroot, head of the U.S. Children's Bureau, and an active participant in the Pan-American child welfare movement.

Unicef's first priority was Europe's postwar famine. The agency organized relief aid according to a model it would use globally in the future, delivering rations to organizations such as schools and clinics that were under government supervision—that is, in partnership with individual governments. Unicef thus took on the role of advisor and supplier, but it was up to each country to distribute the goods according to its own priorities, and the government often made these decisions in conjunction with local committees. This is how Unicef would function later in Latin America—the organization was headquartered in New York, but local Unicef offices were staffed with international and local child welfare specialists.

During the immediate postwar years, the largest proportion of Unicef's dedicated assistance for medical programs went to maternal and child health. The agency provided baby scales, thermometers, lab supplies, incubators, oxygen tents, and other supplies, as well as training. Yet it was Unicef's campaigns against disease, such as its international tuberculosis campaign, that attracted the most notice. These campaigns were to be successful in Latin America as well, and were a harbinger of the region's shift to include rural as well as urban areas in policy on child welfare.

As successful as its work in Europe was, the organization was still held hostage to the politics of the cold war. The United States, Unicef's largest donor, refused to fund the agency if it continued its work in Eastern Europe; Unicef complied with U.S. demands and shut down its operations there in the early 1950s. But this pressure convinced Unicef officials that they had to seek other sources of funding. In 1946 the organization helped

sponsor a campaign to encourage private contributions that would complement government funds. While the success of the campaign varied from
country to country and from year to year (the campaign itself ended in
1950), it nevertheless "left an important legacy," according to Maggie Black's
history of Unicef. This "was the first time that the UN appealed for contributions to private citizens as opposed to governments," writes Black, "and
this imbued it with some of the aura previously reserved exclusively for
charitable and voluntary efforts. In many countries United Nations Associations and national committees for Unicef became successor organizations."

After Unicef had established programs in Europe, it turned its attention
to the war-torn nations of Asia, which presented a special challenge. In
Europe the goal had been to repair the damage caused by the war, to repair
the infrastructure and get the population back on its feet. It quickly became
apparent that in Asia this task would be nearly impossible, because little
charitable infrastructure had existed before the war and the poverty endemic
to the region was exponentially greater than in Europe. The agency simply
did not have the funds to rebuild Asia. Officials studied the situation and
decided to focus on disease prevention, as this could be done without an
infrastructure and more cheaply but would still provide large numbers of
people with an improved quality of life. Therefore, although Unicef did
promote nutrition and maternal and child-care programs in Asia, it focused
primarily on preventing disease. This became the model Unicef would use
in Latin America.

The push to bring Unicef aid to Latin America came from Katherine
Lenroot and from Latin American UN member states. At first, UN officials
balked. They viewed Latin America as a source of funds rather than as an
aid recipient. After all, Latin American nations had not been damaged by
the war; Brazil had even donated a large amount of money to the UNRRA.
Lenroot and Latin Americans disagreed. Lenroot, through her participation
in the Pan-American Child Congresses, had considerable experience in maternal and child welfare issues. Throughout 1948 Lenroot and others lobbied Unicef on behalf of Latin American children. Delegates to the child
congresses placed a lot of faith in Unicef. The agency's focus on vaccinations
and child nutrition campaigns made sense to cash-strapped Latin American
governments. Such programs would provide benefits more cheaply than
previous maternal and child welfare programs had done.

Unicef officials and Latin American policymakers often made assumptions about Latin American populations that shaped attitudes toward Latin
American growth and development. From the beginning, Unicef officials
couched the need for aid programs in racial terms. One contemporary pamphlet said of Unicef's expansion, "Perhaps the most basic reason is simply

that the peoples of Asia and Africa and South America have come to want for their children the same life horizons that the people of Europe and North America have come to expect. Throughout the world there is stirring not only a wish *for* change, but a willingness *to* change, which marks an irrevocable break with the fatalistic past." This statement reflects the racist assumption that Latin American society and culture were static and fatalistic; Latin Americans had to be trained by Westerners to participate in the modern world. "Thus in much of the underdeveloped world," the pamphlet continued, "the desire for healthier and sturdier children is frustrated by the superstitions and traditions of a not-yet-discarded past."[27] Only by discarding these superstitions and backward traditions could Latin American countries effectively modernize.[28] North Americans and Europeans were not the only ones who espoused these views. Prominent Latin American policymakers sat on the Unicef board and approved Unicef projects based on racist notions.

Unicef became well established in Latin America during the 1950s. The Pan-American Child Congress met again in 1955 and 1959 and continued to work toward the goals outlined by the 1948 congress and Unicef. These goals refocused attention on rural areas and reflected a shift in attitude toward mothers. While Unicef emphasized the importance of maternal health and welfare, mothers themselves continued to recede in importance. The organization began to train midwives in Latin America and sponsored heath programs that focused predominantly on nutrition and milk distribution through local mothers' clubs and maternal-child health centers. These clubs and centers were not new; at least in Mexico they had been in existence since the late 1930s, but they focused on pregnant and lactating women. Mothers had a role to play, but only in the strictest of biological senses.[29] As mentioned above, this shift was a result of both international and Latin American circumstances. Unicef started out as an agency designed to minister to the war-torn countries of Europe and Asia, areas where many children were left parentless after the war. In Latin America, internal migration to the cities and endemic poverty also left many children without parents. The increasing number of orphaned and abandoned children necessitated a stronger role for the state. The earlier focus on maternal and child welfare thus shifted away from educational policies to an emphasis on children's legal rights, as we have seen.

These campaigns also reflected inherent biases. Peasants in the rural areas and the poor in the cities had to be trained to overcome their alleged "weaknesses." Concerns about these "weaknesses" reflected middle-class values. For the newly emerging middle classes across Latin America, respect for the law and legal systems, along with faith in education, structured recreation, and training in child rearing was crucial to their conceptions of modernity and their place in a modern nation.

In Mexico, the postwar SSA also increasingly directed its resources toward disease eradication and sanitation, while reformers continued to try and create "model" Mexican families. In the countryside they began to funnel resources for improved sanitation and vaccination programs through rural centers. These centers, co-sponsored with Unicef after 1954, sought to create rural Mexican citizens who would be molded into "middle-class" families, like their urban counterparts. Just as urban families would bolster the industrial project by producing model workers and consumers, rural reforms would produce the disciplined, hardworking agricultural workers needed to feed the cities and produce food for export. The PRI promoted social reform as a way to legitimate itself politically, both in the eyes of its middle-class constituency and internationally.

Alemán and the Rationalization of the Countryside

Alemán and SSA policymakers turned to sanitation and vaccination programs in the hope that improved sanitation would ameliorate some of the more egregious effects of urban industrialization in the cities and also help rural *campesinos*. The health and welfare of the countryside took on increasing importance as Alemán attempted to make Mexico more self-sufficient in food production. Government policymakers firmly linked the health and productivity of the countryside to the modernization project.[30] As one newspaper editorial commented, "It has been proved that unsanitary conditions are the most serious obstacle to the integration of the country—these conditions impede the march of progress. The repercussions are multiple; they are the same in the economic and the social sphere. Without good health, civilization cannot move forward."[31] The SSA turned its focus to aggressively combating smallpox, rabies, polio, tuberculosis, and meningitis, as well as "tropical diseases" like cholera. These campaigns were made possible in part because new vaccines had recently been made available. The SSA, through its newly created Dirección General de Higiene Rural y Medicina Social, and in cooperation with the state governments and municipal authorities, distributed vaccines and, where necessary, built clinics and hospitals.

In addition, the SSA created the Dirección General de Higiene de la Alimentación y Control de Medicamentos, which oversaw the quality and distribution of medicines.[32] It also registered and ensured the safety of food products and beverages, particularly alcoholic beverages. And scientists employed by the SSA worked to improve the Mexican diet, studying in great detail what Mexicans actually ate, and made recommendations on reducing malnutrition.[33] This department worked in cooperation with Unicef and other agencies and reflected postwar concerns with childhood nutrition.

The postrevolutionary Mexican government had a long-standing partnership with the Rockefeller Foundation, whose staff had trained and worked jointly with Mexican doctors and health workers to combat diseases and parasites such as hookworm. Doctors also worked on rural health issues throughout the 1930s as part of government initiatives to improve health in the countryside. Presidents Cárdenas and Ávila Camacho both lauded the government's rural health initiatives in their annual *informes*, linking the progress of Mexico to the political consolidation of the PRM.[34] While the early 1940s saw a shift back to urban areas in the SAP/SSA's welfare programs, sanitation projects and vaccination campaigns in rural areas continued. Once World War II ended, however, the SSA moved to rationalize the countryside for agricultural export and turned to new postwar international agencies such as Unicef to help fund its campaigns.[35]

SSA officials viewed these new investments as complementary to the welfare programs already in existence. The newspaper editorial quoted above also declared, "Really, sanitation is an investment. With just a little we can help many. . . . Whereas previous welfare expenses aided just a few . . . all of these expenses should be thought of as a system in harmony, where welfare complements improved sanitation." By 1955 the SSA was running these programs through rural welfare centers modeled on the welfare centers in Mexico City. These centers promoted a vision of rural life based on the gender and class assumptions of urban middle-class reformers, including the construction of stable families along quasi-scientific lines, with "modern, scientific" gender roles for mothers and fathers.

Centros de Bienestar Rural

Reformers sought to eradicate poverty in order to create a more productive rural workforce that could feed the booming urban centers and produce goods for export—two key elements of the plan to modernize the economy. They argued for the necessity of including the *campesinos*, who, reformers alleged, "have always resisted the harmful impact of our social convulsions, and they have benefited the least from the institutional benefits and advantages of modern life."[36] This statement may reflect a bit of wishful collective amnesia—by the 1950s social workers seem to have forgotten the upheavals of the revolution and the work of the SEP's cultural missions. It may also reflect policymakers' lingering eugenicist attitudes toward the *campesinos*, viewing them not as a threat but as a docile population in need of "expert" guidance. In the late 1940s the SSA established rural service cooperatives under the auspices of the Dirección General de Higiene Rural y Medicina Social. In 1947 the SSA maintained ninety-one cooperatives. By 1952 this number had expanded to 226, extending medical welfare benefits to 61,390 families through the creation of hospitals and maternity centers.[37]

The SSA created several programs, among them the *centros de bienestar rural*, or rural welfare centers, which provided educational programs designed to improve maternal and child health and welfare, environmental and home health, diet, recreation, cultural education, and general economic wellbeing.[38] Social workers defined health to include not only physical but mental and social health as well. Social workers who volunteered to work at these centers required extra training above and beyond their degree. They enrolled in a postgraduate course called Public Health Orientation for Social Workers, offered by the SSA School of Health. This course was followed by a week of practical studies coordinated with visiting nurses and concluded with a roundtable discussion. After this training, social workers were sent to rural centers and might have a week or so to observe before being put to work. Sometimes, however, they had to jump right in.[39]

Social workers continued to believe that women were the key to their efforts. They also focused on group and community social work, although one commented on the necessity of continuing with individual casework, describing the individual as the "index of social needs." She also emphasized the importance of group and community efforts, however, observing that "the most proven action is achieved when groups move themselves to create a collective conscience of their obligations." Personnel at these centers worked in teams consisting of a sanitation official, a sanitation inspector, a social worker, and a doctor or nurse. The team would initially use interviews and questionnaires to establish the needs of the community and then develop programs.[40]

One of the main objectives of community social work was to teach *campesinos* to help themselves. In order to do this, the team initially trained other staff members and eventually community members themselves to teach in these programs. The ultimate goal was to have the community teach itself and organize its own resources without the aid of the centers. To facilitate this training, social workers, much like their urban counterparts, set up women's and children's clubs associated with the centers to provide classes for rural women and their children. These classes taught hygiene, home care, and child care.[41] The SSA also created an *ejido* medical service that focused on maternal and infant care, maternal education, and preventive medical care. These teams traveled to the *ejidos* and tried to persuade the community to use the centers. Like the centers, the service hoped to transform the health and attitudes of rural populations.[42]

By 1954 the cooperatives were working in conjunction with Unicef to establish regional mother-child health and hygiene centers. Six pilot centers were established, two in San Luis Potosí, two in Veracruz, one in Morelos, and one in Coahuila. Their purpose was to provide integrated health care for mothers and their children, to improve agriculture and care of domestic animals with the aim of helping the population better feed itself, to provide education, to inculcate healthy recreational habits through the formation of sports and cultural clubs in order to combat idleness, and to "awaken the spirit of cooperation and sense of responsibility for all community members."[43] The pilot centers comprised nine school breakfast cafeterias, six communal sewing areas, six demonstration kitchens, eight volunteer committees, and one communal bakery. The welfare workers helped plant nineteen communal gardens and thirty-one family plots. They also provided training for commercial cultivation. They conducted immunization campaigns. Finally, the centers created fifteen sports teams and six artists' groups intended to realize the goal of properly structured recreational activities.[44]

As with the urban centers, the focus was on the mother and her children. In contrast to reformers at the Pan-American Child Congress, Mexican social workers seemed to have retained their emphasis not only on a mother's biological role but on her social role as well. As one put it, women were "the directional axis of the family and the administrator of the home. The woman constitutes the best agent for the liberation, direction, and elevation of the community."[45] If stable, agriculturally productive rural families were the goal, then the mother was the agent of change within the rural family.

While all members of the community were immunized and had access to medical care, mothers and children were especially targeted for health and wellness outreach. This in part reflected welfare workers' eugenicist goals: once again, the health of the mother was crucial to the health of the nation. It also reflected Unicef's postwar goals. Other programs were directed at women as well, including model kitchens, communal bakeries, and sewing areas. As in urban areas, the goal of these programs was not to train women to work outside the home but to enable them to participate in a modern economy within the home. Reformers did not intend to rewrite gender norms but to update them and incorporate them into national goals.

Also updated were programs for men, which focused on sports and other constructive recreational activities that would "combat idleness." Although welfare advocates in the 1950s saw the rural population as "docile" and in need of guidance, many of the activities created for men and boys closely resembled programs begun in the 1920s and 1930s, whose aims were specifically to rewrite male gender norms and create a more docile and controllable masculinity. In the 1950s, welfare workers believed that men still needed to be controlled, especially in light of peasant protest movements led by Rubén Jaramillo, whose actions disrupted government plans to do away with the last vestiges of land reform and communal landholding.[46] The move toward more regimented recreational activities also reflected goals articulated in the Ninth Pan-American Child Congress, which reflected international attitudes about controlling populations.

Because government funds were limited, SSA officials looked for ways to expand the scope of their programs without necessarily spending more money. Developing partnerships with agencies like Unicef was one approach. The manner in which personnel at the centers were trained also reflected the need to save money; newly trained community members would then train others. It was also hoped that they could reach more people this way, and it had the added benefit of creating loyal citizens and communities invested in state-sponsored programs.[47]

The six pilot centers were successful, and by 1955 forty-one rural welfare centers had been established, providing multiple services to rural communities.[48] These centers were integral to the SSA's mission in the countryside, which increasingly resembled its programs and policies in the cities. Reformers in rural and urban areas alike centralized their activities in welfare centers and continued to focus on mothers as the key to social transformation, training them to keep their homes clean and hygienic, manage finances responsibly, and participate in a cash economy.

SSA officials continued to co-sponsor projects with Unicef. One such joint venture was a program of integrated health, launched experimentally in Guanajuato, one of the most populous states in Mexico. The program would study the well-being of the community in terms of physical health, economic aptitude, and the "abolition of ignorance," and would provide medical care, education, and job training, once again "elevating the potential of the [rural, agricultural] family."[49]

Unicef also continued to fund disease eradication. In fact, Mexico was the first country to receive Unicef support for a full-scale campaign to eradicate malaria. In 1955 Unicef gave US$7.5 million and in 1959 another $5.5 million, to be matched by the Mexican government. Unicef stressed the importance of disease prevention and child nutrition and sought to support governments committed to increasing economic and social health. As one

Unicef official commented, "Children need not only to be saved from hunger and disease. It is equally important that they be helped to grow up in such a way as to cope with the problems of citizenship in the world of the future."[50] Thus Unicef linked the national with the transnational, as both worked in concert to support children.

Urban Challenges and Expansion of Services

The SSA continued to expand its system of maternal-child welfare centers and day-care facilities in the cities, particularly Mexico City. Between 1947 and 1952 the ministry increased the number of day-care centers from fourteen to thirty-eight and the number of children served from 3,968 to 4,215.[51] SSA-run hospitals increased services as well. In addition, the SSA expanded its mission to include industrial hygiene. The Departamento de Higiene Industrial inspected workplaces and factories throughout Mexico to ensure that these sites were up to standards and that workers had access to health care. This department also ensured through on-site inspections that factories employing more than fifty women installed day-care centers.[52] These services grew because of the SSA's commitment and because of increasing demand. In 1945 SSA facilities served 47,575 persons in Mexico City and in 1950, 51,440. By 1955 this number had increased to 58,563, reflecting in part the population boom.[53] The Mexican government continued to confront inflation and food shortages and to fear urban unrest.

Under President Ruiz Cortines, the government turned to a plan known as "stabilizing development" to address these issues. By the early 1950s, the first part of the original import-substitution industrialization strategy, production of light consumer goods, had been successfully completed. But the Mexican government was not in a position to carry import substitution to its next phase, the production of intermediate goods. In 1955 the rate of inflation was 17 percent, a level not seen since World War II.[54] The new policy of stabilizing development was thus intended to aid the transition to import-substitution industrialization in intermediate and capital goods, a goal that was to be carried out with private capital, both domestic and foreign.[55] The government hoped to increase production without triggering inflation and to promote industry through incentives already in place.

The encouragement of the private sector through tax incentives and subsidies weakened the financial capacity of the government, however, and, together with a drop in export taxes, led to an increase in private debt. As a result, the government turned to foreign capital for this second phase of industrialization. The success of "stabilizing development" was thus contingent upon the availability of external credit. In other words, in order to keep taxes low and government subsidies of industry at current levels, the state had to borrow increasingly from foreign sources to maintain the levels of spending demanded by the developmentalist model. Direct foreign investment thus became an important stimulus to the economy. This, coupled with continued reliance on long-term borrowing from international financial institutions, pushed Mexico deeply into debt.[56]

The economic effects of this approach were predictable. Rural migration to the cities continued unabated—the number of people living in cities with populations of at least a hundred thousand more than tripled between 1920 and 1950, from 5.3 to 17.8 percent. Mexico City's population increased fourfold over this period and by 1950 had a population of more than three million. Migration to the cities continued to exacerbate social problems and inflation, and food shortages persisted. The controversy over the election of Adolfo Ruiz Cortines highlighted the gravity of these issues. His challenger, General Miguel Henriquez Guzmán, capitalized on growing urban discontent with declining standards of living and came close to winning the election. Ruiz Cortines therefore had to address the country's growing crisis.[57] The SSA's expansion of services can be seen also as a reaction to economic woes. Once again, reformers promoted campaigns against vagrancy as part of an overall initiative to combat middle-class anxieties about the urban poor.

The visibility of beggars in Mexico City demanded attention. While the government had fought mendicancy during previous administrations, the public outcry over beggars in the capital city intensified in the 1950s. Many reformers viewed beggars as social parasites and urged the SSA to revamp its programs to encourage work for the poor. Newspaper editorials demanded that the government crack down on beggars. While they conceded that many of the poor were in legitimate need of help, others, they insisted, were not. "Many surprises are in store for researchers," wrote one editorialist, "who will discover that many beggars actually are quite well off, because mendicancy right now has become an industry, and these 'captains of industry' are unlikely to stop just because the state intervenes."[58] Many social commentators believed that the majority of beggars could find work if they wanted to but preferred to take advantage of the system, swindling resources from the government and depriving the truly poor of the aid they needed.

In order to combat what it called "social parasitism" and to aid those it believed were legitimately in need, the SSA, in coordination with the Secretaría de Gobernación, IMSS, and the Mexico City government, launched a winter shelter campaign in 1955. The aim was to provide homeless people with clothing and a place to sleep. Shelters were set up throughout Mexico City, and a phone number was provided that citizens could call if they spotted a person living on the streets. Once the call was placed, an ambulance would arrive to take the person to a shelter, where he or she would be able to sleep for the night and receive food and medical care.[59] Authorities declared the campaign successful, pointing to the fact that the number of professional beggars on the street had appeared to diminish. The shelter program was thus made permanent in order to serve the inhabitants of Mexico City.[60]

The shelter campaign was similar to programs carried out in the 1930s, also as a response to deteriorating economic conditions and middle-class anxieties. Despite years of effort and much rhetoric on the part of welfare workers, middle-class citizens of Mexico City still viewed the poor in terms of deserving and undeserving. Newspapers editorialized about the "fake" poor, people who scammed the system. This concern over abuses also extended to some of the more popular SSA programs, such as the family dining halls. In an era of diminishing resources and rampant inflation, many middle-class families wanted to guard against corruption.

Family Dining Halls

Welfare reformers continued to expand the population served by the family dining halls. The PRI also used the dining halls as a way to provide cheap food to students in the late 1940s. By 1950, however, some had begun to complain that the *comedores* had lost their original purpose—to serve families—and were now attracting parasites. The director of one of the dining halls complained to the head of the dining hall program, calling for stricter eligibility rules and urging that use of the halls be restricted to six months. The SSA denied the request, responding that serving families was the purpose of the halls and that because of the economic crisis families would continue to be allowed to eat there for a full year. Moreover, as long as families were served, single people should also be served in the dining halls and should also receive medical care and job training, provided this did not interfere with services to families.[61]

By the mid-1950s the SSA was supporting six family dining halls, some of which served not only families but a large student population as well (see tables 1 and 2). (The employees listed in the tables were probably those working for the SSA.) The SSA also created six kitchens in México DF, known as *centros femininos de trabajo*, or women's work centers, that served five hundred free meals a day.[62] Families, though supposedly the target of

Table 1   Daily Population of Comedor No. 1, 1953

People in families	426
Students	378
Employees	101
Blind	10
Total	915

Table 2   Daily Population of Comedor No. 2, 1953

People in families	303
Employees	110
Students from the PRI	350
Students from Politécnico	300
Students from the Escuela Amiga de la Obrera No. 5	400
Other students	208
Children from Internado de los Remedios	120
Total	1,791

Source: "Sintesis del informe de las actividades realizadas por la Dirección General de Asistencia Social duránte el periódo comprendido entre 1 de septiembre de 1953 al 31 agosto de 1954," AGN/SSA/Oficialía Mayor, vol. 3, exp. 803.1, pp. 12–13. (This source erroneously gives the total in table 1 as 971; I have corrected it to 915.)

the *comedores*, now made up less than half the population being fed. Students of public schools run by either the SSA or the SEP were the largest group.

The economic crises of the 1950s created demand for subsidized food in many sectors of the population. The PRI became involved in providing free meals, possibly fearing the unrest that could arise if people went hungry, which might endanger its hold on political power. According to SSA statistics, 8,700 university students sponsored by the PRI used Comodor No. 2 on a monthly basis in 1955. The PRI itself also sponsored a number of kitchens. SSA officials noted that as a result of the economic downturn, those who considered themselves middle class were patronizing many of the dining halls and kitchens.[63] The dining halls' ties to the state seem to have diminished any embarrassment that middle-class patrons who needed extra help may have felt. Because the source was the government, they may have viewed the meals as their right, rather than as a handout or act of charity.

By 1950 more than half of all Mexicans lived in cities, and swelling urban populations also increased demand for government services. This influx in population exacerbated worsening conditions for the SSA, which was also dealing with rampant inflation. Inflation not only affected the poor and those members of the middle class who could not afford food; it also meant that the food the SSA purchased was more expensive and consumed a larger portion of the ministry's budget.[64] By the mid-1950s the SSA had moved to streamline urban welfare services, placing them under the aegis of the welfare centers on the grounds that consolidation would be more efficient and in keeping with the recommendations of Pan-American reformers.

Centros de Bienestar Urbano

The rapid increase in Mexico's City's population during the 1950s worried policymakers, who were concerned not only with the population explosion but with population density in the capital city. Reformers cited statistics showing that by 1956 48.2 percent of all of Mexicans lived in Greater Mexico City, and that 40.8 percent of Mexico City's population lived in the *colonias populares*. This meant that the central, poorer areas of the city had a population density of 2,425.4 inhabitants per square kilometer, as compared with a national figure of 15.5. Density concerned reformers because of hygiene issues—the poor could not implement proper cleaning and hygiene standards if they were unable to afford decent housing. Officials may also have worried that a lack of housing would erode the family model they had worked so hard to create—it would have been too expensive to live without help from family or taking in boarders. Welfare workers lamented the lack of services for this population.[65]

Reformers sought to reorganize welfare programs in Mexico City to better serve the swollen population. The SSA established centralized locations where community members could get access to health care, job training, and recreation. The centers still targeted families, and in particular single mothers, who, "owing to their scarce economic resources, carry on their backs multiple physical and moral problems . . . and who will see that their life will change because of this program," as one report put it. Welfare workers hoped that the improvement of women's lives would in turn improve the life of the community.

In 1956 the SSA opened twelve new centers in the lower-class districts of Mexico City. Each was to have a cafeteria and a family club and was to offer workshops for vocational training and provide recreational activities. The centers were also to have a store and to provide legal aid and a job-placement program. In addition, some of the centers had laundry services, irons, sewing machines, and TVs, and gave out food rations. Many sponsored sanitary works such as septic systems and proper drainage. Others had day-care centers and Molina Co-ops (named for the *molinas*, or mills, that are used to grind corn for tortillas). While the centers seem to have been very popular, they nevertheless met with some resistance. SSA workers reported that they had to induce people to use the services by drawing them in with movie nights, TV, and other entertainment.[66] As in the case of the dining halls fifteen years earlier, members of the popular classes did not always want to sacrifice their autonomy to state regulation.

SSA representatives could be their own worst enemies. The director of the center in Santa Julia, María Elena Muzquiz, reported the following altercation:

> I draw your attention to the fact that Sra. Casarín arrived at 8:30 in the evening, accompanied by Sr. Enríque Villafuerte, the son of the former administrator of this center, wanting to control who was allowed to come in to watch the fights playing on the TV. She would not let many in, even after they begged her, declaring that watching the fights was their favorite diversion. Sra. Casarín was very disrespectful to our clients, telling many that they could not enter because they smelled bad. She told wives that they could not enter with their husbands because they should be in their homes, or that they were very dirty, and she would not allow children in with their parents because they were problems.[67]

Casarín protested that she was only following the procedures outlined by Francisca Acosta in order to combat juvenile delinquency. But the point, according to Muzquiz, was to allow children and families in to watch television so that they would not go to the cantinas instead. Muzquiz also said that the center had been selling fruit drinks and soda so as to prevent people from bringing in beer or other alcoholic drinks. She asked if she should continue her policies. In demanding that the clients of the welfare center be treated with respect, Muzquiz invoked official SSA procedures designed to combat juvenile delinquency. She represented the official, "expert" voice of the middle class, whereas Sra. Casarín claimed middle-class status because of her personal relationship and belief system—her ability to define middle-class behavior and mores and to try and enforce them in the center's clientele. Both women based their status on their perceived authority to monitor and regulate the behavior of the popular classes. Their disagreement demonstrates the contested nature of middle-class identity in Mexico City in the 1950s.

Finally, the SSA worked in partnership with Unicef on urban issues. In November 1953, for example, Alice Shaffer, the regional director of Unicef, in response to a request from the secretary of the SSA, Dr. Ignácio Morones Prieto, promised to study the feasibility of a creating a milk-processing plant in partnership with the Mexican government. Morones Prieto had made the request in response to fluctuations in the quality and affordability of milk in the cities, and he was attempting to provide government services to shore up political support in urban areas. Unicef provided US$415,000 for the facility.[68] Unicef also proposed a children's nutrition program, to be sponsored in conjunction with the SSA. Unicef officials envisioned the milk being distributed through the mother-child centers, schools, orphanages, and other institutions to help poor children in need of milk and other staples.[69]

The PRI and the Middle Class

The PRI moved to consolidate its political hold during the 1940s and 1950s. By the end of the period of the "Mexican Miracle" it could count on continued power, even if there were occasional challenges to its authority. It succeeded in part by appealing to the rapidly growing urban middle class—by 1960 17 percent of the Mexican population could be considered middle class (twice the number in 1910), and this group had political clout.[70] The welfare reformers working with the SSA were largely of this class, and their ambitions and goals reflected the desires of this socioeconomic group.

As the PRI garnered more and more power, it used the social welfare programs it had provided—programs popular with middle-class constituents—as the basis for its legitimacy. In 1940 the president of the Congress responded to Cárdenas's opening speech, "Through our public life the middle class has always contributed, both as a group and individually, a body of high human and social value that through authentic representatives has directed our institutional heroic deeds, purified our fights, and lent valuable technological contributions to the edification of the country . . . alongside the workers . . . in the social fight."[71] In his inaugural speech as president, Adolfo Ruiz Cortines said, "[In] the regimen that we are initiating, we will have to multiply our efforts in order to realize the ideals of our collectivity and to unite all Mexicans in the pursuit of social justice. Within the trajectory of our reclaimed social movement [reinvindicador], we will open a new stage in the history of Mexico and confront serenely the grave responsibilities inherent in our investiture."[72] Presidential rhetoric lauded the work of the reformers, and by the 1950s it had begun to signal Mexico's commitment to international health and reform movements.

Welfare workers had long been active in international and Pan-American movements, and in valorizing this participation the government both tipped its hat to middle-class interests and showed Mexicans that their country was respected in the international community. In 1949 President Alemán celebrated the fact that Mexico had hosted the fifth and sixth meetings of the executive committee of the Pan-American Sanitation Organization (OSP), the sixth National Health Directors' conference, and the second meeting of the Directors' Council of the OSP, and had taken part in the seventh meeting of the OSP's executive committee in Washington, D.C.[73] Ruiz Cortines applauded Mexico's participation as well, declaring in a presidential address in 1954 that Mexico had "participated in meetings for health or public hygiene in New York, Washington, D.C., Havana, Bogotá, Albuquerque, Geneva, and Montevideo," and that the following year it would host the seventh assembly of the World Health Organization.[74] Hosting these and other international meetings, such as the Seventh Pan-American Child Congress in 1935, gave Mexico a certain international cachet and reinforced the middle-class conceit that Mexico had succeeded in joining the Western powers on the path to progress and modernity.

State funding may have decreased, but private funding and international partnerships continued, and welfare expanded during this period, allowing the PRI to claim legitimacy in the face of hard economic times. It is noteworthy that two SAP/SSA ministers were prominent members of the PRI prior to heading up that ministry. Gustavo Baz fought in the revolution under Zapata and served as governor of the state of Mexico, and Luis Gamboa, head of the SSA under Alemán, had been the governor of Chiapas. While the SAP/SSA might not have been the most important government ministry in terms of budget allocations, it was important enough for the PRI to make sure that its directors were loyal to the party. The commitment to social welfare policy allowed the government to mitigate political unrest in the cities and gave middle-class reformers, an important political constituency, a voice in the system. It also allowed progressive, middle-class Mexicans to imagine that they were part of the solution rather than part of the problem. Politicians' rhetoric fed the self-image to which many middle-class Mexicans aspired—it allowed them to see themselves as free from poverty and superior to the poor but at the same time as engaged in efforts to improve the lives of their fellow Mexicans.

Many historians have lambasted the PRI for its lack of commitment to social justice. Indeed, it is hard to defend the PRI's relatively meager allocation of resources to fight poverty during this period. Yet as Mexico's population increased and social problems multiplied, the SSA and its policymakers steadily increased the reach of the agency's welfare programs. Mexican presidents saw the importance of public health and welfare. Ávila Camacho dedicated fifty-three points to public health and welfare in his *plan sexenal*.[75] A biography of Ruiz Cortines boasts of his dedication to social welfare as well, pointing out that under his administration the number of mother-child centers in Mexico increased from 396 to 925 and that 315 new hospitals were constructed.[76]

Presidents also used the clout of their First Ladies to reinforce the link between state-sponsored welfare and the social prestige of charity work. Wives of Mexican political leaders had always been associated with charity work, and nineteenth-century women like the empress Carlota and Carmen Romero Rubio de Díaz created and promoted their own, often Catholic, charities. Postrevolutionary First Ladies continued the practice but added their sponsorship to SSA activities as well. Soledad Orozco, the wife of Manuel Ávila Camacho, often distributed toys and other gifts to soldiers and to poor children and their mothers. On Mother's Day she gave poor mothers items such as irons and stoves. One year the government paid off the debts of those who had pawned their sewing machines at the Monte de Piedad, the national pawn shop, returning hundreds of sewing machines to the women who had pawned them.[77] The covers of SSA periodicals often ran pictures of presidents and their wives distributing goods to the poor.

Beatríz Velasco de Alemán, Miguel Alemán's wife, created the Asociación pro Nutrición Infantil (Association for the Improvement of Child Nutrition), which helped the government distribute low-cost school breakfasts. According to the association, it was important that the poor not see this as charity, that mothers received training in hygiene and nutrition, and that both mothers and children got vaccinated. As Beatríz Velasco de Alemán put it, "The well-fed child is the rock, the base of the family. The family is the spirit of a strong race."[78]

Ruiz Cortines's wife, María Izaguirre, also committed herself to welfare activities. In 1953 she organized a group dedicated to the improvement of child nutrition; it sponsored family dining halls, expanded the Escuelas Amigas de la Obrera, and supported day care and discount stores. Izaguirre also founded the Congreso Nacional de Protección a la Infancia, which became the successor to many SSA programs in the 1960s.[79] These First Ladies used the prestige of their position to focus attention on government activities directed at poor children and mothers. They helped staff and raise money for these programs, and their husbands were able to exploit their activities for political gain. Their work also allowed the SSA to expand services during an era of budget cuts.

While the percentage of the national budget devoted to public health and welfare decreased steadily over the period, the SSA managed nevertheless to expand services significantly. How was this possible? The explanation may lie in the role played by the voluntary committees and other private charities linked to the government. Comprehensive statistics on the amount of money raised through private efforts are unavailable, but the amount raised by one campaign may be suggestive. In 1941 the Comite Organizador de la Campaña de Invierno y Navidad a Favor del Niño sin Abrigo, run by Soledad Orozco, spent Mex$31,175.44 to raise $34,346.82, for a net gain of $3,171.38.[80] While some three thousand pesos may not seem like much, all of the money was channeled specifically into welfare services for mothers and children. A portion of the $31,175.44 was used to buy clothing and toys to distribute to children during the fund-raising activities, thereby increasing the percentage of the money that went to children. If this amount was raised several times a year over a twenty-year period, it would help explain the SSA's ability to expand programming.

To sum up, the SSA expanded its mission after World War II to include improved sanitation and disease eradication. This expansion was a response to international dialogue about how developing countries could use limited welfare funds most efficiently. SSA activities mirrored in many ways the efforts of other Latin American reformers and Unicef. Attention was directed to the countryside, and Mexico heeded the call for integrated programming for the rural areas through rural welfare centers. What was unique about Mexico is that the focus on the countryside was not new. The 1920s and 1930s had seen cultural missions and socialist education projects designed to re-create the model Mexican family and the gender roles on which it was based. And sanitation campaigns had been carried out in partnership with the Rockefeller Foundation since the 1920s.

Mexican reformers also consolidated services in the cities, particularly Mexico City, where most of the SSA budget was spent. Urban welfare centers offered pre- and postnatal care, job training, child-rearing classes, and recreation. With the focus on the child, school breakfast programs, family dining halls, vaccination campaigns, and educational opportunities were expanded. Through the SEP, the government expanded its kindergarten program and emphasized the training of professionals to work with preschool children.[81]

Reformers believed that education would transform the poor's role in Mexican society. Through the efforts of the SSA and its army of social workers and volunteers, the poor could aspire to middle-class status—or at least middle-class values—and would embrace hard work, the law, education, and science. Like Fernando and Margarita, whose story began this chapter, they could learn and change. Social workers, and the discipline of social work, would be at the forefront of this campaign to modernize Mexico.

5

THE RISE OF SOCIAL WORK IN MEXICO

In 1941 the American sociologist Norman Hayner interviewed Enelda Fox about Mexican family relations. According to Fox, there were differences between the upper and middle classes, particularly in small towns. She criticized upper-class mothers:

> The [upper-class] Mexican woman must dedicate herself entirely to house, husband, children and church but she has no efficient preparation for these duties and so leaves the real work to the servants, who are untrained, overworked and careless. The children are particularly ill-cared for. The mother has no notion of modern nutritional methods or child hygiene and even less of child psychology. Affection, in the form of cuddling and kisses, is showered on the child, but little time is spent on reading him a suitable book or showing an interest in his interests.

By contrast, middle-class women were educated and were entering professions, which had a positive impact on the family.

> The middle class in provincial towns is more progressive in respect to education. Even comparatively speaking, there are many more university and commercial school students from this group than from the upper class. There is also less prejudice against women acquiring a higher education and working. There is scarcely any professional field

into which women of this group have not entered. . . . Since the middle-class girl, who is driven to study for economic reasons, has more knowledge and experience than the sheltered girl, there is the chance that when she marries she may become less of a bore to her husband and so keep her home intact and her children's minds health- ier and more normal.[1]

Fox's observations reflect the attitudes we have seen in middle-class reform- ers themselves. They saw themselves as superior to and more modern than both the *clases populares* and, because of their modern education, the upper class as well. Despite their money and social status, upper-class women simply did not make good mothers or wives, in Fox's view. They were not trained in modern child-rearing techniques and their lack of education made them boring.

While Fox herself was a working mother (Hayner noted that she had four children), and while her comments may thus be read as defensive, it is true that more women were going to college and entering and the profes- sions in the 1940s and '50s than ever before. As we have seen, government work was particularly attractive for the new class of professional women. The rise of female professionals was concurrent with the expansion and growth of the middle class and the consolidation of the PRI, as social work became an important new career option for women after the revolution. Examining the development of professional social work in Mexico allows us to see how multiple discourses worked together to form class, race, and gender ideologies during this period.

The discipline of social work in Mexico evolved out of a long tradition of women's participation in Catholic charity and social action, influences from U.S. schools of social work, the revolution's call for social justice, Latin American attitudes toward maternal and child welfare emanating from the child congresses, and the postrevolutionary state's own plans for modernization. Social work also reflected class biases. The casework meth- ods adopted by Mexican social workers mitigated many aspects of large- scale social change by placing the blame for poverty squarely on the poor. What emerged in Mexico during the 1930s, 1940s, and 1950s was thus a vision of social welfare that encouraged the poor to help themselves, and urged social workers to see themselves as integral players in the national project to uplift and modernize Mexico. Welfare professionals saw poverty as an obstacle that had to be overcome if Mexico was to progress, and, as we have seen, as a problem that could no longer be addressed effectively by the church. By offering professional women government positions in welfare services, the PRI successfully courted this part of the middle class and demonstrated that the goals of the social reform movement were the goals of the state.

Social workers believed that they were at the forefront of the battle for the hearts and minds of Mexicans, and that they possessed the qualities necessary to win them over to the vision of a modern Mexico. Many of these grew out of traditional beliefs about women's suitability for charity work. Yet the professionalization of the field also gave women access to a degree of status and respect that they had never had before. This chapter relies on SSA documents and on articles and UNAM theses by social workers to trace the outlines of attitudes about the development of social work as a professional occupation in Mexico.

The Professionalization of Social Work

As we have seen, women continued to be active in private charitable organizations after the revolution, but they also began to be incorporated into new postrevolutionary governmental institutions. Many women from "good families," who had suffered such misfortunes as widowhood, became inspectors for Beneficencia Pública, the precursor to the SAP/SSA. These women were not professionally trained and usually had only the rudimentary education available to women at the time.

Social work as a professional occupation began in Mexico in the 1920s. Because the first group of women serving as inspectors had not been trained in social work, Beneficencia Pública undertook their training. A U.S.-trained social worker instructed personnel in the Department of Infant Hygiene, for example. By 1930 many of these inspectors had begun to receive casework training based on U.S. models of welfare work.[2] Because social work in the United States had such an influence on Mexican social work, it is worth examining briefly the early history of social work in Mexico's neighbor to the north.

Social Work in the United States

Although European schools of thought on social work influenced the rise of social work in Mexico, the primary influence outside Latin America was the U.S. casework method, which represented a shift away from the nineteenth-century European charity model.[3] Another important influence was the ideology behind the settlement houses in the United States. What emerged in Mexico was a blend of the two dominant U.S. approaches, combined with the Mexican government's own discourse surrounding development and social justice.

The rise of the social science movement in the United States was a response to high levels of immigration and to rapid industrialization and urbanization. This movement advocated the use of science as a means of combating the social ills created by the influx of European immigrants into American cities. The new academic discipline of sociology and the professionalization of medicine promised to eradicate the social problems urban areas faced at the turn of the century. Social science was billed as a scientific and "modern" way to improve society.[4] The social science movement followed two distinct trajectories. One aimed at radical social transformation on the grounds that social inequities could be resolved only if the fundamental structure of society was changed. The other approach advocated helping the poor to work within existing social structures, that is, "to develop mechanisms to cope with the existing environment and make better use of available resources."

The first approach gave rise to settlement houses for immigrants staffed by middle-class social workers who believed that in order to help the poor, to provide them with useful social and educational services, one had to live among them. The second approach embraced a philosophy known as the "stewardship of wealth." The premise here was that the well off had an obligation to share their wealth through the creation of jobs and direct philanthropy. The group that advocated this approach created philanthropic agencies to distinguish the truly deserving poor from those who could be rehabilitated for productive work. The main organization representing this group's interest was the Charity Organization Society.

Casework practice grew out of this second tradition, first as a method of determining whether a client had a right to assistance. Clients would either come to the agency or be visited at home by a social worker, who assessed the problems the client and the family faced and what services could be provided to help them. This practice became known as diagnostic social work, and it assumed that a client was poor because of a specific social or psychological problem that could be solved by a well-trained social worker. Diagnostic social work relied on the professionalizing discourse of psychology and medicine, offering a scientific "solution" to a client's problems. These social workers believed that poverty was a result of an internal pathogen rather than an external structural problem, and their "scientific" orientation to solving the problem justified their professional training.

By the 1930s social work in the United States was dominated by an extreme version of diagnostic casework. Known as the functionalist school of casework theory, it was based on Rankian psychology and held that a client's poverty could be directly traced to the client's psychological outlook. Functionalists believed that the root of the problem was that the client was unable or unwilling to make the decisions necessary to pull himself or herself out of poverty or to meet his or her needs. It was the role of the social worker to help clients progress psychologically to the point of being able to help themselves. All poverty was attributed to a poor person's psychological state. The caseworker did not offer or recommend services or help in any form. Her role was only to help the client psychologically. Functionalism called for intense professional training and also drew upon the field of psychology, which helped to legitimize social work as a profession.

Both the diagnostic and the functionalist schools of social work rejected the concept of social reform. Instead, they pathologized poverty and believed that the poor created their own problems. The popularity of this approach encouraged an attitude that blamed the victim and did not seek social change as a means of grappling with the predominant social issues of the day. Attitudes toward the professionalization of social work in Mexico blended both the casework method and the settlement house ideology, combining them with existing attitudes about women's work in welfare activities as well as revolutionary calls for social justice. Social workers in Mexico pursued a casework approach, but they also maintained that many social problems had their roots in structural economic dislocations.

Mexican Social Work

Mexican welfare reformers explicitly linked the use of the case file to their desire for social transformation. Many of the welfare advocates who argued for the professionalization of social work in Mexico had been given scholarships from a variety of agencies to train and study in the United States.[5] Social reformers championed this policy but were troubled by some aspects of the training. They complained that welfare professionals trained in the United States had difficulty applying what they had learned to Mexico's social situation and could be a little "egotistical."[6] Policymakers argued for a specific definition of what came to be known as social therapy, which Mexicans defined as their approach to social work.

Social therapy was "the scientific art that studies the poorly socialized with the object of promoting socialization, and with the goal of reincorporating the socially weak into the processes of production. . . . Social therapy classifies the socially weak in to the following categories: socially weak because of physical incapacities, psychiatric incapacities, as well as ethical, economic or educational incapacities."[7] In the 1930s Mexican social reformers sought social change on a larger social level yet still maintained that the casework method was the best way to uncover the roots of social ills. As Josefina Gaona, the head of social workers for Mexico City's Department of Social Therapy (part of Beneficencia Pública), put it, "Modern social work requires a perfect knowledge of society and individuals, of sociology and psychology and the connected social sciences; it requires the perfect knowledge of the places where social problems germinate and an intimate treatment with the people who live in these communities."[8] Another welfare worker maintained that "the casework file also shows us, after much research, the causes of social ills, and this is the only way to cure them, as any other way only treats the symptoms, not the causes. In social science statistics alone teach us; only with statistics can we reach logical conclusions, and the individual case file is the only way to reach these conclusions."[9]

Unlike U.S. social workers, who used the case file to determine an individual pathology, Mexican social workers advocated the use of the file to compile the statistics necessary to pursue larger social reform. While welfare workers did not deny that individual psychoses explained some poverty, they also saw broader social forces at work. Like their Latin American counterparts at the Pan-American Child Congresses, Mexican social workers saw social transformation as their fundamental goal and scientific statistics as the best way to reach it. They therefore focused on integrating the poor as a class into the "processes of production."[10]

In the quest to modernize and industrialize Mexico, poverty had to be eradicated, insofar as possible. As one reformer commented,

> Social and economic weakness does not allow people to take care of themselves or their families. . . . This weakness deserves the special attention of the government, because of the fact that this [weakness] is inconvenient for individuals and their families. . . . It is bad for society that these people do not enjoy full well-being, because they cannot be active consumers, they cannot be part of the processes of production, they represent a burden on society. The socially weak live in conditions that do not facilitate the development of the country. . . . In addition, these weak people cannot raise children with the vigor necessary for the future of the country.[11]

As we have seen, poverty was no longer viewed as a moral dilemma with a religious solution but as an obstacle to Mexican development. Indeed, not just the reform movement but the discipline of social work itself was imbued with the revolution's antireligious spirit. Social workers criticized both the upper classes' private charitable activities and what they saw as the poor's religious superstition. "In our country social help has not quite reached the completely technical stage," wrote Berta Alanís Cebrián, a student of the Mexican social work movement, in 1957. "Some continue to give alms, and sometimes philanthropists—'our millionaires'—give just enough to make sure the people do not starve, or they give to make a name for themselves. Their private charities may help some, but meanwhile the misery under which most of the people live continues."[12] The critique of Catholic social action was implicit, a critique made all over Latin America by reformers in the 1930s. Social workers viewed private charitable activities as a stopgap measure at best, and they questioned the motives of the rich. According to Mexican reformers, the poor had to be more fully integrated into the economy; they had to make enough money to become the active consumers industrialization necessitated—especially since the first stage of import-substitution industrialization proposed to create an industry dedicated to the production of light consumer goods. The older social action model simply could not accomplish this task. As one professor of social work at UNAM wrote in the June 1942 issue of *Asistencia*:

> The concept of social service has been transformed after a long and interesting evolution. The well-being and happiness of the individual, the development and progress of the community, is the ideal that modern social service tries to realize. In order to achieve this ideal, [we need] to intelligently mobilize all of the resources of individuals and communities. Modern social service does not refer only to the aid given to the beggar under the influence of a charitable impulse, but to the organization that proposes to improve and enrich the lives of all and to achieve social equilibrium.[13]

The religious superstitions of the poor had to be combated as well. In particular, social workers criticized the poor's reliance on *curanderos*, Mexican folk healers. "With the *curanderos*, so many mothers have lost their health or their life, and have sacrificed their children to these absurd curative practices," wrote Dolores Palácios de Fuentes, an SSA social worker. "It is known the credulity and trust that the people have in these charlatans. . . . The women trust them with their health and the health of their families. . . . They have more trust in these *curanderos* than in their own doctors."[14] Palácios may have overestimated a poor woman's access to a medical doctor, but her opinion of the poor's reliance on *curanderos* is clear. If Mexico was to progress, the poor had to be weaned from their superstitions; modern, "scientific" medicine was the key to the health of the nation's children.

As noted earlier, the eugenicist belief that public health programs contributed to racial "improvement" was also linked explicitly to the economic and social progress of the nation. As Palácios observed in her UNAM licenciatura thesis, the point of social work was "to improve the race and enhance social accommodation of future generations."[15] The racial inferiority of the Mexican populace was of urgent concern to social workers. In Alanís Cebrián's words, "Mexico is a country of passive resistance. Our people, with few exceptions, are docile and submissive, indifferent and apparently unworried. They do not know how to make use of all that social services have to offer. They are used to depending on alms or charity or public benevolence; they don't know that it is their right to participate in social service programs that the state has an obligation to provide."[16] Social work in Mexico therefore had to break a vicious cycle: the people were already hereditarily "unfit"—they were docile and passive—and "old-fashioned" Catholic charity did nothing to improve the situation. Only social workers could break this cycle and help transform Mexico.

The therapy of social work could be applied to three targets—the individual, the group, or the community. Individual social work relied on the casework method. Social workers assumed that an individual in need of help was experiencing a temporary hardship—perhaps the client was sick, or had recently lost his job. Readjustment came through addressing whatever specific temporary problems the client faced. They did not think that this type of social work was helpful for people whose poverty stemmed from structural factors, but they did believe that the statistics compiled from the case files could form the basis for structural change. To address these larger structural issues, social workers recommended group or community social work.[17]

When applied to a group, social work took the form of education. Social workers considered group therapy most effective when problems transcended the individual level, or when many of the group's members could benefit from training in personal and social development. Groups could be made up of family members or formed from school, work, religious, or recreational cohorts. A social worker initially directed the group, but the ultimate goal was to teach group members to educate themselves, to teach the group members social skills so that they could get along with one another and "unite their forces for a common good."[18]

The third target of social work—the community—involved structural problems faced by a community as a whole. Social workers, in conjunction with members of the community, studied the area's social and geographical problems and resources. They then helped community members organize the area in order to make the most efficient use of its resources. Community social work emphasized the need of the community as a whole to take an active role in promoting its own welfare. Communities could expect to receive some government aid, but here, too, the point was to teach people to improve their communities through their own efforts.[19]

While all three levels of social work acknowledged that poverty could stem from conditions beyond the individual's control, they also emphasized that poverty could be overcome only through the efforts of the individual, group, and/or community. In one way, this might have been very empowering for the poor. Social workers taught poor people that although their poverty might not be their fault, they could do something to improve their circumstances. This attitude stood in opposition to pre-Vatican II Catholic attitudes, which exhorted the poor to suffer on earth and receive their reward in heaven. It also reflected the psychological basis of the profession. Social workers believed that if only people could learn to be socially well adjusted, many of their problems would be mitigated.

This approach did not really attempt to solve structural social problems. Social reformers as a group did not agitate for social justice, nor did they (after 1940) blame capitalism for the conditions suffered by the poor. To the contrary, their vision of social transformation was quite narrow. It is easy to criticize this vision retrospectively, but it is important to remember that these welfare professionals had limited governmental resources. While their faith in the transformative power of individual effort may have been unrealistic, their attitude nevertheless represented a dramatic change in the way the poor were viewed. These women advocated an ethic of personal strength, which must have aided their own efforts to define themselves personally and professionally as they entered into this new type of work.

Professional Training in Mexico

In the 1930s Mexican social workers who had been trained in the United States advocated the professionalization of social work in Mexico and fought to set up social work programs in Mexico City. In 1933 the SEP instituted the first course in social work, taught by Professor Julia Nava de Ruisánchez, in the Escuela de Enseñanzas Especiales No. 6, also known as the Escuela Doméstica.[20] This school emphasized the training of poor women, both in and outside their homes, on the grounds that "ill-formed families" and poor economic conditions were the seeds of all other problems. The course of study was four years long. After 1937, when secondary school was included, the training took five years. The school taught some theory but primarily offered practical classes in sewing, cooking, embroidery, preserving fruit, and other manual work. In order to be admitted, a student needed a primary school certificate, a transcript, and a letter certifying her good conduct. Neither age nor socioeconomic class was important. In fact, most of the students were very young and from the working class. This program closed in 1945, but it included a variety of programs while it lasted. Social workers and their students created a small center where they taught people how to read and write and founded work centers for women (for example, one had sewing machines that women could come and use) and sport centers for children, adolescents, and adults.

In 1937 Mathilde Rodríguez Cabo successfully petitioned the secretary of state for a program that would "scientifically train" employees of the children's court. This two-year program was created under the auspices of UNAM's Facultad de Derecho y Ciencias Sociales. Its classes in empirical social work began in 1937 but were suspended two years later for lack of students. In 1940 the program was reinstated under the new name School of Social Workers.[21]

While the U.S.-trained women who were the first teachers in this program almost certainly were middle class, the students at the Escuela Doméstica were not. In 1938, 634 women[22] and 10 men were enrolled, only 7 percent of whom could be said to come from the upper class; these were students whose parents (presumably their fathers) were landowners or were wealthy enough that they did not have to work. Roughly half of the students were the daughters of clerks, office workers, and police officers, and another 20 percent were the daughters of manual laborers, peasants, or artisans (see table 3). This suggests that these women's families were not poor, but they certainly were not wealthy, either. They were middle class, but perhaps not firmly so, which may explain the willingness of these families to allow their daughters to pursue a professional career—the family

Table 3 Parental Occupations for Students at the Escuela Doméstica, 1938

Occupation of Parents	Number of Students	Percentage of Student Body
Servants, domestics, waiters, etc.	14	2.17
Workers, peasants, and artisans	124	19.25
Clerks, including police	285	44.26
Military personnel	16	2.49
Merchants, traders, farmers, and ranchers	124	19.25
Housewives	2	0.31
Landowners or professionals without official employment	45	6.99
Misc. (journalists, students, etc.)	13	2.02

Source: AHSSA/BP, Sección Asistencia, serie Dirección General de Asistencia, leg. 5, exp. 3, record 68. In addition to the students listed in table 3, twenty-one students, or 3.26 of the student body, were not dependent on their parents and thus are not included in the table.

may have needed the money. It may also have been a way for these women to become more firmly entrenched in the middle class themselves. Although social workers in Chile tended to be upper-class women seeking to professionalize their status as former charity workers, the Escuela Doméstica offered women of a more humble class access to a professional career. In 1944 women working for the SSA as visiting nurses (an occupation similar to social work) made a monthly salary (at the highest level) of Mex$240. The chief of visiting nurses made $300 a month.[23] This put the *jefas* in the marginal middle class (in 1950 pesos), and the visiting nurses themselves technically in the lower middle class. Yet it is important to remember that social work at this time was a professional career, so that even if women were not making salaries equivalent to those of middle-class men, they were nevertheless middle class in social terms.[24]

The SEP revised the program in 1948 to include more of the material covered by the UNAM program.[25] Graduates, if they chose, could go on to study social work at the university level. The students continued, for the most part, to be young women from the lower middle class. Many students did not finish the program. Between 1946 and 1956, 445 students enrolled, 118 finished the coursework, but only twenty actually received the degree.[26]

Women continued to dominate the profession throughout the 1940s and 1950s. In 1940 the social work program was reinstated at UNAM's Facultad de Derecho y Ciencias Sociales.[27] The program itself was not welcomed by the other UNAM departments, which considered the School of Social Work "a badly placed patch on our faculty." Between 1940 and 1956 only nine men applied to the program: three in 1940, one in 1941, and five in 1956. The average age of the students was between twenty and twenty-five.[28] The attrition rate for this program was high as well. Between 1940 and 1956, 446 students enrolled but only sixty-five students actually graduated and received their degrees. Most of the graduates found employment at the SSA, the Departamento de Prevención Social, Mexico City's Department of Social Action, the Hospital Infantíl, or the IMSS. Some of them went into rural service. Others went into administration, working in the offices of these agencies or at universities and schools.[29]

Social workers worked to professionalize their status. The inclusion of social work in the university curriculum shows the difficulties they faced. Social work as a discipline was not as well respected as professions like medicine were, in large part because the profession was dominated by women. Attitudes toward working women were often contradictory and conflicted during this period. In addition, some critics devalued social work because they claimed that the prerequisites for entrance to the program were less rigorous than those of other schools and departments.[30]

The 1940s saw the establishment of other schools of social work in addition to the degree offered by UNAM. Many of these schools were part of the Catholic Church and offered slightly different training. One was the Autonomous Institute of the School of Social Service, a part of the International Catholic Union of Social Service, founded in 1945 by Rosa Velasco Zimbrón and a group of members interested in social service work. The Catholic Church and private donations funded the school, which received no money from the government. The founders based the coursework on the curricula of schools in Peru, Belgium, and Canada. They agreed that U.S. models of casework were excellent but ill suited to the idiosyncrasies of Latin America, although they did not specify why.[31] The coursework provided training for both urban and rural areas and offered a mixture of theoretical methods and practical application. Contemporary observers noted that this school was just as prestigious as the UNAM program, and its graduates filled many of the same positions as UNAM graduates. According to the school's own statistics, its students came from all social levels. Another program founded in the 1940s was the social work program at the Universidad Femenina. Originally a "short course" offered in 1943, the school did not offer a full degree until 1952. The university served a wealthy student body—the social workers trained in this program came from an elite background.

In Mexico City two other religious orders created social work programs in the 1950s. One of these was the Escuela de Trabajo Social "Vasco de Quiroga," founded in 1955. It was run by nuns and boasted a student population from all socioeconomic levels, even offering scholarships for students from rural areas. The coursework was modeled on the classes offered at UNAM. Another group of nuns, the Sisters of Charity, created the Marillac School of Social Work. This was also incorporated into the UNAM school, offering classes based on the UNAM School of Social Work.

One social worker commented on the fact that the "Vasco de Quiroga" and the Marillac School demonstrated the Catholic Church's attempt to move away from older notions of charity and toward a more "scientific" version of social work. While it is beyond the scope of this study to delineate the specific differences between a Catholic vision of social work and the state-sponsored vision, I would argue that at this level of training there was probably very little difference at all. While U.S.-based casework methods were popular in Mexico during this period, it is important to remember that Mexican social work had its foundation in Catholic social action. Women had long participated in charitable activities not in spite of but because of their religious nature. Thus, I argue, professional social work became specifically Mexican during this period because of its dual heritage—both Catholic social action and the revolutionary government's anticlerical calls for secular reform. It is also important to differentiate between professional social workers and "charity ladies," women of an elite background who participated in philanthropic activities. Upper- and middle-class women were active in voluntary committees (discussed in chapters 2 and 3), which gave elite women a venue for their work. While voluntary committees worked under the aegis of the SSA, they did not provide committee women with specific training in social work.

The Social Workers

Much of existing research on the history of social work and welfare reform is informed by the social control school, exemplified by such historians as Michel Foucault, who viewed asylums and other institutions for the poor as systems of control and discipline. While control and discipline might have been the original intent of the founders, historians have shown that the poor and other groups often were able to modify the original goals.[32] In this model of thought, social workers have also been considered agents of state control. As Karen Tice comments, "Despite the harsh and often unfair judgments made by protective workers, social workers should not be caricatured as heartless detectives of a therapeutic state, driven to trample the lives of the poor and working-class clients in search of evidence that would confirm existing middle-class assumptions of deviance and transgression."[33] In Mexico as well as the United States, the story of social workers and social work is much more complicated.

One complicating factor is the class backgrounds of social workers themselves. In a departure from the pattern both in the United States and in other Latin American countries, social workers in Mexico did not necessarily come from elite families. Historians like Rosemblatt, Tice, and Guy have commented on the difficulties class differences presented to the creation of any cross-class feminist alliance, or even to any form of gendered solidarity. Certainly this was the case in Mexico. Welfare work there, however, rather than solidifying existing class disparities, served as a conduit for some women from humble families to the middle class. In essence, the system created a two-tiered class of social workers. Given the cost of attending the university and the loss of income involved, many welfare professionals, particularly those who could afford a university degree in the 1940s and 1950s, probably came from solidly middle-class or elite families. Yet many social workers were trained in vocational high school programs and Catholic schools. These programs had higher rates of attendance among women of poorer backgrounds; they also had more flexible class schedules, allowing their students to work part-time.

How did this class background affect Mexican social reform? It is difficult to say, since many factors influenced the development of Mexican social work. In many ways it is a chicken-and-egg question. Did Mexican welfare workers emphasize social justice because many of them came from humble backgrounds, or did Mexican revolutionary ideology attract more lower middle-class women to this career? Social workers themselves saw social work as a vocation.[34] They believed they were at the forefront of a fight to help Mexico progress and modernize. As Palácios de Fuentes observed, "One must note that every case that comes into the center is an object of social investigation. This shows that social work is just as important as medical, hygiene, and social services. These services are based on the work of social workers or visiting nurses, who rely upon this research to complete their work."[35]

Women who chose social work also saw themselves as having very special characteristics. "A social worker should be scientific, persuasive, intelligent, have an aptitude for working with others, [and she should have] an attractive personality, free of misunderstood sentimentalism, free of prejudice," wrote one social worker. The social worker should also be "objective and realistic in order to penetrate modern society's social problems. She should have the ability to inspire, a sense of organization, [and] balance and emotional stability, [and should] be a dynamic and mentally healthy person with an aptitude for social work."[36] Welfare workers were to be modern women, free of superstition and sentimentality, whose hard work and discipline would help Mexico become the modern country social reformers envisioned. One social worker declared that "social work and social action do not distinguish nationalities, religions, or political creeds; it is a work of harmony and love of humanity."[37] The law agreed that social workers were professionals, equal to doctors and nurses. In 1945 the Reglamentación de la Ley de Profesiones made social work a technical-scientific profession that required a degree.[38] Nevertheless, many social workers complained that they did not receive enough professional training through their university programs. Specifically, many demanded less theoretical study and more practical training.[39]

The professionalization of social work allowed social workers to claim middle-class status. This professionalization was embedded within the rise of the postrevolutionary state, which relied on "experts" to legitimate itself. Just as economic experts could guide development, social welfare experts could help transform a population fit for an industrial miracle. Social workers were middle class because they were professional, and they derived this definition from their education and degrees. But they also derived this status from the tradition of Catholic charity work dating back to the Porfiriato. The charity ladies were empowered to make decisions on behalf of their clients, and it was this ability to distinguish between the deserving and undeserving poor that gave them social power. Professional social workers, while deriding religious charity, nevertheless also drew social capital from this tradition. This can be seen in the language they used when they talked about themselves and their choices. They were "called" to social work; they saw it as a "vocation." This language had religious overtones—indeed, with their talk of a "work of harmony and love of humanity," it has much in common with the language of social Catholicism.

In the mid-twentieth century social workers thus achieved status through both education and the tradition of women's charitable work. They also derived social power from their continuing ability to define and mediate class. Social workers not only helped the poor; they had power to define what was middle class as well. Women like Enelda Fox had the ability to write and administer programming designed to "uplift" the poor, which gave them leeway to document and enforce what they considered "appropriate" middle-class standards, including definitions of appropriate motherhood. Motherhood could no longer be seen as "natural" or "eternal"; it had to be appropriately defined, monitored, and regulated. Mothers were the key to the development of a modern Mexico, and therefore motherhood had to be constructed to aid in this development. Mothers had to be scientific yet instinctive, disciplinarians yet affectionate. Even supposedly middle-class mothers—those who served as foster mothers, for example—were scrutinized and taken to task if not up to standards.

As Enelda Fox stated, middle-class mothers would be the exemplars of modernity. With proper tutelage, mothers of all classes could become modern and could help create a modern Mexico. Social workers, with their ability to define and regulate these values, had what they saw as a crucial task. Interestingly, although they focused on mothers, they did not seek to overthrow male authority in the household. They simply sought to update that authority, as Mary Kay Vaughan and others have shown, by modernizing patriarchy. They sought to domesticate men and train women to be scientific mothers.[40]

Social workers occupied a complicated position in Mexican society. On the one hand, they did interfere in and attempt to change the lives of the poor. Sometimes their advice and recommendations reflected class biases, and their women-focused programs were not necessarily friendly toward women. On the other hand, social work offered women of different classes the opportunity to participate in a professional career that must have been liberating. It allowed women to enter the workforce in nontraditional ways and be considered important and professional. This move was contested, but it led to greater female participation in the workforce. It also opened to the door to creating greater female sociability through the centers and mothers' clubs.

Elí Evangelista argues that the development of Mexican social work was inherently linked to the growth and centralization of the modern postrevolutionary state and its needs to satisfy the revolution's calls for social justice.[41] Social work is thus a postrevolutionary phenomenon that arose because of the way the modern Mexican state was formed. While professional social work certainly developed in Mexico as the postrevolutionary governments consolidated, Evangelista's analysis ignores the long tradition of women's participation in welfare activities. Particularly since the mid-nineteenth century, elite women had founded and administered charitable and philanthropic programs and organizations throughout the country. These were largely of a religious nature, since male professionals dominated state-run agencies. Mexican society viewed elite women's charitable activities as a natural extension of their maternal characteristics and inherent moral superiority to men. Although social work as a profession renounced religion and superstition, attitudes about women's involvement in this career evolved out of these older attitudes regarding women's charitable work. After the revolution, women who wanted to continue this kind of work, and be paid for it, exploited the belief that social work was considered particularly well suited to women. Women worked hard to ensure the professional status of social work. The influence of the casework method, which blamed the individual for being poor and was popular in the United States, extended beyond the field of social work and informed the attitudes of anthropologists such as Oscar Lewis and his "culture of poverty" thesis.[42]

Unlike Lewis and other casework advocates, Mexican reformers championed a version of "social therapy" that emphasized social transformation and development. This focus was result of both dominant Latin American discourses regarding child and maternal welfare and the revolution's calls for social justice. Evangelista argues that the blend of these influences resulted in "a superficial collage and an unreflexive amalgamation of different theoretical parts, different ideas of social action, and inarticulate fragments of various schools of thought."[43] While Mexican social thought can indeed be seen as a blend of different attitudes toward social welfare, it had its own internal logic. Mexican social reformers argued that economic development was impossible without social transformation. Poverty was a result of many factors, some individual, others rooted in economic dislocations. In order for Mexico to progress, social workers argued, all of these factors had to be addressed. Thus social workers used the casework method in conjunction with educational programs to achieve their goals of social uplift.

Social workers themselves saw social work as a vocation and considered their work part of a national project in social transformation and reform. They believed in developmentalist goals that saw import-substitution industrialization as the route to modernization. Social workers and social reformers in general believed that these goals could only be met through the "uplift" of the population as a whole. Social work, and by extension female social workers, thus played a large role in the government's modernization policies. Women were also the primary target of social work strategies. By examining the emphasis placed on women in these dual roles, we can begin to see how the very concept of modernization in Mexico was gendered in specific ways. The political economy of the time was linked to very specific notions of gender—for example, the male family wage earner, as well as changing attitudes about women's place in this new society.

EPILOGUE

Mexican reformers were an integral part of the international maternal child welfare movement. Mexican teachers, doctors, social workers, and other professionals attended Pan-American and other international meetings and helped shape discourses about gender, race, class, and the role of the emerging welfare state in Mexico. They also helped shape international, especially Pan-American, views on maternal and child welfare. Examining the proceedings of these meetings is one key to understanding how the Mexican welfare state developed and why it focused on mothers and children.[1]

The Mexican emphasis on motherhood in the 1940s and 1950s represented the convergence of several discourses surrounding welfare and poverty. On the one hand, elite women, active in such organizations as the Union de Damas Católicas Mexicanas since Porfirian times, argued that their social position as mothers should give them a voice in debates regarding social welfare. Their activities centered on religious as well as vocational training for poor women; their goal was to provide the poor with improved living standards while at the same time imparting a clear moral message. Theirs was a class-based vision—elite women could participate in the public sphere through religious charitable activities that emphasized their inherent maternal nature. Working women, however, had to be taught their proper role in society. While these "ladies" created day-care centers for working mothers, they never suggested that their own children be cared for outside the home.

At the same time, eugenics, as a means of "scientifically" improving the population through public health and education measures that targeted mothers, was also an influential discourse. Eugenicists clearly linked modernization to improved social welfare, arguing that in order to develop, Mexico had to guard its most important national resource—children. They maintained that since a mother provided most of a child's education, a mother's education assumed great importance as well. While these ideas echoed Enlightenment ideals of republican motherhood, eugenicists took this idea of motherhood one step further by linking it to science. Mothers had to be trained to raise their children scientifically, using the most progressive child-rearing techniques available. Medicine also assumed new importance. Eugenicists believed that diseases like syphilis and conditions such as alcoholism could be passed down genetically to children. It was not just that a syphilitic mother would give birth to a child with syphilis but that the vice itself would corrupt the next generation. Therefore, even if doctors could cure a child of syphilis, his or her genes would be forever weakened, and these deficiencies would be in turn passed down to the next generation. Mothers, in both their medical and social capacities, took on added significance. If Mexico was to be a part of "modern civilization," mothers would have to be monitored. Arguably, this was a class-based vision as well. Reformers did not propose to regulate all mothers, only poor mothers. According to reformers, this would help build a new, "revolutionary" Mexico.

One factor that distinguished Mexico from other Latin American nations was its commitment to rural as well as urban transformation. Educational programs were administered by the SAP in the 1920s and 1930s and expanded by the SSA in the 1940s and 1950s. These agencies recognized the necessity of the countryside to the state's project of modernization. To aid in this project, the SSA established schools in Mexico to train professional social workers, offering a mix of theoretical and practical training and giving women of all social classes access to a professional career. These programs also provided specific training for rural social workers.

While much has been written about postrevolutionary state formation in Mexico, scholars have only just begun to explore how this process was gendered. Historians and political scientists alike have argued about the significance of the Mexican Revolution in the creation of the twentieth-century Mexican political system. Was the PRI the "inheritor" of revolutionary values and aspirations? Or did the Mexican government betray the revolution? Similarly, political economists have analyzed twentieth-century nationalist economic policy. Was import-substitution industrialization a legitimate attempt to modernize Mexico? Or did the PRI merely sell out its *patria* in an attempt to maintain its own power and hegemony?

Studies of these questions highlight important debates in Mexican history. Yet by posing such either/or questions, historians have missed the many ways in which the PRI did exercise control and authority. As many historians have pointed out, this authority was not simply exercised from above; rather, it was a dialectical process.[2] And, I argue, this process was fundamentally gendered.[3]

Scholars are also beginning to examine the ways in which international movements influenced the process of Mexican state formation. Historians in particular have looked at how international currents shaped issues of women's reproductive rights, women's sexuality, and maternal and child welfare, and have shown how these processes were linked to issues of post-revolutionary state formation. Katherine Bliss argues persuasively that social welfare reform movements in Mexico, particularly those targeting prostitution, not only reflected the contingencies of the Mexican Revolution itself but were consistent with international movements regarding "social conditions of modernization, human rights and public health reform" during the same period. Social reform in Mexico gave middle-class activists a way to differentiate themselves from the poor and affiliate themselves with revolutionary principles.[4]

Mexican women began to increase in importance to the state because of the expansion of the welfare sector in the postrevolutionary government. Nineteenth-century notions of republican motherhood intersected with newer discourses of science and modernity to create a new social role for mothers. Scientific motherhood linked women with the state through the SAP/SSA, and allowed reformers to rewrite not only women's role within the family but the relationship of the family vis-à-vis the postrevolutionary government. Welfare policy redefined the border between the public and the private, as welfare workers asserted their rights to monitor and regulate families to achieve a "modern" Mexico. According to the Mexican government, women had a central role to play within their own families and within the larger Mexican body politic. The significance the postrevolutionary regime attached to motherhood altered reformers' visions of the traditional patriarchal family but did not fundamentally change patriarchy at the larger social level. It merely updated and modernized patriarchal arrangements, inserting the state as the paternal figure within the family.

Women were able slowly to take advantage of new government goals to put a female face on the postrevolutionary state. Social work, a new profession in the 1930s and 1940s, allowed women to participate in welfare work on a professional level. The professionalization of social work built on the notion that women were "naturally" fit for work in the public health and welfare field, although, ironically, in order to professionalize, they had to be properly trained and educated to perform this role. While male policymakers were firmly in control of the administrative hierarchy within the SAP/SSA, it was predominantly women, as social workers, visiting nurses, and volunteers, who implemented policy. Thus women regulated, monitored, and helped other women. Social work developed in an era when women began to equate professional status with membership in the middle class. Thus the rise of professional women in Mexico can be seen as part of the ascendancy of both the middle class and the PRI itself.

The women who ran social welfare programs never directly challenged the norm of the male-headed family. Instead, they established family dining halls and similar programs that allowed men to provide for their families more effectively, and they encouraged marriage and male responsibility through campaigns against *amasía*, or common-law marriage. Yet they also managed programs that helped single mothers find employment and raise their children without men. Thus professional women acting on behalf of other women may have subtly challenged and undermined male patriarchal authority, not only in the home but in the political sphere as well. When women gained the suffrage and began to vote, their concerns became more relevant to the maintenance of PRI authority, which was based on political stability and economic growth.

Social reformers and economic policymakers alike believed that Mexico could become modern through a combination of social and economic policy. Welfare programs were meant to complement policies such as import-substitution industrialization. Many reformers asserted that economic policy would fail on its own unless the population was educated enough to participate productively in modern life. Indeed, the number of welfare agencies and programs increased throughout the 1940s and 1950s, a period many scholars see as more conservative than the years immediately following the revolution. This expansion continued until the economic crisis of the 1980s.

In 1961 the government reorganized maternal and child welfare programs under the National Institute for Child Protection (INPI), which reiterated the state's dedication to the protection of childhood but refocused policy to support the whole family rather than just mothers and children. In 1968 the Mexican National Institute for the Care of Children was established to organize and direct all welfare activities. Both agencies were dedicated to the protection of children, but the INPI concentrated on child nutrition programs. In 1974 all welfare activities were recentralized under the INPI, which again rededicated its commitment to children, families, and communities. The INPI was the precursor to the Agency for the Integrated Development of the Family (DIF), which remains the state agency that serves mothers, children, and families today.

Private charities and international agencies continued their work on behalf of mothers and their children. After 1954 Unicef sponsored many public health initiatives, such as vaccination and sanitation programs, as well as clinics for pregnant and lactating mothers, which continue to work in conjunction with the DIF today. The health and welfare of mothers and children was of central importance to both reformers and the Mexican government throughout the twentieth century. The economic crisis of the 1970s and 1980s, however, necessitated a shift in the government's economic planning. Capital flight provoked the nationalization of the banking system in 1982, as inflation reached previously unheard-of levels. The election of Miguel de la Madrid as president in 1982 meant the implementation of a neoliberal attempt to deal with the economy. The older import-substitution industrialization model was dead.

De la Madrid launched the Immediate Program for Economic Recovery to combat the nation's problems and lay the groundwork for long-range development. According to the government, its principal objectives were to lower inflation, protect employment, and reestablish basic conditions for economic growth and development. De la Madrid's administration identified the rate of inflation, which exceeded 100 percent, as the most important threat facing the economy and concluded that only drastic cuts in public expenditures could bring it under control. Beginning in 1983 the state's participation in the economy as a percentage of GDP dropped. Budget cuts affected not only welfare expenditures but also agriculture, infrastructure, the oil industry, and public-sector manufacturing investments. Excluding debt service, public expenditures declined by 62.9 percent between 1982 and 1987.[5]

Cuts were made for both practical and ideological reasons. International lenders, led by the IMF, demanded that Mexico, like other developing nations hit by the world economic crisis, adopt adjustment policies that would "give creditors grounds for confidence in their capacity to bring their external obligations and resources into better alignment."[6] Both the IMF and the technocrats agreed that the adoption of structural adjustment policies would strengthen Mexico's economy in the long term. Public spending cuts were the hallmark of structural adjustment. Social spending on areas such as public health and welfare had been an important part of the Mexican welfare state and were particularly targeted.

It should come as no surprise that the dismantling of the welfare state has had particularly harmful effects on women. As women have increasingly moved into the workforce over the past thirty years, much of their labor has been concentrated in low-paying work in manufacturing. Transnational corporations have preferred female labor, arguing that women are better suited to this work and that their "innate" passivity and docility make them less likely to challenge management and organize unions. The "feminization of employment" has resulted not only in more women in the workforce but in changing types of work, including temporary, part-time, and home-based work—work that is normally poorly paid.[7] Without the help of public assistance, women must make up for aid previously offered through educational programs, day-care programs, and school breakfasts. As three decades' worth of neoliberal policy has systematically dismantled social assistance, adversely affecting women in particular, it is important that we understand how central gender was to the creation of the postrevolutionary Mexican welfare state. Current social policy and social ills, such as unequal income distribution, access to health care, and housing, have their roots in the way social reformers conceived of welfare, reform, and charity after the revolution.

In fact, since the economic crisis of 1994, Mexican reformers have once again targeted mothers in an attempt to ameliorate extreme poverty. Begun in the 1990s as a program called Progreso, this effort has continued in the 2000s as Oportunidades, a program that gives rural mothers cash payments for keeping their children (especially daughters) in school and additional money for food if mothers bring their children in for preventive care check-ups and vaccinations at a local clinic. (Mothers are also required to attend a monthly workshop on a health-related topic in exchange for this assistance.) This successful program has been widely emulated, and not just in Latin America—Mayor Bloomberg in New York City has looked into it as well.[8] It seems that once again mothers are the key to economic development, and that once again Mexico is leading the way in innovative programs to challenge extreme poverty.

NOTES

The following abbreviations appear in the notes.

AGN   Archivo General de la Nación (National Archives)
AHSSA   Archivo Histórico de la Secretaría de Salubridad y Asistencia
          (Historical Archive of the Ministry of Health and Welfare)
BP   Beneficencia Pública (Mexico City Department of Public Be-
          nevolence, precursor of the SAP)
DAS   Dirección de Asistencia Social (Office of Social Welfare)
DGHAMI   Dirección General de Higiene y Asistencia Materno-Infantil
          (Office of the Director-General of Hygiene and Maternal and
          Child Welfare)
exp.   expediente (file)
leg.   legajo (folder)

INTRODUCTION

1. All translations are my own unless otherwise indicated.

2. According to James Wilkie, the upper class (which he defines as managerial and professional) and the middle class (defined as small tradesmen, semiskilled artisans, miners, petroleum
labor, and service employees) both expanded during the period 1940–1960. In 1940, the upper class
made up 2.9 percent of the population and the middle class, 12.6. By 1960 the upper class constituted
6.5 percent of the population and the middle class, 33.5 percent. Wilkie, *Mexican Revolution*, 203; see
also Ervin, "1930 Agrarian Census in Mexico."

3. Aguilar Camín and Meyer, *Shadow of the Mexican Revolution*, 109.

4. Buck, "Activists and Mothers," 369–70.

5. Scott, "Gender." For an excellent discussion of gender, see also French and Bliss, *Gender,
Sexuality, and Power*, especially the introduction.

6. Koven and Michel, *Mothers of a New World*, 24–25.

7. See Guy, *Women Build the Welfare State*; Rosemblatt, *Gendered Compromises*; Ehrick, "*Madrinas* and Missionaries"; Blum, *Domestic Economies* and "Conspicuous Benevolence." Donna Guy's work
on the Pan-American Child Congresses is an exception to the national focus.

8. Vaughan makes this compelling argument about the PRI's rural education project during
the same time period, in "Modernizing Patriarchy." Susan Besse makes the same argument in her
pathbreaking work *Restructuring Patriarchy*.

9. Jean Franco makes a similar argument by analyzing films in *Plotting Women*, 147–74. See also Lavrín, *Women, Feminism, and Social Change*; Blum, *Domestic Economies*.

10. Stepan, *Hour of Eugenics*, 44–45, 89.

11. Ibid., 37.

12. Rosemblatt, "Other Americas," 612.

13. Stern, "Responsible Mothers and Normal Children," 370.

14. Ibid.

15. Ibid., 369, 371–72. Reformers all over Latin America challenged the unfettered control men had over their families. For example, see Guy, "Parents Before the Tribunals," 173–90.

16. De Grazia, *How Fascism Ruled Women*, 3.

17. Fuentes, *Asistencia social en México*, 74–76.

18. Hellman, *Mexico in Crisis*, 56.

19. See, for example, Camp, *Politics in Mexico*; Cockcroft, *Mexico*; Levy and Székely, *Mexico*; Aguilar Camín and Meyer, *Shadow of the Mexican Revolution*; Looney, *Economic Policymaking in Mexico*; Glade and Anderson, *Political Economy of Mexico*; Hellman, *Mexico in Crisis*; Hansen, *Politics of Mexican Development*; Newell and Rubio, *Mexico's Dilemma*; and Teichman, *Policymaking in Mexico*.

20. Middlebrook, *Paradox of Revolution*, 210.

21. Labor unions also provided women with opportunities to fight patriarchal assumptions. See Fernández Aceves, "Struggle Between the *Metate* and the *Molinos de Nixtamal*." For gender and company welfare, see Gauss, "Working-Class Masculinity and the Rationalized Sex." See also Snodgrass, *Deference and Defiance in Monterrey*.

22. Incháustegui Romero, "Cambio de la asistencia social," 114.

23. By way of comparison, in 1938 education received 13 percent of the budget (falling to 9.6 percent in 1958), and the Department of Labor received 0.4 percent in 1938 and 0.2 percent in 1958. Wilkie, *Mexican Revolution*, 160–61, 166–67, 171, 174. The SAP/SSA was also funded in part by the national lottery.

24. Incháustegui Romero, "Cambio de la asistencia social," 119.

25. González Navarro, *Pobreza en México*, 267–69.

26. Dirección de Pensiones Civiles de Retiro, *Tercer censo de empleados federales*, 36, 41.

27. Rubenstein, *Bad Language, Naked Ladies*, 42.

28. Tice, *Wayward Girls and Immoral Women*, 205n19.

29. Quoted in Fuentes, *Asistencia social en México*, 54–55.

30. Manrique Castro, *De apostoles a agentes de cambio*, 44, 49.

31. Schell, "Honorable Avocation for Ladies," 79.

32. González Navarro, *Pobreza en México*, 74–75.

33. Pedersen, *Family Dependence and the Origins of the Welfare State*.

34. For an excellent discussion of Catholic social action in Mexico, see Curley, "Sociólogos peregrinos"; and Ceballos Ramírez, *Catolicismo social*.

35. Porter, *Working Women in Mexico City*, 55–60.

36. Blum, "Conspicuous Benevolence." For a discussion of male reformers' attempts to control the social ill of prostitution, see Bliss, *Compromised Positions*, 23–62.

37. For a discussion of Argentina's Beneficent Society, see Mead, "Beneficent Maternalism."

38. Blum, "Conspicuous Benevolence," 22.

39. "La viuda de Díaz dona fuerte suma," *El Nacional*, March 28, 1941.

40. Blum, "Conspicuous Benevolence," 22–23.

41. Schell, "Honorable Avocation for Ladies," 81, 84–93.

42. Ibid., 79.

43. Guy, *White Slavery*, 38.

44. "Contestación del Dip. Manuel Martínez Sicilia, Presidente del Congreso" (1938), in *Presidentes de México ante la nación*, 139.

CHAPTER I

1. "Las ponencias del congreso del niño en esta capital: La delegación norteamericano leería interesantes temas de utilidad social," *El Nacional*, October 1, 1935; advertisement announcing October 3 as "Dia de Beneficencia" sponsored by Asociación Francesa, Suiza y Belga de Beneficencia y Previsión, *El Nacional*, October 4, 1935; R. Ezqueero Peraza, "Yo quiero mi jacalito: Corrido ranchero," *El Nacional*, October 6, 1935; "Importantes trabajos para discutirse en el congreso del niño, en esta capital," *Excélsior*, October 1, 1935; "Destacadas personalidades figuran como delegados al septimo congreso del niño," *Excélsior*, October 11, 1935.

2. "Inauguro sus labores el congreso del niño," *El Nacional*, October 13, 1935; "No más niños epilépticos," *El Nacional*, October 17, 1935; "La nueva generación revolucionaria del país," *El Nacional*, October 18, 1935.

3. "Apertura del VII Congreso Panamericano del Niño," *Excélsior*, October 13, 1935.

4. "Hasta en el congreso del niño hace irrupción el bolchevismo," *Excélsior*, October 16, 1935.

5. "Hoy clausura sus trabajos el VII congreso panamericano del niño, en forma solemne," *Excélsior*, October 19, 1935; "La liberación del niño proletario," *El Universal*, October 18, 1935.

6. "La mortalidad en la infancia," *Excélsior*, October 17, 1935; "La castidad es prejuicio burgues, y el capitalismo culpable de muchos males," *Excélsior*, October 18, 1935.

7. Guy, *White Slavery*, 36–37.

8. The Mexican case stood in contrast to authoritarian regimes such as Franco's in Spain, which embraced national Catholicism.

9. See Loaeza, *Clases medias y política*; Porter, "Empleadas públicas."

10. *Memoria del VII Congreso Panamericano del Niño*, 1:5. Katherine Lenroot had been an active participant in the U.S. Children's Bureau, serving as its director during the 1930s. For a discussion of Lenroot's U.S. activities, see Gordon, *Pitied but Not Entitled*, 101, 103, 256, 268–72. For Lenroot's activities in Latin America, see Guy, *White Slavery*, 54–71.

11. Scholars have discussed the role U.S. companies played in attempting to "civilize" Latin American working classes. See, for example, Klubock, *Contested Communities*; O'Brien, *Revolutionary Mission*. I argue, by contrast, that Latin American, not U.S., elites spearheaded this effort.

12. Lavrín, *Women, Feminism, and Social Change*, 97.

13. Simons, "Trabajo social," 838.

14. Ibid., 840.

15. Vázquez and Loyo, "Programa mínima de preparación," 849–50.

16. Lavrín, *Women, Feminism, and Social Change*, 97, 118–19.

17. Simons, "Trabajo social," 839–40.

18. Ibid., 841.

19. Rosemblatt, *Gendered Compromises*, 4.

20. Simons, "Trabajo social," 841.

21. This is the casework method of social work, discussed more fully in chapter 5.

22. Simons, "Trabajo social," 840.

23. AHSSA/BP, Sección Asistencia, leg. 3, exp. 4. This kind of complaint is discussed more fully in chapter 3.

24. Simons, "Trabajo social," 843.

25. Lavrín, *Women, Feminism, and Social Change*, 100–102.

26. Simons, "Trabajo social," 843.

27. Rivera de Rangel, "Colaboración de la familia y de la escuela," 322.

28. Fox, "Coordinación y desarrollo de los trabajos," 891.

29. Ibid., 892.

30. Torres was active in both the Mexican and the Pan-American women's movement. She served as vice president of the Pan-American Association for the Advancement of Women in 1922,

she was the chief of Mexico's Bureau for Cultural Missions in the 1920s, and she helped found the National Council of Mexican Women in 1918. See Miller, *Latin American Women*, 87, 92–93.

31. Torres, "Servicio social infantil," 887.

32. Hernández, "Coordinación y desarrollo de los trabajos," 897.

33. Ibid., 898–99, 902.

34. Ibid., 903.

35. *Congresos Pan-Americanos del Niño*, 83.

36. Quevedo L., "Protección de la madre soltera," 103.

37. Sainz Trejo, "Protección a los hijos ilegítimos," 135.

38. Quevedo L., "Protección de la madre soltera," 106.

39. Domínguez Navarro, "Investigación de la paternidad," 127.

40. Ibid., 128. Domínguez had been working on this issue since the 1920s in Cuba. She was exiled in Mexico during the 1930s. For a brief biography, see Stoner, "Ofelia Domínguez Navarro."

41. Blum, *Domestic Economies*, 111.

42. Quevedo L., "Protección de la madre soltera," 104.

43. Sainz Trejo, "Protección a los hijos ilegítimos," 137–38.

44. Thorp, *Progress, Poverty, and Exclusion*, 128.

45. Rock, "War and Postwar Intersections," 16–18. The quotation is from Abarca, *Industrialización de Argentina*, 17–32, quoted in ibid., 18.

46. Bethell and Roxborough, "Postwar Conjuncture in Latin America," 13.

47. Wilkie, *Mexican Revolution*, 184; Rock, "War and Postwar Intersections," 17–18.

48. Mathilde Rodríguez Cabo, "Informe de la labor desarrollada por la delegación de México en el VIII Congreso Panamericano del Niño," *Asistencia*, July–August 1942, 10.

49. Ibid., 10–11.

50. "Acta Final del VIII Congreso Panamericano del Niño," *Asistencia*, July–August 1942, 25.

51. Mink, *Wages of Motherhood*, 155; "Acta Final del VIII Congreso," 25.

52. "Acta Final del VIII Congreso," 25.

53. For a discussion of food shortages and urban unrest in Mexico, see Ochoa, *Feeding Mexico*, 71–98.

54. "Acta Final del VIII Congreso," 25. The information and quotations in the following eight paragraphs are from this work, 20–21, 24.

55. For a discussion of changing attitudes toward child labor in Mexico, see Blum, *Domestic Economies*, 255–56.

CHAPTER 2

1. Doremus, "Indigenism, Mestizaje, and National Identity," 381–83.

2. Ochoa, "Coercion, Reform, and the Welfare State," 41–42.

3. One indicator of how the economic downturn hurt the poor and working class was the rapid increase in the number of loans taken from the Nacional Monte de Piedad. Between 1905 and 1927 an average of 476,796 loans per year were made. In 1929 that figure jumped to 613,111; in 1932, to 1 million; and in 1933, to 1.5 million. González Navarro, *Pobreza en México*, 228.

4. Knight, "Cardenismo: Juggernaut or Jalopy?" 79–80.

5. Garrido, *Partido de la revolución*, 235–36.

6. There are various interpretations of the insurrection. Robert Quirk and David Bailey see the events as a reaction between the church hierarchy and the postrevolutionary state, whereas Jean Meyer argues that the Cristero Rebellion was deeply religious in nature and was largely a rural insurgency rather than a clash between elites. See Quirk, *Mexican Revolution and the Catholic Church*; Bailey, *Viva Cristo Rey*; and Meyer, *Cristiada*, vol. 2, *El conflicto entre la iglesia y el estado*.

7. Porter, "Espacios burocráticos." Porter notes that the SAP had a larger number of female employees (57 percent) than any other federal agency in 1938 (195).

8. The SAP defined beggars as those who were homeless or who regularly sought alms on the street rather than work.

9. For an excellent discussion of campaigns against begging in Mexico City, see Ochoa, "Coercion, Reform, and the Welfare State."

10. Between 1910 and 1940 Mexico City's population expanded from 535,745 to 1,565,626. In 1930, 55.8 percent of the Mexican population lived in rural villages; by 1940 that number had dropped to approximately 52 percent. See Wilkie, *Latin American Population*, 328–29, 337.

11. Francisco Palacios, "Hacia la justicia social," *Asistencia Social*, November 20, 1938, 11.

12. Miguel A. Quintana, "La asistencia pública como complemento del salario," *Asistencia Social*, March 1, 1938, 1.

13. Editorial, "Los origenes económicos y sociales de la mendicidad," *Asistencia Social*, February 15, 1938, 14.

14. Editorial, "Mision de la Secretaría de Asistencia Pública," *Asistencia Social*, April 1, 1938, 1.

15. Piccato, *City of Suspects*, 15.

16. Guerrero's radio address was reprinted as "Cristeleza un patriótico llamamiento para la organización del comité nacional por la madre y el niño, como obra de asistencia pública," *Asistencia Social*, June–July 1939; the quotation appears on p. 5.

17. *Estadísticas históricas de México*, 13.

18. Stepan, *Hour of Eugenics*, 3.

19. Bliss, *Compromised Positions*, 108–9.

20. Historians and political scientists have traditionally understood import-substitution industrialization as a phenomenon of the 1940s in Mexico. Scholars such as Enrique Cárdenas have shown, however, that ISI had its beginnings in the 1930s and was practiced in other Latin American countries, and that Ávila Camacho continued already existing policies. See Cárdenas, *Hacienda pública*.

21. Teichman, *Policymaking in Mexico*, 34.

22. Cypher, *State and Capital in Mexico*, 51.

23. Ávila Camacho, "Arenga dirigida a los oficiales graduados en los planteles de la dirección general militar, el 19 de enero de 1941," in *Seis mensajes a la nación* (México: Secretaría de Gobernación, 1941), 7.

24. Wilkie, *Latin American Population*, 337–38.

25. Ochoa, *Feeding Mexico*, 71–74.

26. Dr. Baz began his career at the beginning of the revolution, studying medicine in Mexico City. The violence interrupted his studies, and he soon left the city to fight with Emiliano Zapata. By the end of the revolution Zapata had promoted him to the rank of general. The new constitutional government also named him provisional governor of the state of México. He was named governor again in 1958 under President Ruiz Cortines. In 1920 Baz left the army and his post as governor and rededicated himself to the study of medicine. By 1938 he had been named rector of UNAM. He left UNAM to serve as minister of the SAP in 1940. See Baz's memoir, *Gustavo Baz: Anecdotario e ideas*.

27. Interestingly, FBI reports from 1940 state that Baz was "the closest thing to being pro-Nazi as anyone else in the cabinet." Niblo, *Mexico in the 1940s*, 90.

28. "Bases para la organización de los comités voluntarios de asistencia infantil," 1941, AGN/SSA/SAP/DAS, vol. 17, exp. 096.1/5.

29. P. E. Reina Hermosillo, "Organización de la asistencia: Patrimonio y técnica, resumen de la actuación del estado," *El Nacional*, August 26, 1943.

30. The cooperation between the government and private philanthropic agencies was not new in Latin America, but in many countries (e.g., Argentina and Uruguay), by the 1940s the state had essentially taken over all welfare activities, making Mexico's newly created partnerships unique. See Ehrick, "Affectionate Mothers and the Colossal Machine."

31. Reina Hermosillo, "Organización de la asistencia."

32. Gabino A. Palma, "Hacia el derecho asistencial: 150 millones sin trabajo en la post-guerra," *El Universal*, April 4, 1944.

33. In 1940, under Cárdenas, 6.4 percent of the national budget was dedicated to public health and welfare. This figure declined over the next twenty years, reaching a low of 2.5 percent in 1952, under Alemán. By 1958 the percentage had increased to 3.3 percent. Wilkie, *Mexican Revolution*, 166–67.

34. As noted above, private philanthropy continued throughout the period; the SAP was trying to persuade some of these charities to direct their energies and money toward government-sponsored welfare.

35. Editorial, "Asistencia pública y privada," *Excélsior*, March 22, 1941.

36. Manuel Carcamo Lardizabal, "La basura humana," *Grafico* (afternoon edition), April 12, 1941.

37. "Primer Congreso Nacional de Asistencia Pública: Se efectuará en esta capital de 15 al 20 de mayo de este año—Temario de importancia," *El Nacional*, February 16, 1943. Interestingly, when the congress was first proposed four years earlier, in 1939, a planning document reflected the Cárdenista emphasis on integrating the socially weak into the processes of production. It did not specifically mention mothers and children. See "Proposición para realizar el primer congreso de la asistencia pública," AHSSA/BP, Departamento de Acción Educativo y Social, leg. 13, exp. 6.

38. "Será trascendental el Primer Congreso Nacional de Asistencia: El temario y el programa de la reunión," *El Nacional*, May 10, 1943.

39. Messersmith quoted in "Continuo su labor el congreso de asistencia," *El Nacional*, August 18, 1943.

40. Dore, "One Step Forward, Two Steps Back," 23. See also Varley, "Women and the Home in Mexican Family Law."

41. Lavrín, *Women, Feminism, and Social Change*, 229. See also chapters 6 and 7.

42. Blum, *Domestic Economies*, 111.

43. While concubinage was socially accepted at all class levels, middle-class and elite women had the "protections" offered by a legal marriage.

44. "Informe de labores presentado a H. ejecutivo de la unión por el Dr. Gustavo Baz secretario del ramo," AGN/SSA/SAP, vol. 1, exp. 2, p. 261. See also Roberto García Formenti, "Una tarea moral de asistencia," *Asistencia*, May 1942, 19; and Roberto Parra Gómez and Rafael Vela Najar, "El registro civil de la población (necesidad de la adopción de un programa de propaganda educativa)," *Asistencia*, April 1942, 36.

45. For a discussion of the reform of Mexican family law that encouraged nuclear families, see Varley, "Women and the Home in Mexican Family Law."

46. Ibid., 243–44.

47. "Resumen de las actividades de la Secretaría de Salubridad y Asistencia, en el periodo comprendido 1 de diciembre de 1946, al 31 de agosto de 1947," AGN/SSA/Oficialía Mayor, vol. 4, exp. 03/803.1/1, p. 9.

48. "Informe de las actividades realizadas por le Dirección General de Asistencia Social durante el período comprendido entre 1 de septiembre de 1955 al 31 de agosto de 1956," ibid., vol. 8, exp. 03/803.1/1, p. 26.

49. The *informe* specifically states that it gave aid to women divorced because of domestic abuse, thereby legitimating some forms of divorce, but not all. "Informe de las actividades realizadas por le Dirección General de Asistencia Social durante el período comprendido entre 1 de septiembre de 1953 al 31 de agosto de 1954," ibid., exp. 03/803.1, p. 20.

50. Lewis, *Children of Sanchez*, 58–59.

51. For more on Domínguez Navarro, see K. Lynn Stoner's essay, "Ofelia Domínguez Navarro."

52. "La obra de comedores familiares," *Asistencia*, November–December 1941, 5.

53. Ibid., 5–6.

54. Ibid., 7.

55. Dr. José Quintín Olascoaga, "Comedores populares en la América del Sur," *Asistencia*, November–December 1941, 31.

56. Ibid., 27.

57. F. de P. Miranda, "Soluciones al pensamiento de los comedores familiares," *Asistencia*, November–December 1941, 22.

58. For an excellent discussion of the *comedores'* locations and services, see Rodríguez, "Cooking Modernity."

59. Miranda, "Soluciones al pensamiento," 20.

60. "Reglamento Exterior del Comedor No. 1," *Asistencia*, November–December 1941, 76–78.

61. "Obra de comedores familiares," 8.

62. Isaías Balanzario, "Labor médico-dietológica y de trabajo social," *Asistencia*, November–December 1941, 61.

63. Ibid., 71.

64. "Trabajo social en el comedor familiar num. 2," *Salubridad y Asistencia*, January–February 1946, 4.

65. "Composición humana del comedor," *Asistencia*, November–December 1941, 72–73.

66. Ibid., 73–74.

67. Arrom, *Containing the Poor*, 189–90.

68. AGN/SSA/DAS, vol. 64, exp. 50/231.1/119.

69. "Comedores familiares: Anteproyecto," AGN/SSA, Dirección General de Asistencia, vol. 49, exp. 103/014/10.

70. "Opiniones de algunas personas que han visitado el Comedor Familiar 1," AGN, Ramos Presidenciales, Manuel Ávila Camacho, vol. 517, exp. 463.4/1.

71. For more on this process, see Vaughan, "Modernizing Patriarchy."

72. Blum, *Domestic Economies*, 3–4; Blum, "Conspicuous Benevolence," 23, 34–35.

73. Blum, *Domestic Economies*, 10.

74. Ibid., 33.

75. Ibid., 168–69.

76. "Informe sobre los hogares sustitutos," 1942, AGN/SSA/SAP/DAS, vol. 17, exp. 1/161(04)/1, pp. 1–2.

77. Ibid., p. 2.

78. Problems also existed between those running *hogares colectivos* and those running the newly formed *hogares sustitutos*, or foster homes. Many of the families running collective homes did not understand that eventually all of the children would be placed with foster families, and they thought this was a bad idea. According to social workers, the families running the homes felt superior to the foster families and would create scenes on payday at the *pagaduría general*. Ibid., pp. 3–6.

79. Ibid., pp. 6–7.

80. "Resumen de las actividades de la Secretaría de Salubridad y Asistencia, en el periodo comprendido del primero de septiembre de 1945 al 31 de agosto de 1946," AGN/SSA/Oficialía Mayor, vol. 4, exp. 03/803.1/1, p. 25.

81. Memorandum, DGHAMI–Hogares Sustitutos to foster mother, October 5, 1942, AGN/SSA/DGHAMI, vol. 20, exp. 105/151.3/52–54.

82. Dolores Torres, social worker, report to DGHAMI–Hogares Sustitutos, May 26, 1947, August 9, 1947, ibid.

83. "Informe sobre los hogares sustitutos," 1942, AGN/SSA/SAP/DAS, vol. 17, exp. 1/161(04)/1, pp. 8–10.

84. Dolores Torres, report to DGHAMI–Hogares Sustitutos, November 8, 1946, AGN/SSA/DGHAMI, vol. 20, exp. 105/151.3/52–54.

85. Dolores Torres, report to DGHAMI–Hogares Sustitutos, November 22, 1946, ibid.

86. "Curso para las encargadas de hogares substitutos," 1941, AGN/SSA/SAP/DAS, vol. 17, exp. 1/303/7.

87. Memorandum, Maria Luisa Diaz Lombardo to foster mother, August 8, 1942, AGN/ SSA/DGHAMI, vol. 20, exp. 105/151.3/5254.

88. Maria L. de Lanz, social worker, report to DGHAMI–Hogares Sustitutos, January 13, 1942, ibid.

89. Maria L. de Lanz, report, April 24, 1942, ibid.

90. Maria L. de Lanz, report to DGHAMI–Hogares Sustitutos, n.d., ibid.

91. Maria L. de Lanz, reports to DGHAMI–Hogares Sustitutos, July 28, 1942 and August 12, 1942, ibid.

92. Dolores Torres, report to DGHAMI–Hogares Sustitutos, August 26, 1947, ibid.

93. Mercedes García González, social worker, report to DGHAMI, October 3, 1946, ibid.

94. Luz A de Cortés, social worker, reports to DGHAMI, June 2, 16, and 28, July 15, and September 29, 1955, ibid.

95. Memorandum, Bernardo Sepúlveda to Directora del Hogar Colectivo #9, June 18, 1941, AHSSA/BP, Sección Asistencia, Dirección General de Asistencia, leg. 2, exp. 1.b

96. Eglantina Rámos to Jefe de Asistencias Diversas, June 1, 1941, ibid., leg. 2, exp. 1.

97. "Informe: Dirección General de Higiene y Asistencia Infantiles; Departamento de Acción Social Infantil y Maternal," AGN/SSA/Oficialía Mayor, vol. 4, exp. 03/803.1/2, p. 6.

98. Fernanda Jones-Vargas to Enelda Fox, April 2, 1944, AGN/SSA/SAP/Dirección de Asistencia Infantil, vol. 18, exp. 50/303/16.

99. See advertisement in Marriage and Family Living, November 1956, 307.

100. Rafael Alvares Alva, "Proyecto de instructivo de labores para trabajadores sociales de hogares substitutos," June 6, 1950, AGN/SSA/Dirección General de Asistencia, vol. 49, exp. 103/014/16.

101. For a discussion and critique of this historiography, see Dore, "Holy Family." See also Cicerchia, "Charm of Family Patterns"; for Brazil, see Kuznesof, Household Economy and Urban Development.

102. For Chile, see Rosemblatt, Gendered Compromises; for Brazil, see Besse, Restructuring Patriarchy.

CHAPTER 3

1. "De los casos de solicitud de asistencias, según el estado civil y condiciones sociales de los solicitantes," in "Memoria," 1941, AGN/SSA/SAP, vol. 1, fig. 26.

2. "De los casos de solicitud de asistenciales, según quien sostiene económicamente el hogar," ibid., fig. 27

3. "De los casos de solicitud de asistencias, por ocupaciones y salarios de las madres jefes del hogar," ibid., fig. 29 (female workers), fig. 28 (male workers).

4. "Protección de la niñez, a la maternidad y las clases debiles," AGN/SSA/Oficialía Mayor, vol. 5, exp. 03/803.1/1, p. 49.

5. "Informe narrativo de labores del Centro Materno-Infantil 'Gral. Maximino Ávila Camacho,' durante el periodo comprendido del 1 de septiembre de 1954 al 31 de agosto de 1955," ibid., vol. 10, exp. 03/803.1/1, pp. 3-4.

6. Ibid.

7. "Informe Sintético," 1951, ibid., vol. 4, exp. 03/803.1/1.

8. "Dirección General de Higiene y Asistencia Materno-Infantil: Informe de sus labores practicadas durante el tercer trimestre de 1954," ibid., vol. 7, exp. 03/803.1/1.

9. "Bases para la organización de los comités voluntarios de asistencia infantil," 1941, AGN/ SSA/SAP/DAS, vol. 17, exp. 096.1/5.

10. In the 1940s there were twelve.

11. For a discussion of other government-sponsored feminine leagues in the 1930s, particularly agrarian leagues, see Olcott, "'Worthy Wives and Mothers.'"

12. "Memoria," AGN/SSA/Dirección de Asistencia Pública, vol. 1, exp. 2, p. 272.

13. Ibid.

14. Memorandum, Mathilde Rodríguz Cabo to Dr. Salvador Zubirán, Subsecretario de Asistencia Pública, August 20, 1941, AGN/SSA/SAP/Dirección de Asistencia Infantil, vol. 16, exp. 161(072)/5.

15. Many of the committees were part of a wave of feminist organizing. See Buck, "Activists and Mothers."

16. The photo appears on p. 8 of the February 1942 issue of *Asistencia*.

17. "Datos para Informe Presidencial, junio 1955," AGN/SSA/Oficialía Mayor, vol. 7, exp. 03/ 803.1/1, pp. 4-7.

18. Guadalupe P. de la Lara and G. Ramirez, secretarias del Comité Voluntario "Juan Ma. Rodríguez," to Francisco Sánchez, September 30, 1941, AGN/SSA/SAP/DAS, vol. 17, exp. 096.1/5.

19. For a discussion of women's work and similar programs in Brazil, see Weinstein, "Unskilled Worker, Skilled Housewife."

20. For a discussion of vocational training, see Schell, "Gender, Class, and Anxiety."

21. "Proyecto de organización de trabajo social de la 'Casa de la Madre,'" 1942, AGN/SSA/ SAP/DAS, vol. 17, exp. 1/303/7. The information in the following four paragraphs is from this source.

22. "Cooperación privada y acción social," 1938, AGN/SSA/SAP/DAS, vol. 17, exp. 303/10; "Lista de madres que asisten a los diferentes clubes," 1945, ibid.

23. "Programa de actividades en los clubs de madres," n.d. (in 1943 documents), ibid.

24. Enelda G. Fox, "Industrias para los clubs de madres," 1942, ibid.

25. "Programa de actividades en los clubs de madres," n.d. (in 1943 documents).

26. For a discussion of elite women's charitable activities during an earlier period, see Schell, "Honorable Avocation for Ladies."

27. Memorandum, 1943, AGN/SSA/SAP/Dirección de Asistencia Infantil, vol. 16, exp. 50/ 161(02)/20.

28. Club de Madres Joel Luévano to Leonora Yac, 1945, ibid., vol. 16, exp. 161/725.1/7.

29. Estela Jimenez Esponda, Secretary-General of the Bloque Nacional de Mujeres Revolucionarios, to Gustavo Baz, February 9, 1946, AGN/SSA/Dirección General de Higiene y Asistencia Infantil, box 1, exp. 58/113.1/2-50/402/20.

30. Sociedad de Padres de la Escuela "Alberto Correa" to Director-General de Asistencia Infantil, 1944, ibid., exp. 2311/10.

31. Isabel J. de Domínguez to Guillermo Lechuga, June 12, 1940, ibid., vol. 17, exp. 303/10.

32. De Domínguez to Lechuga, July 3, 1940, ibid.

33. Memorandum, Enelda Fox to Federico Gómez, Director-General de Asistencia Infantil, May 13, 1938, ibid. See chapter 5 for discussion of the connection many professional social workers made between being an educated professional and devotion to the work, a sentiment with religious overtones.

34. Villarespe Reyes, *Solidaridad*, 29-30.

35. AHSSA/BP, Sección Asistencia, Departamento de Acción Educativa, box 7, exp. 1. Thirteen Casas Amigas were in operation by the end of the 1950s.

36. "Proyecto de Reglamento," July 13, 1939, ibid.

37. "Informe," 1939, AHSSA/BP, Sección Asistencia, Dirección General de Asistencia, leg. 2, exp. 1, February 28, 1938.

38. "Informe," 1939, AHSSA/BP, Sección Asistencia, Departamento de Acción Educativa y Social, box 7, exp. 1.

39. Sociedad de Madres de la "Casa Amiga de la Obrera #1," to Gustavo Baz, May 13, 1937, AHSSA/BP, Sección Asistencia, Dirección General de Asistencia, leg. 3, exp. 4.

40. AHSSA/BP, Sección Asistencia, Departamento de Acción Educativa y Social, box 7, exp. 1.

41. Stern, *Secret History of Gender*, 301.

CHAPTER 4

1. Manuel González Rivera, "El tesero mas grande," *Salud*, June 1945, 8–10.

2. Ochoa, *Feeding Mexico*, 99.

3. Vaughan, "Modernizing Patriarchy," 197.

4. For more on this subject, see Becker, *Setting the Virgin on Fire*; Loyo, *Maestros y la cultura nacional*; Torres Septién, *Historia de la educación*; Vaughan, *State, Education, and Social Class* and *Cultural Politics in Revolution*; Vázquez, *Nacionalismo y educación*.

5. Rock, "War and Postwar Intersections," 29. See also Vernon, *Dilemma of Mexico's Development*, 138–42.

6. Thorp, "Latin American Economies," 51; Rock, "War and Postwar Intersections," 30–31.

7. Thorp, "Latin American Economies," 55–56.

8. "Recomendaciones: El IX Congreso Panamericano del Niño; Sección Primera—Organización y financiamiento de los servicios de higiene materno-infantiles," AGN/SSA/Oficina de Asuntos Internacionales, exp. 01-III-050(87)/4, p. 67.

9. Ibid., "Sección Segunda/VI/VIII—De los alimentos," 79.

10. Ibid., "Sección Tercera/XVII—Protección y distracción del niño fuera de la escuela," 112–15. For a discussion of the censorship of comic books in Mexico during this period, see Rubenstein, *Bad Language, Naked Ladies*, 110–22.

11. "Recomendaciones: Sección Tercera/XIV—La educación en el medio rural," 105–7.

12. Ibid., 106.

13. For a discussion of this trend in Mexico, see Cockcroft, *Mexico*, 145–85. For Nicaragua, see Gould, *To Lead as Equals*; for Chile, see Tinsman, *Partners in Conflict*.

14. "Recomendaciones: Sección Tercera/XIV—La educación en el medio rural," 107.

15. Ibid., "Sección Tercera/XV—La educación del preescolar," 109. The U.S. government refused to contribute to Unicef in the immediate postwar period because it operated in eastern bloc countries; U.S. officials accused the agency of aiding the Communists.

16. Ibid.

17. Ibid., "Sección Segunda/IV—El problema de la infancia abandonada y la organización de su asistencia," 69.

18. Ibid., "Sección Segunda/VI—El código de menores," 71.

19. Ibid., "Sección Segunda/II/II—Declaración de derechos del menor," 73.

20. Ibid., "Sección Segunda/II/III—Deberes y derechos del estado," 74.

21. Ibid., "Sección Segunda/VI/IV—De los institutos oficiales de protección de menores," 75.

22. Ibid., "Sección Segunda/VI/XIV—Bases generales sobre tribunales de menores," 88–89.

23. Unicef increased in importance throughout the 1950s, as the influence of the Pan-American Child Congresses diminished. Guy, *White Slavery*, 52.

24. Calder, "Growing Up with Unicef," 14–15.

25. In 1949 the board included members from Argentina, Brazil, Colombia, Ecuador, and Peru. Grant, "For the Children of Three Decades," 9.

26. Black, *Children and the Nations*, 2–3. The information in the following six paragraphs is from this source, specifically pp. 4–8, 33, 45, 66–67 (quotation), 70, 74.

27. Heilbroner, *Mankind's Children*, 3, 12.

28. For discussion of how European colonizers used racial ideas about colonial populations to justify their own imperial policies, see McClintock, Mufti, and Shohat, *Dangerous Liaisons*. For Latin American racial attitudes, see Stepan, *Hour of Eugenics*; Graham, *Idea of Race in Latin America*.

29. Hazzard, *Unicef and Women*, 3.

30. For agricultural policy, see Torres, *Historia de la Revolución Mexicana*, 57–86. See also Cárdenas, *Política económica en México*.

31. Editorial, "La salubridad y la asistencia en el primer año del periodo presidencial," *El Universal*, December 2, 1947.

32. Armando Arevalo Macias, "Los beneficios sanitarios se han extendido a todo el país en el actual periódo oficial," *Novedades*, September 1, 1947.

33. "Salubridad y la asistencia en el primer año."

34. See, for example, "El Gral. Lázaro Cárdenas, al abrir el Congreso sus sesiones ordinarios, el 1 de septiembre de 1936," in *Presidentes de México ante la nación* 4:59, 80.

35. For a discussion of the Rockefeller Foundation, see Anne-Emmanuelle Birn, "Revolution, the Scatological Way." On doctors and rural health, see Kapelusz-Poppi, "Physician Activists and the Development of Rural Health." The Rockefeller Foundation continued to work with the SSA through its Institute of Nutrition.

36. "Informe Sinóptico de las labores técnicas y administrativas realizadas en el periodo comprendido entre el 1 de septiembre de 1955 al 31 agosto de 1956," AGN/SSA/Oficialía Mayor, vol. 8, exp. 03/803.1/1, p. 2.

37. "Resumen de las actividades de la SSA, en el periodo comprendido del 1 de diciembre de 1946 al 31 de agosto de 1947," ibid., vol. 4, exp. 03/803.1/1; and "Informe," ibid., vol. 5, exp. 03/803.1/ 1, p. 8.

38. Alanís Cebrián, "Como se enseña y se practica el trabajo social," 166; Gonzalez Alfaro, "Consideraciones de trabajo social en el medio rural," 13.

39. Gonzalez Alfaro, "Consideraciones de trabajo social en el medio rural," 13–14; "Plan del segundo cursillo de orientación para trabajadores sociales y educadores," AGN/SSA/DAS, vol. 65, exp. 103/303/44.

40. Gonzalez Alfaro, "Consideraciones de trabajo social en el medio rural," 44–45, 15; see also Alanís Cebrián, "Como se enseña y se practica el trabajo social," 166–67.

41. "Informe annual de la Dirección de Enfermería y Trabajo Social," AGN/SSA/Oficialía Mayor, vol. 7, exp. 03/803.1/1, p. 13.

42. Alanís Cebrián, "Como se enseña y se practica el trabajo social," 166.

43. "Informe annual de actividades técnicas de la SSA realizadas durante el periodo compredido del primero de septiembre de 1953 al 31 de agosto de 1954," AGN/SSA/Oficialía Mayor, vol. 16, exp. 03/807.3/1, pp. 19–20, 47–48.

44. "Informe que rinde la SSA ante el C. presidente de la república, en relación con las labores desarrolladas por esta dependencia en el periodo comprendido entre el primero de septiembre de 1953 y 31 diciembre del mismo año," ibid., vol. 10, exp. 03/803.1/1, pp. 26, 36–37.

45. Alanís Cebrián, "Como se enseña y se practica el trabajo social," 167.

46. Niblo, *Mexico in the 1940s*, 185–86.

47. Alanís Cebrián, "Como se enseña y se practica el trabajo social," 167.

48. "Informe de las Labores Técnicas y Administrativas durante el 3er. trimestre de 1955," AGN/SSA/Oficialía Mayor, vol. 7, exp. 03/803.1/1, p. 3.

49. "Informe de las Labores Técnicas y Administrativas durante el 40. [*sic*] trimestre de 1955," ibid., pp. 3–5.

50. "Statement by the Chairman of the UNICEF Executive Board, Mr. J. E. Ryan (Australia) to the Economic and Social Council, 23 April 1959," Archivo de la Secretaría de Relaciones Exteriores, XII/413 (XXVII)/ 17.

51. "Personas atendidas en el Distrito Federal, en los establecimientos y servicios de asistencia social con fines educativos," AGN/SSA/Oficialía Mayor, vol. 5, exp. 03/803.1/1.

52. "Salubridad y la asistencia en el primer año."

53. "60,000 personas reciben asistencia social," *Excélsior*, November 25, 1956.

54. Cypher, *State and Capital in Mexico*, 59.

55. Teichman, *Policymaking in Mexico*, 37.

56. Millor, *Mexico's Oil*, 35; Cypher, *State and Capital in Mexico*, 61.

57. Ochoa, *Feeding Mexico*, 128.

58. Editorial, "Parásitos sociales," *El Universal*, December 11, 1955.

59. "Ni un anciano, ni un niño, ni un mendigo, sin abrigo," *El Nacional*, December 16, 1955.

60. "Ni un muerto de frío o de hambre en las calles," *El Nacional*, December 23, 1955. In order to be released from the shelters, people picked up by these ambulances had to sign a statement swearing that they would not resume begging. AGN/SSA/DAS, vol. 67.

61. Director of Comedor #2 to Dr. Manuel Carcamo Lardizabal, SSA, April 28, 1950; Lardizabal to director of Comedor #2, May 20, 1950, both in AGN/SSA, Dirección General de Asistencia, vol. 49, exp. 103/014/10.

62. "Sintesis del informe de las actividades realizadas por la Dirección General de Asistencia Social durante el periódo comprendido entre 1 de septiembre de 1953 al 31 agosto de 1954," AGN/SSA/Oficialía Mayor, vol. 3, exp. 803.1, pp. 12–13.

63. "Aspecto administrativo del informe de las actividades realizadas por la Dirección General de Asistencia Social durante el período comprendido entre el 1 de septiembre de 1954 al 31 de agosto de 1955," ibid., vol. 7, exp. 03/803.1/1, pp. 11–13.

64. Ibid.

65. "Datos para el informe presidencial: Junio de 1956," ibid., vol. 8, exp. 03/803.1/1. The information in the following two paragraphs is also from this source.

66. "Sintesis e información de las actividades realizadas durante el periodo comprendido entre 1 de septiembre de 1956 al 31 agosto de 1957," ibid., vol. 10, exp. 03/803.1/1, pp. 24–44.

67. Report from Centro Social No. 1, Santa Julia, May 24, 1952, AGN/SSA/DAS, vol. 64, exp. 103/231.1/94.

68. "Ryan to Economic and Social Council, 23 April 1959," 17.

69. Memorandum, Alice Shaffer to Dr. Ignácio Morones Prieto, "Sugestiones sobre un programa cooperative del UNICEF y de la FAO con el Gobierno de México para la producción, conservación y distribución de leche y sus derivados, en relación con los proyectos de asistencia social y alimentación escolar de esa Subsecretaría," AGN/SSA/Oficina de Asuntos Internacionales, vol. 64, exp. 01/III 715.2/6. For background on controversies surrounding milk and the Mexican government's role in milk regulation, see Ochoa, "Reappraising State Intervention."

70. Aguilar Camín and Meyer, *Shadow of the Mexican Revolution*, 176.

71. "Contestación del Dip. Manuel Martínez Sicilia, Presidente del Congreso," in *Presidentes de México ante la nación*, 4:139.

72. "Discurso del Sr. Adolfo Ruiz Cortines, al protestar como Presidente de la República ante el Congreso de la Unión, el 1 de diciembre de 1952," ibid., 4:518.

73. "El Lic. Miguel Alemán, al abrir el Congreso sus sesiones ordinarios, el 1 de septiembre de 1949," ibid., 4:414.

74. "El Sr. Adolfo Ruiz Cortines, al abrir el Congreso sus sesiones ordinarios, el 1 de septiembre de 1954," ibid., 4:547.

75. Amezquita et al., *Historia de la salubridad*, 2:447.

76. Rodríguez Prats, *Adolfo Ruiz Cortines*, 149.

77. Sefchovich, *Suerte de la consorte*, 278–79.

78. Quoted in ibid., 292–93.

79. Aguilar Castro, *Primeras Damas*, 126.

80. "Comité Organizador de la Campaña de Invierno y Navidad a Favor del Niño sin Abrigo," AGN/SSA/SAP, vol. 22.

81. Ford, "Children of the Mexican Miracle," 70–124.

CHAPTER 5

1. Fox quoted in Hayner, "Notes on the Changing Mexican Family," 493.

2. Valero Chávez, *Trabajo social en México*, 47, 49–51.

3. See Evangelista Ramírez, *Historia del trabajo social en México*, 79; Guy, *White Slavery*, 58; Valero Chávez, *Trabajo social en México*, 86.

4. Rothman, *Philanthropists, Therapists, and Activists*, 10; the following four paragraphs rely on this source, especially pp. 10–11, 50, 25, 57. See also Leighninger, *Social Work*; Lubove, *Professional Altruist*; and Wenocur and Reisch, *From Charity to Enterprise*. On U.S social workers, see also Gordon, *Pitied but Not Entitled*; Koven and Michel, *Mothers of a New World*.

5. Ernesto Martínez Mejia, "Un verdadero clamor demanda la creación del Instituto de Trabajo Social," *Asistencia Social*, September 15, 1938, 13. See also "Nuevas becas para estudiantes Mexicanas," June 30, 1942, AGN/SSA/SAP/DAS, vol. 17, exp. 303/10.

6. Martínez Mejia, "Verdadero clamor demanda," 13.

7. Jorge Ramirez Esteva, "Delincuentes que deben ser sujetos de terapia social," *Asistencia Social*, November 1, 1937, 7.

8. Josefina Gaona, "Tipos de establecimientos recomendables según la zona patógena que sea," *Asistencia Social*, October 15, 1937, 7.

9. Romulo V. Ramírez, "La importancia de la ficha individual en terapia social," *Asistencia Social*, September 15, 1937, 6.

10. The SSA kept very careful statistics generated by case files, noting monthly how many cases had been seen by each department or agency. See, for example, "Informe anual de la Dirección de Enfermería y Trabajo Social," June 10, 1955, AGN/SSA/Oficialía Mayor, vol. 7, exp. 03/803.1/1. Alan Knight comments that the 1930s saw an explosion of officials traveling throughout Mexico to measure and quantify all aspects of Mexican life. According to Knight, these officials were rarely welcomed. Knight, "Weight of the State in Modern Mexico," 216–17.

11. Palácios de Fuentes, "Importancia de la trabajadora social," 22–23.

12. Alanís Cebrián, "Como se enseña y se practica el trabajo social," 34.

13. Esperanza Balmaceda de Josefé, "Adiestramiento de personal para servicios sociales," *Asistencia*, June 1942, 121.

14. Palácios de Fuentes, "Importancia de la trabajadora social," 37.

15. Ibid., 23.

16. Alanís Cebrián, "Como se enseña y se practica el trabajo social," 34–35.

17. "Memoria," AGN/SSA/SAP, vol. 1, exp. 2, p. 271.

18. "Proyecto de organización de trabajo social de la 'Casa de la Madre,'" AGN/SSA/SAP/DAS, vol. 17, exp. 1/303/7.

19. Alanís Cebrián, "Como se enseña y se practica el trabajo social," 29.

20. Ibid., 59. See also Valero Chávez, *Trabajo social en México*, 81–83.

21. Alanís Cebrián, "Como se enseña y se practica el trabajo social," 60–65.

22. The source cited in table 3 gives a total of 636 women, but the correct figure is 634.

23. "Distribución de las enfermeras de la Dirección General de Higiene y Asistencia en los estados y territorios en las entidades Federativas—1944," AGN/SSA/DAS, vol. 60, exp. 103/161.3(72)/1.

24. In 1950, according to tables compiled by Stephanie Granato and Aída Mostkoff, a stable middle-class worker would have made a monthly salary of Mex$600, while a marginal middle-class person would have made half that. A person in the transitional class, somewhere between the middle and popular classes, would have earned $200 a month. See Granato and Mostkoff, "Class Structure of Mexico," 106–8.

25. Valero Chávez, *Trabajo social en México*, 87.

26. Alanís Cebrián, "Como se enseña y se practica el trabajo social," 93–95.

27. Evangelista Ramírez, *Historia del trabajo social en México*, 92.

28. Alanís Cebrián, "Como se enseña y se practica el trabajo social," 65, 69.

29. Ibid., 77.

30. Muller Arizmendi, "Escuela de trabajo social," 9.

31. Alanís Cebrián, "Como se enseña y se practica el trabajo social," 109–10. The material in this and the following two paragraphs are from this source, 111–23.

32. See Arrom, *Containing the Poor*, 4.

33. Tice, *Wayward Girls and Immoral Women*, 127.

34. Gutiérrez Zambrano, "Influencia de la familia," 13.

35. Palácios de Fuentes, "Importancia de la trabajadora social," 27.

36. Alanís Cebrián, "Como se enseña y se practica el trabajo social," 40.

37. Mercedes Mondragón, "Intervención de la investigadora y de la trabajadora social, en el tratamiento de la situación de necesidad," *Asistencia*, June 1942, 140.

38. Alanís Cebrián, "Como se enseña y se practica el trabajo social," 50.

39. Muller Arizmendi, "Escuela de trabajo social," 9; Gonzalez Alfaro, "Consideraciones de trabajo social en el medio rural," 45.

40. Vaughan, "Modernizing Patriarchy," 201.

41. Evangelista Ramírez, *Historia del trabajo social en México*, 132.

42. Tice, *Wayward Girls and Immoral Women*, 205n4.

43. Evangelista Ramírez, *Historia del trabajo social en México*, 133–34.

EPILOGUE

1. Katherine Lenroot quotes a report that highlights Mexican reform measures and states that "original experiments of great interest are being made." Lenroot, "Child Welfare in Latin America," 339.

2. See, for example, Vaughan, *Cultural Politics in Revolution*; Joseph and Nugent, *Everyday Forms of State Formation*; Falcón, *Revolución y caciquismo*; Hernández Chávez, *Anenecuilco*.

3. I am not the first to make this point. For discussions of how women, as teachers, feminists, and organizers, affected the creation of the postrevolutionary Mexican regime, see, for example, Buck, "Activists and Mothers"; Fernández Aceves, "Political Mobilization of Women"; Macias, *Against All Odds*; Olcott "'Worthy Wives and Mothers'"; Tuñon Pablos, *Mujeres que se organizan*; and Tuñon Pablos, *Women in Mexico*. For a discussion of Catholic women's organizing, see Boylan, "Mexican Catholic Women's Activism"; and Schell, *Church and State Education*.

4. Bliss, *Compromised Positions*, 13, 5. For a discussion of how international movements influenced Mexican discussions of birth control and pronatalism, see Buck, "Control de la natalidad."

5. Centeno, *Democracy Within Reason*, 192–93.

6. International Monetary Fund, *Annual Report, 1983*, 1.

7. Bergeron, "Political Economy Discourses," 990. See also Nash and Fernández-Kelly, *Women, Men, and the International Division of Labor*; and Tinsman, "Reviving Feminist Materialism," 145.

8. Tina Rosenberg, "A Payoff Out of Poverty?" *New York Times*, December 21, 2008.

BIBLIOGRAPHY

ARCHIVES AND LIBRARIES

Archivo de la Secretaría de Relaciones Exteriores, Mexico City
Archivo General de la Nación, Mexico City
    Galería Presidencial
    Secretaría de Salubridad y Asistencia
Archivo Histórico de la Secretaría de Salubridad y Asistencia, Mexico City
Biblioteca Miguel Lerdo de Tejada de la Secretaría de Hacienda y Crédito Público, Mexico City
Biblioteca Nacional, Universidad Nacional Autónoma de México, Mexico City
Centro de Estudios de Historia de México (Condumex), Mexico City
Fundación Miguel Alemán, Mexico City
Instituto José María Luis Mora, Mexico City
Nettie Lee Benson Library, University of Texas, Austin

MEXICAN NEWSPAPERS AND PERIODICALS
(ALL PUBLISHED IN MEXICO CITY)

Asistencia
Asistencia Social
Eugenesia
Excélsior
Grafico
Higiene
El Nacional
Novedades
La Prensa
Puericultura
Salubridad y Asistencia
Salud
El Universal
Vida

SECONDARY SOURCES

Abarca, Mariano. *La industrialización de Argentina*. Buenos Aires: Ministerio de Agricultura de la
    Nación, 1944.

Agostoni, Claudia. "Discurso médico, cultura higiénica y la mujer en la ciudad de México al cambio de siglo (XIX–XX)." *Mexican Studies/Estudios Mexicanos* 18, no. 1 (2002): 1–22.

Aguilar Camín, Héctor, and Lorenzo Meyer. *In the Shadow of the Mexican Revolution: Contemporary Mexican History, 1910–1989.* Austin: University of Texas Press, 1993.

Aguilar Castro, Alicia. *Primeras Damas, las ausentes presentes: Historias de mujeres mexicanas.* Mexico City: Demac, 2006.

Agustín, José. *Tragicomedia mexicana: La vida en México, 1940 a 1970.* Mexico City: Planeta, 1990.

Alanís Cebrián, Berta. "Como se enseña y se practica el trabajo social en México y en América Latina." Licenciatura thesis, UNAM, 1957.

Alarcón-Gónzalez, Diana, and Terry McKinley. "The Adverse Effects of Structural Adjustment on Working Women in Mexico." *Latin American Perspectives* 26, no. 3 (1999): 103–17.

Amezquita, José Alvarez, Miguel Bustamante, Antonio López, and Francisco Fernández del Castillo. *Historia de la salubridad y de la asistencia en México.* Vol. 2. Mexico City: Secretaría de Salubridad y Asistencia, 1960.

Arrom, Silvia Marina. *Containing the Poor: The Mexico City Poor House, 1774–1871.* Durham: Duke University Press, 2000.

———. *The Women of Mexico City, 1790–1857.* Stanford: Stanford University Press, 1985.

Arrom, Silvia Marina, and Servando Ortoll, eds. *Riots in the Cities: Popular Politics and the Urban Poor in Latin America, 1765–1910.* Wilmington, Del.: Scholarly Resources, 1996.

Azuela, Mariano. *The Underdogs.* New York: Signet Classics, 1962.

Bailey, David. *Viva Cristo Rey! The Cristero Rebellion and the Church-State Conflict in Mexico.* Austin: University of Texas Press, 1974.

Bantjes, Adrian A. *As If Jesus Walked on Earth: Cardenismo, Sonora, and the Mexican Revolution.* Wilmington, Del.: Scholarly Resources, 1998.

Baz, Gustavo. *Gustavo Baz: Anecdotario e ideas.* Mexico City: Estado de México, 1978.

Becker, Marjorie. *Setting the Virgin on Fire: Lázaro Cárdenas, Michoacán Peasants, and the Redemption of the Mexican Revolution.* Berkeley and Los Angeles: University of California Press, 1995.

Beezley, William, and Judith Ewell, eds. *The Human Tradition in Latin America.* Wilmington, Del.: Scholarly Resources, 1987.

Bergeron, Suzanne. "Political Economy Discourses of Globalization and Feminist Politics." *Signs: Journal of Women in Culture and Society* 26, no. 4 (2001): 983–1006.

Bergmann, Emilie, ed. *Women, Culture, and Politics in Latin America.* Berkeley and Los Angeles: University of California Press, 1990.

Bergquist, Charles. *Labor in Latin America: Comparative Essays on Chile, Argentina, Venezuela, and Colombia.* Stanford: Stanford University Press, 1986.

Besse, Susan. *Restructuring Patriarchy: The Modernization of Gender Inequality in Brazil, 1914–1940.* Chapel Hill: University of North Carolina Press, 1996.

Bethell, Leslie, and Ian Roxborough. "Introduction: The Postwar Conjuncture in Latin America." In *Latin America Between the Second World War and the Cold War, 1944–1948,* ed. Leslie Bethell and Ian Roxborough, 1–32. New York: Cambridge University Press, 1992.

Birn, Anne-Emmanuelle. *Marriage of Convenience: Rockefeller International Health and Revolutionary Mexico.* Rochester: University of Rochester Press, 2006.

———. "Revolution, the Scatological Way: The Rockefeller Foundation's Hookworm Campaign in 1920s Mexico." In *Disease in the History of Modern Latin America: From Malaria to AIDS,* ed. Diego Armus, 158–82. Durham: Duke University Press, 2003.

Black, Maggie. *The Children and the Nations: The Story of Unicef.* New York: Unicef, 1986.

Blanco Moheno, Roberto. *Tata Lázaro: Vida, obra y muerte de Cárdenas, Múgica y Carillo Puerto.* Mexico City: Editorial Diana, 1972.

Bliss, Katherine. *Compromised Positions: Prostitution, Public Health, and Gender Politics in Revolutionary Mexico City.* University Park: Pennsylvania State University Press, 2001.

Blum, Ann. "Conspicuous Benevolence: Liberalism, Public Welfare, and Private Charity in Porfirian Mexico City, 1877–1910." *Americas* 58, no. 1 (2001): 7–38.

————. *Domestic Economies: Family, Work, and Welfare in Mexico City, 1884–1943*. Lincoln: University of Nebraska Press, 2009.

Bock, Gisela, and Pat Thane. *Maternity and Gender Policies: Women and the Rise of the European Welfare States, 1880s–1950s*. New York: Routledge, 1991.

Boylan, Kristina. "Mexican Catholic Women's Activism, 1929–1940." PhD diss., St Cross College, Oxford University, 2001.

Buck, Sarah. "Activists and Mothers: Feminist and Maternalist Politics in Mexico, 1923–1953." PhD diss., Rutgers University, 2002.

————. "El control de la natalidad y el día de la madre: Pólitica feminista y reaccionaria en México, 1922–1923." *Signos Históricos* 3, no. 5 (2001): 9–53.

Calder, Ritchie. "Growing Up with Unicef." Public Affairs Pamphlet no. 330. New York: Public Affairs Committee, 1962.

Camp, Roderic. *Politics in Mexico*. New York: Oxford University Press, 1993.

Cárdenas, Enrique. *La hacienda pública y la política económica, 1929–1958*. Mexico City: Fondo de Cultura Económica, 1994.

————. *La política económica en México, 1950–1994*. Mexico City: Fondo de Cultura Económica, 1996.

Ceballos Ramírez, Manuel. *El Catolicismo social: Un tercero en discordia; Rerum Novarum, la "cuestión social" y la movilización de los católicos mexicanos, 1891–1911*. Mexico City: El Colegio de México, 1991.

Centeno, Miguel Ángel. *Democracy Within Reason: Technocratic Revolution in Mexico*. University Park: Pennsylvania State University Press, 1997.

Cicerchia, Ricardo. "The Charm of Family Patterns: Historical and Contemporary Change in Latin America." In *Gender Politics in Latin America: Debates in Theory and Practice*, ed. Elizabeth Dore, 118–33. New York: Monthly Review Press, 1997.

Cockcroft, James. *Mexico: Class Formation, Capital Accumulation, and the State*. New York: Monthly Review Press, 1990.

Collier, Simon, and William F. Sater. *A History of Chile, 1808–1994*. New York: Cambridge University Press, 1996.

Congresos Pan-Americanos del Niño: Ordenación sistemática de sus recomendaciones, 1916–1963. Montevideo, Uruguay: Instituto Interamericano del Niño, 1965.

Curley, Robert. "Sociólogos peregrinos: Teoría social católica en el fin-de-régimen porfiriato." In *Catolicismo social en México: Teoría, fuentes e historiografía*, ed. Jaime del Arenal Fenochio, Manuel Ceballos Ramírez, and Alejandro Garza Rangel, 195–237. Mexico City: Academia de Investigación Humanística, 2000.

Cypher, James M. *State and Capital in Mexico: Development Policy Since 1940*. Boulder: Westview Press, 1990.

Davin, Anna. "Imperialism and Motherhood." *History Workshop Journal* (Spring 1978): 9–14.

De Grazia, Victoria. *How Fascism Ruled Women: Italy, 1922–1945*. Berkeley and Los Angeles: University of California Press, 1992.

Dirección de Pensiones Civiles de Retiro. *Tercer censo de empleados federales sujetos a la Ley General de México*. Mexico City: M. L. Sánchez, 1938.

Domínguez Navarro, Ofelia. "La investigación de la paternidad como medida de protección al niño." In *Memoria del VII Congreso Panamericano del Niño*, 2 vols., 2:123–28. Mexico City: Talleres Gráficos de la Nación, 1937.

Dore, Elizabeth. "The Holy Family: Imagined Households in Latin American History." In *Gender Politics in Latin America: Debates in Theory and Practice*, ed. Elizabeth Dore, 101–17. New York: Monthly Review Press, 1997.

————. "One Step Forward, Two Steps Back: Gender and the State in the Long Nineteenth Century." In *Hidden Histories of Gender and the State in Latin America*, ed. Elizabeth Dore and Maxine Molyneaux, 3–32. Durham: Duke University Press, 2000.

Doremus, Anne. "Indigenism, Mestizaje, and National Identity in Mexico During the 1940s and 1950s." *Mexican Studies/Estudios Mexicanos* 17, no. 20 (2001): 375–402.

Dunkerly, James, ed. *Studies in the Formation of the Nation-State in Latin America*. London: Institute of Latin American Studies, 2002.

Ehrenreich, Barbara, and Deirdre English. *For Her Own Good: 150 Years of the Experts' Advice to Women*. Garden City, N.Y.: Anchor Press, 1978.

Ehrick, Christine. "Affectionate Mothers and the Colossal Machine: Feminism, Social Assistance, and the State of Uruguay, 1910–1932." *Americas* 58, no. 1 (2001): 121–39.

———. "*Madrinas* and Missionaries: Uruguay and the Pan-American Women's Movement." *Gender and History* 10, no. 3 (1998): 406–26.

Eighth Pan-American Child Congress: Washington D.C., May 2–9, 1942. Washington, D.C.: U.S. Government Printing Office, 1942.

Ervin, Michael. "The 1930 Agrarian Census in Mexico: Agronomists, Middle Politics, and the Negotiation of Data Collection." *Hispanic American Historical Review* 87, no. 3 (2007): 537–70.

Esping-Andersen, Gøsta. *Politics Against Markets: The Social Democratic Road to Power*. Princeton: Princeton University Press, 1985.

———. *The Three Worlds of Welfare Capitalism*. Cambridge: Polity Press, 1990.

Evangelista Ramírez, Elí. *Historia del trabajo social en México*. Mexico City: UNAM Escuela de Trabajo Social, 1998.

Falcón, Romana. *Revolución y caciquismo: San Luis Potosí, 1910–1938*. Mexico City: El Colegio de México, 1984.

Fernández Aceves, María Teresa. "The Political Mobilization of Women in Revolutionary Guadalajara, 1910–1940." PhD diss., University of Illinois, Chicago, 2000.

———. "The Struggle Between the *Metate* and the *Molinos de Nixtamal* in Guadalajara, 1920–1940." In *Sex in Revolution: Gender, Politics, and Power in Modern Mexico*, ed. Jocelyn Olcott, Mary Kay Vaughn, and Gabriela Cano, 147–61. Durham: Duke University Press, 2006.

Fildes Valerie, Lara Marks, and Hilary Marland, eds. *Women and Children First: International Maternal and Infant Welfare, 1870–1945*. New York: Routledge, 1992.

Ford, Eileen. "Children of the Mexican Miracle: Childhood and Modernity in Mexico City, 1940–1968." PhD diss., University of Illinois, Urbana-Champaign, 2008.

Fox, Enelda G. "La coordinación y desarrollo de los trabajos encaminados a preparar a las madres para la debida protección de sus hijos." In *Memoria del VII Congreso Panamericano del Niño*, 2 vols., 1:890–95. Mexico City: Talleres Gráficos de la Nación, 1937.

Franco, Jean. *Plotting Women: Gender and Representation in Mexico*. New York: Columbia University Press, 1989.

French, William E. *A Peaceful and Working People: Manners, Morals, and Class Formation in Northern Mexico*. Albuquerque: University of New Mexico Press, 1996.

French, William E., and Katharine Elaine Bliss. *Gender, Sexuality, and Power in Latin America Since Independence*. New York: Rowman and Littlefield, 2007.

French, William E., and Daniel James, eds. *The Gendered Worlds of Latin American Women Workers: From Household and Factory to the Union Hall and Ballot Box*. Durham: Duke University Press, 1997.

Fuentes, Mario Luís. *La asistencia social en México: Historia y perspectivas*. Mexico City: Ediciones del Milenio, 1998.

Garduño Valdéz, Carmen. "El trabajo social en el Centro Materno Infantil General Maximino Ávila Camacho." Licenciatura thesis, UNAM, 1953.

Garrido, Luís Javier. *El partido de la revolución institucionalizada: La formación del nuevo estado en México*. Mexico City: Siglo Veintiuno Editores, 1982.

Gauss, Susan. "Working-Class Masculinity and the Rationalized Sex: Gender and Industrial Modernization in the Textile Industry in Postrevolutionary Puebla." In *Sex in Revolution: Gender, Politics, and Power in Modern Mexico*, ed. Jocelyn Olcott, Mary Kay Vaughn, and Gabriela Cano, 181–98. Durham: Duke University Press, 2006.

Gentleman, Judith. *Mexican Oil and Dependent Development*. New York: Peter Lang, 1984.

Gilly, Adolfo. *El cardenismo, una utopía mexicana*. Mexico City: Cal y Arena, 1994.

———. *La revolución interrumpida, México, 1910–1920: Una guerra campesina por la tierra y el poder*. Mexico City: Ediciones el Caballito, 1971.

Gilman, Amy. "From Widowhood to Wickedness: The Politics of Class and Gender in New York City Private Charity, 1799–1860." *History of Education Quarterly* 24, no. 1 (1984): 59–74.

Glade, William P., and Charles W. Anderson. *The Political Economy of Mexico*. Milwaukee: University of Wisconsin Press, 1963.

Gonzalez Alfaro, Carmen. "Consideraciones de trabajo social en el medio rural, Comarca Lagunera, Centro de Bienestar Social Rural." Licenciatura thesis, UNAM, 1955.

González Navarro, Moisés. *La pobreza en México*. Mexico City: El Colegio de México, 1985.

Gordon, Linda. *Pitied but Not Entitled: Single Mothers and the History of Welfare*. Cambridge: Harvard University Press, 1994.

Gould, Jeffrey L. *To Lead as Equals: Rural Protest and Political Consciousness in Chinandega, Nicaragua, 1912–1979*. Chapel Hill: University of North Carolina Press, 1990.

Gould, Stephen Jay. *The Panda's Thumb: More Reflections in Natural History*. New York: W. W. Norton, 1980.

Graham, Richard, ed. *The Idea of Race in Latin America, 1870–1940*. Austin: University of Texas Press, 1990.

Granato, Stephanie, and Aída Mostkoff. "Class Structure of Mexico, 1895–1980." In *Society and Economy in Mexico*, ed. James W. Wilkie, 103–16. Los Angeles: UCLA Latin American Center Publications, 1990.

Grant, Kenneth E. "For the Children of Three Decades: Unicef in the Americas." New York: Unicef, 1986.

Gutiérrez Zambrano, Amalia. "La influencia de la familia en la sociedad y la actividad de la trabajadora social en este campo." Licenciatura thesis, Escuela Trabajo Social de la Clínica y Maternidad "Conchita," UNAM, 1955.

Guy, Donna J. "The Pan-American Child Congresses, 1916 to 1942: Pan-Americanism, Child Reform, and the Welfare State in Latin America." *Journal of Family History* 23, no. 3 (1998): 272–91.

———. "Parents Before the Tribunals: The Legal Construction of Patriarchy in Argentina." In *Hidden Histories of Gender and the State in Latin America*, ed. Elizabeth Dore and Maxine Molyneaux, 172–93. Durham: Duke University Press, 2000.

———. *White Slavery and Mothers Alive and Dead: The Troubled Meeting of Sex, Gender, Public Health, and Progress in Latin America*. Lincoln: University of Nebraska Press, 2000.

———. *Women Build the Welfare State: Performing Charity and Creating Rights in Argentina, 1880–1955*. Durham: Duke University Press, 2009.

Haber, Stephen H. *Industry and Underdevelopment: The Industrialization of Mexico, 1890–1940*. Stanford: Stanford University Press, 1989.

Hamilton, Nora. *The Limits of State Autonomy: Post-Revolutionary Mexico*. Princeton: Princeton University Press, 1982.

Hamilton, Nora, and Timothy F. Harding, eds. *Modern Mexico: State, Economy, and Social Conflict*. Beverly Hills: Sage Publications, 1986.

Hansen, Roger D. *The Politics of Mexican Development*. Baltimore: Johns Hopkins University Press, 1971.

Hart, John Mason. *Revolutionary Mexico: The Coming and Process of the Mexican Revolution*. Berkeley and Los Angeles: University of California Press, 1987.

Hayner, Norman S. "Notes on the Changing Mexican Family." *American Sociological Review* 7, no. 4 (1942): 489–97.

Hazzard, Virginia. *Unicef and Women: A Historical Perspective*. New York: Unicef, 1987.

Heilbroner, Robert L. *Mankind's Children: The Story of Unicef*. New York: Public Affairs Committee, 1959.

Hellman, Judith Adler. *Mexico in Crisis*. New York: Holmes and Meier, 1983.

Hernández, Nieves. "La coordinación y desarrollo de los trabajos encaminados a preparar a las madres para la debida protección de sus hijos: Protección de madres obreras." In *Memoria del VII Congreso Panamericano del Niño*, 2 vols., 1:896–903. Mexico City: Talleres Gráficos de la Nación, 1937.

Hernández Chávez, Alicia. *Anenecuilco: Memoria y vida de un pueblo*. Mexico City: El Colegio de México, 1991.

———. *La mecánica cardenista*. Mexico City: El Colegio de México, 1979.

Hidalgo, Berta. *El movimiento femenino en México*. Mexico City: Edamex, 1980.

Incháustegui Romero, Teresa de Carmen. "El Cambio de la asistencia social en México 1937–97." PhD diss., FLACSO-SEDE, 1997.

Instituto Nacional de Estadística, Geografía e Informática. *Estadísticas históricas de México*. Mexico City: Instituto Nacional de Estadística, Geografía e Informática, 1985.

International Monetary Fund. *Annual Report, 1983*. Washington, D.C.: International Monetary Fund, 1984.

James, Daniel. *Resistance and Integration: Peronism and the Argentine Working Class, 1946–1976*. New York: Cambridge University Press, 1988.

Joseph, Gilbert M. *Revolution from Without: Yucatán, Mexico, and the United States, 1880–1924*. Durham: Duke University Press, 1988.

Joseph, Gilbert M., and Daniel Nugent, eds. *Everyday Forms of State Formation: Revolution and the Negotiation of Rule in Modern Mexico*. Durham: Duke University Press, 1994.

Kapelusz-Poppi, Ana María. "Physician Activists and the Development of Rural Health in Postrevolutionary Mexico." *Radical History Review* 80 (Spring 2001): 35–50.

Katz, Friedrich. *The Secret War in Mexico: Europe, the United States, and the Mexican Revolution*. Chicago: University of Chicago Press, 1981.

Klubock, Thomas. *Contested Communities: Class, Gender, and Politics in Chile's El Teniente Copper Mine, 1904–1951*. Durham: Duke University Press, 1998.

Knight, Alan. "Cardenismo: Juggernaut or Jalopy?" *Journal of Latin American Studies* 26, no. 1 (1994): 73–107.

———. *The Mexican Revolution*. 2 vols. Lincoln: University of Nebraska Press, 1986.

———."The Weight of the State in Modern Mexico." In *Studies in the Formation of the Nation-State in Latin America*, ed. James Dunkerly, 212–53. London: Institute of Latin America Studies, 2002.

Koven, Seth, and Sonya Michel, eds. *Mothers of a New World: Maternalist Politics and the Origins of the Welfare State*. New York: Routledge, 1993.

Kuznesof, Elizabeth Anne. *Household Economy and Urban Development: São Paulo, 1765 to 1836*. Boulder: Westview Press, 1986.

LaFeber, Walter. *The American Age: United States Foreign Policy at Home and Abroad Since 1750*. New York: W. W. Norton, 1989.

Lavrín, Asunción. *Women, Feminism, and Social Change in Argentina, Chile, and Uruguay, 1890–1940*. Lincoln: University of Nebraska Press, 1995.

Leighninger, Leslie. *Social Work: Search for Identity*. New York: Greenwood Press, 1987.

Lenroot, Katherine. "Child Welfare in Latin America." *Bulletin of the Pan American Union* (June 1939): 336–48.

Levy, Daniel, and Gabriel Székely. *Mexico: Paradoxes of Stability and Change*. Boulder: Westview Press, 1987.

Lewis, Oscar. *The Children of Sanchez*. New York: Random House, 1960.

Loaeza, Soledad. *Clases medias y política en México: La querella escolar, 1959–1963*. Mexico City: El Colegio de México, 1999.

Looney, Robert. *Economic Policymaking in Mexico: Factors Underlying the 1982 Crisis*. Durham: Duke University Press, 1985.

Loyo, Engracia. *Los maestros y la cultura nacional, 1920–1952*. Mexico City: Secretaría de Educación Pública, 1987.

Lubove, Roy. *The Professional Altruist: The Emergence of Social Work as a Career, 1880–1930*. Cambridge: Harvard University Press, 1965.

Macias, Anna. *Against All Odds: The Feminist Movement in Mexico to 1940*. Westport, Conn.: Greenwood Press, 1982.

Manrique Castro, Manuel. *De apostoles a agentes de cambio: El trabajo social en la historia latinoamericana*. Lima: Celats Ediciones, 1982.

McClintock, Anne, Aamir Mufti, and Ella Shohat, eds. *Dangerous Liaisons: Gender, Nation, and Postcolonial Perspectives*. Minneapolis: University of Minnesota Press, 1997.

McGann, Thomas. *Argentina, the United States, and the Inter-American System, 1880–1914*. Cambridge: Harvard University Press, 1957.

Mead, Karen. "Beneficent Maternalism: Argentine Motherhood in Comparative Perspective, 1880–1920." *Journal of Women's History* 12, no. 3 (2000): 120–45.

Medina Peña, Luís. *Hacia el nuevo estado, México, 1920–1994*. Mexico City: Fondo de Cultura Económica, 1994.

Memoria del VII Congreso Panamericano del Niño. 2 vols. Mexico City: Talleres Gráficos de la Nación, 1937.

Meyer, Jean. *La cristiada*. 3 vols. Mexico City: Siglo Veintiuno Editores, 1973–74.

Middlebrook, Kevin J. *The Paradox of Revolution: Labor, the State, and Authoritarianism in Mexico*. Baltimore: Johns Hopkins University Press, 1995.

Miller, Francesca. *Latin American Women and the Search for Social Justice*. Hanover: University Press of New England, 1991.

Millor, Manuel R. *Mexico's Oil: Catalyst for a New Relationship with the U.S.?* Boulder: Westview Press, 1982.

Mink, Gwendolyn. *The Wages of Motherhood: Inequality in the Welfare State, 1917–1942*. Ithaca: Cornell University Press, 1995.

Modesto Martínez, Socorro. "El trabajo social en la prevención de la sífilis pre-natal en la ciudad de México." Licenciatura thesis, UNAM, 1956.

Moreno, Julio. *Yankee Don't Go Home! Mexican Nationalism, American Business Culture, and the Shaping of Modern Mexico, 1920–1950*. Chapel Hill: University of North Carolina Press, 2003.

Muller Arizmendi, Martha. "Escuela de trabajo social." Licenciatura thesis, UNAM, 1956.

Nash, June, and María Patricia Fernández-Kelly, eds. *Women, Men, and the International Division of Labor*. Albany: State University of New York Press, 1983.

Newell, Roberto G., and Luís F. Rubio. *Mexico's Dilemma: The Political Origins of Economic Crisis*. Boulder: Westview Press, 1984.

Niblo, Steven. *Mexico in the 1940s: Modernity, Politics, and Corruption*. Wilmington, Del.: Scholarly Resources, 1999.

Obregón, Alvaro. *Ocho mil kilometres en la campaña*. Mexico City: Fondo de Cultura Económica, 1959.

O'Brien, Thomas. *The Revolutionary Mission: American Enterprise in Latin America, 1900–1945*. New York: Cambridge University Press, 1996.

Ochoa, Enrique C. "Coercion, Reform, and the Welfare State: The Campaign Against 'Begging' in Mexico City During the 1930s." *Americas* 58, no. 1 (2001): 39–64.

———. *Feeding Mexico: The Political Uses of Food Since 1910*. Wilmington, Del.: Scholarly Resources, 2000.

———. "Reappraising State Intervention and Social Policy in Mexico: The Case of Milk in the Distrito Federal During the Twentieth Century." *Mexican Studies/Estudios Mexicanos* 15, no. 1 (1999): 73–99.

Olcott, Jocelyn. *Revolutionary Women in Postrevolutionary Mexico*. Durham: Duke University Press, 2005.

———. "'Worthy Wives and Mothers': State-Sponsored Women's Organizing in Postrevolutionary Mexico." *Journal of Women's History* 13, no. 4 (2002): 106–31.

Orloff, Ann. "Gender in the Welfare State." *Annual Review of Sociology* 22 (1996): 51–78.

Palácios de Fuentes, Dolores. "Importancia de la trabajadora social en los centros de higiene de asistencia infantil." Licenciatura thesis, UNAM, 1943.

Parker, D. S. *The Idea of the Middle Class in Peru.* University Park: Pennsylvania State University Press, 1998.

Pateman, Carole. *The Sexual Contract.* Stanford: Stanford University Press, 1988.

Pedersen, Susan. *Family Dependence and the Origins of the Welfare State: Britain and France, 1914–1945.* New York: Cambridge University Press, 1993.

Piccato, Pablo. *City of Suspects: Crime in Mexico City, 1900–1931.* Durham: Duke University Press, 2001.

Porter, Susie. "Empleadas públicas: Normas de feminidad, espacios burocráticos e identidad de la clase media in México durante la década de 1930." *Signos Históricos* 6, no. 11 (2004): 41–63.

———. "Espacios burocráticos, normas de feminidad e identidad de la clase media en México durante la década de 1930." In *Orden social e identidad de género, México, siglos XIX y XX,* ed. María Teresa Fernández Aceves, 189–213. Mexico City: CIESAS, Universidad de Guadalajara, 2006.

———. *Working Women in Mexico City: Public Discourses and Material Conditions, 1879–1931.* Tucson: University of Arizona Press, 2003.

Los presidentes de México ante la nación: Informes, manifiestos y documentos de 1821 a 1966. Vol. 4. Mexico City: XLVI Legislatura de la Camara de Diputados, 1966.

Quevedo L., V. Fernando. "Protección de la madre soltera." In *Memoria del VII Congreso Panamericano del Niño,* 2 vols., 2:103–8. Mexico City: Talleres Gráficos de la Nación, 1937.

Quirk, Robert. *The Mexican Revolution and the Catholic Church, 1910–1929.* Bloomington: Indiana University Press, 1973.

Rivera de Rangel, Judith. "Colaboración de la familia y de la escuela en beneficio de los niños." In *Memoria del VII Congreso Panamericano del Niño,* 2 vols., 2:322–29. Mexico City: Talleres Gráficos de la Nación, 1937.

Rock, David. *Argentina, 1516–1987.* Berkeley and Los Angeles: University of California Press, 1987.

———. "War and Postwar Intersections: Latin America and the United States." In *Latin America in the 1940s: War and Postwar Transitions,* ed. David Rock, 15–40. Berkeley and Los Angeles: University of California Press, 1994.

Rodríguez, Sandra Aguilar. "Cooking Modernity: Nutrition Policies, Class, and Gender in 1940s and 1950s Mexico City." *Americas* 64, no. 2 (2007): 177–205.

Rodríguez Prats, Juan José. *Adolfo Ruiz Cortines.* Mexico City: Gobierno del Estado de Veracruz, 1990.

Rosemblatt, Karin. *Gendered Compromises: Political Cultures and the State in Chile, 1920–1950.* Chapel Hill: University of North Carolina Press, 2000.

———. "Other Americas: Transnationalism, Scholarship, and the Culture of Poverty in Mexico and the United States." *Hispanic American Historical Review* 89, no. 4 (2009): 603–41.

Rothman, Gerald C. *Philanthropists, Therapists, and Activists: A Century of Ideological Conflict in Social Work.* Cambridge, Mass.: Schenkman, 1985.

Rubenstein, Anne. *Bad Language, Naked Ladies, and Other Threats to the Nation: A Political History of Comic Books in Mexico.* Durham: Duke University Press, 1998.

Ruiz, Ramón. *The Great Rebellion: Mexico, 1905–1924.* New York: W. W. Norton, 1980.

Sainz Trejo, A. "Protección a los hijos ilegítimos." In *Memoria del VII Congreso Panamericano del Niño,* 2 vols., 2:134–38. Mexico City: Talleres Gráficos de la Nación, 1937.

Sandoval, Miranda. "La familia: La sociedad y el estado como factores educativas." Licenciatura thesis, UNAM, 1959.

Schell, Patience. *Church and State Education in Revolutionary Mexico City.* Tucson: University of Arizona Press, 2003.

———. "Gender, Class, and Anxiety at the Gabriel Mistral Vocational School, Revolutionary Mexico City." In *Sex in Revolution: Gender, Politics, and Power in Modern Mexico,* ed. Jocelyn

Olcott, Mary Kay Vaughn, and Gabriela Cano, 112–26. Durham: Duke University Press, 2006.

———. "An Honorable Avocation for Ladies: The Work of the Mexico City Union de Damas Catolicas Mexicanas, 1912–1926." *Journal of Women's History* 10, no. 4 (1999): 78–103.

Schlesinger, Stephen, and Stephen Kinzer. *Bitter Fruit: The Story of the American Coup in Guatemala.* Cambridge: Harvard University Press, 1982.

Scott, Joan. "Gender: A Useful Category of Historical Analysis." *American Historical Review* 91, no. 5 (1986): 1053–75.

Seed, Patricia. *To Love, Honor, and Obey in Colonial Mexico: Conflicts over Marriage Choice, 1574–1821.* Stanford: Stanford University Press, 1988.

Sefchovich, Sara. *La suerte de la consorte: Las esposas de los gobernantes de México; Historia de un olvido y relato de un fracaso.* Mexico City: Océano, 1999.

Simons, Marisabel. "El trabajo social como redentor en la sociedad." In *Memoria del VII Congreso Panamericano del Niño,* 2 vols., 1:838–46. Mexico City: Talleres Gráficos de la Nación, 1937.

Skocpol, Theda. *Protecting Soldiers and Mothers: The Political Origins of Social Policy in the United States.* Cambridge: Harvard University Press, 1992.

Smith, Peter. *Democracy in Latin America: Political Change in Comparative Perspective.* New York: Oxford University Press, 2005.

Snodgrass, Michael. *Deference and Defiance in Monterrey: Workers, Paternalism, and Revolution in Mexico, 1890–1950.* New York: Cambridge University Press, 2003.

Stepan, Nancy Leys. *The Hour of Eugenics: Race, Gender, and Nation in Latin America.* Ithaca: Cornell University Press, 1991.

Stern, Alexandra Minna. "Responsible Mothers and Normal Children: Eugenics, Nationalism, and Welfare in Post-Revolutionary Mexico, 1920–1940." *Journal of Historical Sociology* 12, no. 4 (1999): 369–97.

Stern, Steve J. *The Secret History of Gender: Women, Men, and Power in Late Colonial Mexico.* Chapel Hill: University of North Carolina Press, 1995.

Stoner, K. Lynn. "Ofelia Domínguez Navarro: The Making of a Cuban Socialist." In *The Human Tradition in Latin America: The Twentieth Century,* ed. William Beezley and Judith Ewell, 119–40. Wilmington, Del.: Scholarly Resources, 1987.

Teichman, Judith. *Policymaking in Mexico: From Boom to Bust.* Boston: Allen and Unwin, 1988.

Thorp, Rosemary. "The Latin American Economies in the 1940s." In *Latin America in the 1940s: War and Postwar Transitions,* ed. David Rock, 41–58. Berkeley and Los Angeles: University of California Press, 1994.

———. *Progress, Poverty, and Exclusion: An Economic History of Latin America in the Twentieth Century.* Washington, D.C.: Inter-American Development Bank, 1998.

Tice, Karen W. *Tales of Wayward Girls and Immoral Women: Case Records and the Professionalization of Social Work.* Urbana: University of Illinois Press, 1998.

Tinsman, Heidi. *Partners in Conflict: The Politics of Gender, Sexuality, and Labor in the Chilean Agrarian Reform, 1950–1973.* Durham: Duke University Press, 2002.

———. "Reviving Feminist Materialism: Gender and Neoliberalism; Pinochet's Chile." *Signs: Journal of Women in Culture and Society* 26, no. 1 (2000): 145–88.

Topik, Steven C. *Trade and Gunboats: The United States and Brazil in the Age of Empire.* Stanford: Stanford University Press, 1996.

Torres, Blanca. *Historia de la Revolución Mexicana, 1940–1952: Hacia la utopía industrial.* Mexico City: El Colegio de México, 1984.

Torres, Elena. "Servicio social infantil y de higiene doméstica." In *Memoria del VII Congreso Panamericano del Niño,* 2 vols., 1:885–89. Mexico City: Talleres Gráficos de la Nación, 1937.

Torres Septién, Valentina. *Historia de la educación: Perpectivas de analysis.* Toluca, Mexico: Instituto Superior de Ciencias de la Educación del Estado de México, 1991.

Tuñon Pablos, Esperanza. *Mujeres que se organizan: El Frente Unico pro Derechos de la Mujer, 1935–1938.* Mexico City: Grupo Editorial Miguel Angel Porrúa, 1992.

Tuñon Pablos, Julia. *Women in Mexico: A Past Unveiled*. Austin: University of Texas Press, 1987.

Valero Chávez, Aída. *El trabajo social en México: Desarrollo y perspectivas*. Mexico City: UNAM, Escuela Nacional de Trabajo Social, 1994.

Varley, Ann. "Women and the Home in Mexican Family Law." In *Hidden Histories of Gender and the State*, ed. Elizabeth Dore and Maxine Molyneaux, 238–61. Durham: Duke University Press, 2000.

Vaughan, Mary Kay. *Cultural Politics in Revolution: Teachers, Peasants, and Schools in Mexico, 1930–1940*. Tucson: University of Arizona Press, 1997.

———. "Modernizing Patriarchy: State Policies, Rural Households, and Women in Mexico, 1930–1940." In *Hidden Histories of Gender and the State*, ed. Elizabeth Dore and Maxine Molyneaux, 194–214. Durham: Duke University Press, 2000.

———. *The State, Education, and Social Class in Mexico, 1880–1928*. DeKalb: Northern Illinois University Press, 1982.

Vázquez, Jénaro V., and Gilberto Loyo. "Programa minima de preparación de las enfermeras visitadoras y de las trabajadores sociales." In *Memoria del VII Congreso Panamericano del Niño*, 2 vols., 1:847–67. Mexico City: Talleres Gráficos de la Nación, 1937.

Vázquez, Josefina. *Nacionalismo y educación*. Mexico City: El Colegio de México, 1970.

Vernon, Raymond. *The Dilemma of Mexico's Development: The Roles of the Private and Public Sectors*. Cambridge: Harvard University Press, 1965.

Villarespe Reyes, Verónica Ofelia. *La solidaridad: Beneficencia y programas; Pasado y presente del tratamiento de la pobreza en México*. Mexico City: UNAM, 2001.

Voekel, Pamela. *Alone Before God: The Religious Origins of Modernity in Mexico*. Durham: Duke University Press, 2002.

Wassserman, Mark. *Persistent Oligarchs: Elites and Politics in Chihuahua, Mexico, 1910–1940*. Durham: Duke University Press, 1993.

Weiner, Richard. "Competing Market Discourses in Porfirian Mexico." *Latin American Perspectives* 26, no. 1 (1999): 44–64.

Weinstein, Barbara. "Unskilled Worker, Skilled Housewife: Constructing the Working-Class Woman in São Paulo, Brazil." In *The Gendered Worlds of Latin American Women Workers: From Household and Factory to the Union Hall and Ballot Box*, ed. William E. French and Daniel James, 72–99. Durham: Duke University Press, 1997.

Wenocur, Stanley, and Michael Reisch. *From Charity to Enterprise: The Development of American Social Work in a Market Economy*. Urbana: University of Illinois Press, 1989.

Wilkie, James W. *The Mexican Revolution: Federal Expenditure and Social Change Since 1910*. Berkeley and Los Angeles: University of California Press, 1967.

———, ed. *Society and Economy in Mexico*. Los Angeles: UCLA Latin American Center Publications, 1990.

Wilkie, Richard W. *Latin American Population and Urbanization Analysis: Maps and Statistics, 1950–82*. Los Angeles: UCLA Latin American Center Publications, 1984.

Winn, Peter. *Weavers of Revolution: The Yarur Workers and Chile's Road to Socialism*. New York: Oxford University Press, 1986.

INDEX